The Arkansas Delta Oral History Project

Writing, Culture, and Community Practices
Steve Parks and Eileen Schell, *Series Editors*

Syracuse University Press's Writing, Culture, and Community Practices series is distinguished by works that move between disciplinary identity and community practices to address how literacies and writing projects empower a population and promote social change.

Other titles in Writing, Culture, and Community Practices

Writing Suburban Citizenship: Place-Conscious Education and the Conundrum of Suburbia
Robert E. Brooke, ed.

The Arkansas Delta Oral History Project

Culture, Place, and Authenticity

David A. Jolliffe,
Christian Z. Goering,
Krista Jones Oldham,
and James A. Anderson Jr.

S|U

Syracuse University Press

Syracuse, New York 13244-5290

First Edition 2016
16 17 18 19 20 21 6 5 4 3 2 1

∞ The paper used in this publication meets the minimum requirements of the American National Standard for Information Sciences—Permanence of Paper for Printed Library Materials, ANSI Z39.48-1992.

For a listing of books published and distributed by Syracuse University Press, visit www.SyracuseUniversityPress.syr.edu.

ISBN: 978-0-8156-3481-2 (hardcover)
978-0-8156-3466-9 (paperback)
978-0-8156-5378-3 (e-book)

Library of Congress Cataloging-in-Publication Data
Available upon request from the publisher.

Manufactured in the United States of America

Contents

Foreword

UNIVERSITIES, AND WRITING PROGRAMS IN PARTICULAR, have long experimented with classes and projects that take students into local communities. Under certain conditions (Mathieu 2005), such endeavors can result in the genuine transformation of both university students and the communities in which they serve. Frequently, though, community-engaged teaching prioritizes student learning—in forms that fit neatly into a semester, and whose successes are meant to be assessed within the college classroom context—over creating actual change in communities beyond the college classroom (Stoecker 2016).

The Arkansas Delta Oral History Project (ADOHP) documents the experimentation, commitment, and continual self-reflection required to create a program that has the potential to change both university students and the communities in which they undertake literacy work. But the ADOHP also asks us to extend our vision beyond the local university community to consider the entire region that a university serves. In doing so, this book helps us see what universities owe not only to the cities and towns in which they are located, but also to the rural areas—often vast rural areas—that are typically overlooked in community-based teaching and learning. As the authors note, beyond agricultural extension offices, many state university systems have little to no presence in the rural regions of their states.

As you read this book, consider these two questions: What do we, as literacy scholars and teachers, owe to the regions where we teach? What do our students owe to the regions where they learn? When it comes to rural places, one critical need is helping youth negotiate relationships with their home regions and with hopes for their futures. The authors detail the pressures for out-migration that high school students face in the Arkansas Delta, and others have documented the ways rural students (Corbett 2007; Carr and Kefalas 2009) and adults (Donehower 2013) feel pulled between leaving, staying, or trying to negotiate some other kind of relationship with the place they call home. Literacy projects, such as the ADOHP, have the potential to encourage strong partnerships between rural schools and local colleges and universities.

The type of literacy that emerges in the ADOHP is akin to what Ursula Kelly, in *Migration and Education in a Multicultural World: Culture, Loss, and Identity* (2009), calls a "critical civic emotional literacy." Kelly argues that we need such a literacy to explore the emotional and ethical effects of neoliberalism, industrialization, and postcolonialism on attachments to both place and personal identity—particularly to places, many of them rural, that have been radically altered by these forces. Kelly acknowledges the emotional work, as well as the critical consciousness, needed to go beyond feelings of nostalgia or solastalgia about threatened places and to move toward "the urge to do right by that which has been lost, or gone: to repair" (109). (Whereas nostalgia is generally a positive emotion toward what has been lost, solastalgia involves feelings of anger or blame about places that have been destroyed.)

The possibilities of repair are greatly enhanced when literacy work can build coalitions among the people from a particular place and people who have come to feel connected to that place, and who wish to explore ways to stay connected to it. Critical civic emotional literacy needs to be experienced by all participants in the community project, from the Brown Chair in English Literacy that heads up the ADOHP, to the other university faculty and administrators involved in the project, to the graduate and undergraduate students who participate, to the K–12 teachers in the Delta schools, to the Delta students themselves.

Too often, however, scholarship about local contexts and the potential unwieldiness of bringing participants together can either remain abstract or so particular that imagining transferability can be difficult for readers. Not so with the ADOHP. From sharing candidly the logistical challenges of literally bringing college students and high school students together from far-flung places—and the pedagogical impact of such challenges—to grounding readers in the important historical and cultural context of the Delta, readers are able to witness negotiations and collaborations by various stakeholders as they seek critical civic emotional literacy. Even the structure of the book itself enacts the collaborative, participatory work by all involved, as the authors situate readers not just with theoretical underpinnings of the ADOHP but also with local histories themselves in ways that supplement, rather than overtake, the student projects.

The themes of the projects highlighted in the body of the book—religion, food, and race—allow the authors to best showcase how a critical civic emotional literacy was sought or achieved. To do so, the work is framed through the lens of David Gruenewald's (2003) reciprocal processes of "decolonization and reinhabitation," or challenging the education of dominant culture in seeking to repair inhabitation amid damaged spaces. Though not without challenges described along the way, readers learn about the process and products of the literacy endeavors with the goal of fostering change within classrooms and communities. The university student Laine Gates, for example, analyzes the impact for Delta residents of Act 1220, passed by the Arkansas legislature to reduce obesity. Gates conducted research on the histories of local and regional foodways, underscored by two interviews she did with high school women in the Delta that led her to concretely challenge the recommendations in Act 1220.

In chapter 5, highlighting ADOHP projects on race relations, the authors openly, and with an awareness of their own privileged positions, reveal the realities for many Delta students invested in studying race: the opportunity had simply not been provided to them a half century after desegregation. Resulting projects, such as a portfolio about a 1971–72 local boycott, demonstrates well how the structure of a program like the ADOHP invites work that engages decolonization. In the final chapter, the authors specifically address ideas of reinhabitation, or how projects like the ADOHP can move beyond its parameters to foster real economic change in a region, focusing on the ways storytelling and personal relationships are critical to efforts for sustainability on a range of fronts.

We first became aware of the work of the ADOHP when its organizers submitted a chapter describing the work in process to our edited collection *Reclaiming the Rural* (2011). We saw then that a project this bold in scope and purpose, bringing together many different constituencies across boundaries of place, race, socioeconomic class, and education, was likely to be fraught with many tensions. We know from our own work with college students that getting them to adequately conceptualize poverty, the challenges and possibilities of rural life, and literacy without resorting to stereotypes or "othering" is a tall order. The creators of ADOHP knew all of this, and they jumped into the fray nonetheless. You'll see that the ADOHP gave way to other exciting projects, which the authors describe as branches on the ADOHP tree. Not content to merely wrap up a successful five-year project, the ADOHP is being translated into further rural sustainability projects. As the authors argue, "Connecting community or region to a group of students holds tremendous potential for all parties involved." Creating learning opportunities like these should be the measure of schools much more than standardized tests. Dreaming big, plunging in, staying alert and aware of tensions and difficulties—and of possibilities—are all modeled for us here.

What we can most gain from reading this book is the kind of attitude required to undertake such work. It comes through, particularly in David Jolliffe's voice, on every page. We must be continually aware of the pitfalls of such projects, and go forth and do the work anyway. We must be ready to compromise some of our intellectual purity for achievements on the ground—perhaps cultivating a bit of nostalgia is a necessary part of sustainability work in rural places. We must stay optimistic and energized, and we can maintain these feelings by paying close attention to all the constituencies of projects such as these—to what they say, to what they want, to how they feel, to what they know, and to what we can learn.

Kim Donehower
Charlotte Hogg
Eileen Schell

Acknowledgments

THE FOUR COAUTHORS owe a debt of gratitude to the many people who supported the Arkansas Delta Oral History Project and the development of this book. We specifically note our debt to the other members of the ADOHP instructional team: Anne Pearson Raines, Catherine Roth-Baker, and Laine Gates. We humbly acknowledge the students, teachers, university students, and university personnel. Each gave their all so that this work could happen, ultimately providing worthy and interesting subjects about which to write: thank you.

David Jolliffe gratefully acknowledges the support of the Brown Foundation, the Walton Family Foundation, the J. William Fulbright College of Arts and Sciences, and the Department of English at the University of Arkansas. He particularly thanks Joy Lynn Bowen and Steven Collier of ARCare for their constant collaboration, and he deeply appreciates the assistance several colleagues have offered, particularly Eli Goldblatt of Temple University and Steve Parks and Eileen Schell of Syracuse University. He notes with love the unwavering support of his sisters—Joyce Wilcox, Ruth Ellen Parks, and Judy Fox—and his spouse, Gwynne Gertz.

Christian Goering thanks the fine staff at JJ's Bar and Grill in Fayetteville, Arkansas, who provided encouragement and nourishment that helped in the planning, organization, divvying up of tasks, and writing of sections of the book. Most of all, Christian thanks the people who were (Nana before she passed), are (Emily, Mom, and Dad), or will be (Katie and Zach) proud of this accomplishment.

Krista Jones Oldham thanks her family for their constant support: her parents, Michael and Ruth Jones; her sister, Jacqueline Jones; and her husband, Scot Oldham, whose support and guidance has proved immeasurable. Thank you for being supportive and caring throughout the whole process.

James Anderson thanks the members of the Department of English and the Program in Rhetoric and Composition at the University of Arkansas for their support, especially Patrick Slattery. James is forever thankful for his past teachers, especially Amelia Merritt, his aunt and high school English teacher, and Joan Smith Anderson, his mother and role model, both of whom taught in rural schools in North Carolina for over thirty years. Lastly, James would like to thank Dusty and Mirabelle for growing love and flowers at their home.

Introduction

THERE'S AN OLD ADAGE about writing about cultural immersion experiences, a pithy maxim that used to be invoked in the 1970s and 1980s when the People's Republic of China was gradually opening up to American scholars and to joint ventures with US universities. "If you go to China and stay a week, you think you know everything you need to know about the culture and you write a book about it," the saying went. "If you go to China and stay a month, you think you know a good bit about the culture and you write an article about it. If you go to China and stay longer than a month, you realize you really don't understand anything about the culture and you never write a word about it." Perhaps the same could be said about visiting and writing about any cultural milieu.

We, the authors of this book and a substantial team of collaborators, went to a region of Arkansas called the Arkansas Delta and essentially stayed for five years—though many of us continue to return to the Delta and work with blossoming projects that were planted in our initial foray in the region. We are not so bold to assert that we now know everything about the socio-political-economic-educational culture of the region, and sometimes when we look back over the years that our project ran, we wonder what we really do know for sure about the Delta. So perhaps we can characterize this book as encompassing what we *started to learn* and *continue to learn* about this fascinating, fecund, and fraught-with-trouble strip of east, central, and south Arkansas.

This book is about the Arkansas Delta Oral History Project, a five-year initiative led by the office of the Brown Chair in English

Literacy, an endowed position housed in the Department of English at the University of Arkansas. We began the project with a relatively simple, straightforward question: what happens when you ask high school students from small towns in the Delta to select a topic that they think is essential to the history, heritage, and quality of life in the region and then, mentored by University of Arkansas students, read, talk, and write about that topic as oral historians and "essayists," in the broadest sense of that term?

We quickly realized that a simple answer to this question could not do justice to the intellectual, psychological, social, and emotional work that these students would put into their projects. We learned several important concepts that we discovered we had to unpack in the book:

- When you give students the choice of writing about anything they want to write about, as long as it connects in some way to the region where they live, they tend to select topics that have an extensive social text—a history of legend, lore, conversation, iconography, and documentation—that the students realize they can write themselves into. Their topics tended to be like streams or rivers into which they could dive and swim and out of which they could jump and then describe the experience.
- A major, but considerably overlooked, source of invention for academic writers is just talking to people. As academics, we usually ask students to consult other texts and write about them, or less frequently to look into their own lives and write expressively about their thoughts and feelings. We too seldom say to students, "Go talk to someone who has an informed perspective on your topic and write about what you learned from talking to that person."
- Although some students say they can't wait "to get the hell out of Dodge"—to leave their hometowns or regions as soon as they can—not all feel this way, and even if they see themselves leaving home someday, they are mostly committed to making their towns and regions better places to live.
- Students—both high schoolers and university students—have had precious few opportunities to propose substantial projects

> of their own design, to carry out these projects over an extended period, and to produce "new knowledge" about their topics rather than simply reproducing knowledge they find in other texts.

Given all this, the terrain of *The Arkansas Delta Oral History Project: Culture, Place, and Authenticity* does indeed cover what happens when young writers are given relatively free choice of topics, but it also aims to explain the topical "streams" in which the students chose to swim, to show the importance of having young writers talk to informed and interested adults, to promote academic projects that could revitalize a troubled region, and to argue for the exigency of authentic work on the part of all students.

It would be easy for us to claim that the book comprises what we *learned* in response to these questions, but we think it more honest for us to admit that we have simply opened up veins of inquiry that continue to pump insights and perspectives into our consciousness. As we explain in chapter 1, the project, which we abbreviate as ADOHP throughout this book, raised thorny questions about the sociopolitics of any outreach program that might be construed as a school-to-college articulation and transition program, about the perceptions that university faculties and administrators apparently hold about what it means to "go to college," and the mismatches and tensions that arise when largely successful and affluent college students mentor high school students from generally poor milieus, from which relatively few students proceed to matriculate and graduate from college. While we introduce (and wrestle with) these questions in chapter 1, we would not be so bold as to claim we have come up with pat answers and easy fixes.

Similarly, it would be easy for us to claim from the outset that we knew specifically the nodes of literacy, composition, and rhetorical theory that the ADOHP would be draw on and contribute to, but that also would be an oversimplification. To be sure, as we explain in chapter 2, since the project would require students to consult nontraditional and noncanonical sources and to generate products that veered from normal school-based work, we knew that the ADOHP would tap into and speak to the literature of cultural studies. But we were delighted to learn along the way about the subfield of *youth* cultural studies and to discern that the identity-forming and shape-shifting functions that the subfield's scholars describe were indeed being manifest in the ADOHP participants' work. Because the project asked students to choose their own topics and to create *new* knowledge about them, we knew that we would be contributing material to theoretical discussions of student engagement and authentic intellectual achievement. We were pleased to learn, along the way, that our participants' engagement in the history, economics, politics, and social fabric of their home region linked our project solidly to a strong body of theoretical work on the relation between critical pedagogy and place. We knew from the outset that ADOHP student work, examining stories and lore from the region's past, might evoke a brand of nostalgia that could potentially impede critical examinations of the Delta's present and deliberations about its future. But we were delighted to formulate, along the way, a new (for us, as least) conceptual and theoretical node that explained a connection between the sense of loss that examinations of rural America often embody and a version of epideictic, celebratory discourse, examples of which abounded in ADOHP student work, that pointed to aspects of the region's life and culture that are worth preserving.

Chapters 3, 4, and 5—the heart, the core, the *coeur* of the book—give us the opportunity to showcase student work that fleshes out and exemplifies the energies, tensions, and theoretical nodes introduced in the first two chapters, but a prefatory note about these middle chapters is warranted: there is no way we could write about the scores of topics in the dozens of categories that students chose to write about, so we selected three topical areas—religion, food, and race—that we believe exemplified the best, most authentic place-based knowledge work in the project. Because we came to realize and admire the way the students wrote themselves into the social text of their topics, we devote considerable energy in each chapter to explain the "stream" in which the students are swimming as well as examine the student work.

Finally, as we explain in chapter 6, we are still growing projects that encourage engaged literacy work in the Delta, and we continue to learn about the palpable sources of energy and productive tensions that attach to literacy in these communities, and we strive to contribute to the several theoretical nodes. We hope you'll enjoy joining us on the journey that this book represents.

Part One
Foundations

1

Origins, Pedagogy, Potholes, and Fixes

IT'S A LOVELY APRIL DAY in Helena/West Helena, Arkansas, a city of about 12,000 people, with a handsome (but in need of renovation) downtown and a working (if not terribly active) shipping port on the Mississippi River. About 150 people are gathered in Helena, a sizeable crowd for any event there other than the annual King Biscuit blues festival. Two-thirds of the group comes from several small, mostly rural high schools in central and eastern Arkansas—students, teachers, parent chaperones, and their trusty bus drivers. The other third—college students and an instructional team—hails from the University of Arkansas at Fayetteville, five and a half hours by car and a figurative world away from the lives of many of the high school students.

In one room, a group of students from a media production class at Forrest City High School performs its original play, based on a true incident, about a white man who takes grief from his neighbors in the 1960s for selling his property to an African American family. Down the street in a second location, Katie Lambert, a University of Arkansas junior, screens her documentary video about Lily Peter, the first woman ever to manage a large farm on her own in the Arkansas Delta. At yet another site, a young man from Brinkley High School, dressed

Portions of this chapter first appeared as "The Arkansas Delta Oral History Project: Understanding Poverty through Literacy Outreach," in Kim Donehower, Charlotte Hogg, and Eileen E. Schell, eds., *Reclaiming the Rural: Essays on Literacy, Rhetoric, and Pedagogy* (2011). Reprinted by permission of Southern Illinois University Press.

in a vintage 1940s zoot suit, does his best imitation of Louis Jordan, a native of Brinkley, Arkansas, who gained international fame forty years before this youngster was born by "making the blues jump." On a stage overlooking the main downtown street, still another large aggregation, students in a domestic and consumer science (home economics) class from Marvell High School perform their original play, based on interviews, about how families in Marvell fixed and enjoyed regular dinners together in the 1950s, and how the families would make a special dinner when the preacher was coming over—and then they serve the fancy meal, which they cooked themselves, to the spectators. The high school and university students move from site to site, taking in the performances and celebrations of their classmates' and peers' projects.

This day and other iterations of it happened every spring from 2007 through 2012 as the annual culmination of the Arkansas Delta Oral History Project, a regional literacy initiative and a collaboration between the University of Arkansas and several high schools in a largely rural area of central, east, and south Arkansas known as the Arkansas Delta. The project combined service to the region with critical inquiry, not only into its history, traditions, and cultural patterns but also into its prospects and plans for the future—the "agenda, assumptions, and interpretations" (Flower 2008, 156) of the students, teachers, and citizens who populate the area.

The Arkansas Delta Oral History Project (ADOHP) was designed in part to confront a peculiar paradox in American literacy education. One of the tenets of the New Literacy Studies is that literacy is "always embedded in social practices, such as those of a particular job market or a particular educational context, and the effects of learning that particular literacy will be dependent on those particular contexts" (Street 2003, 78), yet literacy education does its darnedest to become generic. The educational testing movement—think the Iowa Test of Basic Skills, the National Assessment of Educational Progress, assessments emerging from the Common Core Standards movement—inherently says that every student in every location ought to be reading and writing about the same things and learning to read and write in exactly the same way. Pre-college programs (Advanced Placement, International Baccalaureate, and concurrent enrollment), articulation and transfer agreements, and all the online instructional programs essentially argue that it doesn't matter where or when you study reading and writing, the "skills" are all the same, and these school-based skills allegedly "transfer" to other arenas: jobs, citizenship forums, personal contexts.

Whether and how literacy "skills" transfer from one context to another—for example, from "general skills" reading and writing courses to reading- and writing-intensive courses in particular fields or disciplines—is a sticky issue, one that many educators tend to oversimplify (see Salomon and Perkins 1989.) It's not the brief of this book, however, to argue that literacy education needs to eliminate "general skills" reading and writing instruction (see Petraglia-Bahri 1995) or to speculate whether literacy education can ever hope to prepare students for all the contexts within which they might find themselves that call for extensive reading and writing.

It is the brief of this book—one of its purposes, at least—to argue that students, particularly secondary and postsecondary, ought to have at least some opportunity to learn about literacy-in-use-in-context, that is, to learn about reading and writing by engaging in a sustained, focused project in which their literacy education is both influenced by and in turn affects the social, political, economic, and cultural structures of a specific milieu. Educators have rarely realized the potential for a group of students in a particular location to take up a literacy project that can both capitalize on the educational abilities of the students, at their particular stage of life, and transform the cultural landscape of that location.

That's one of the things the ADOHP attempted to do. In the project, initiated by the Brown Chair in English Literacy at the University of Arkansas, undergraduate (and occasionally graduate) students who were studying the history, literature, and politics of the Arkansas Delta served as online and face-to-face writing coaches and mentors for students who attended primarily small, poor, rural high schools in the Delta. All the participating students—University of Arkansas mentors and Delta high school student mentees—engaged in the same process. They identified a topic exigent within the culture of the Delta. They engaged in a carefully orchestrated oral history project that led them to connect with residents—not only "institutional" people such as elected officials and teachers but also everyday, ordinary citizens who lived in the Delta—and to produce verbatim transcripts of their interactions. Then—and here is where we think the project achieved its leading edge—they got "literacy license." They wrote about their project in whatever genre they chose: an academic essay, a piece of historical fiction, a poem or series of poems, a play for stage or screen, a brochure, a webpage. Finally, they "performed" their final project for their colleagues and peers throughout the state, thereby raising to a conscious level and making available for inspection and discussion a broad array of historical and cultural issues about this region of the state that is struggling through an era of stark economic decline.

Our dual purposes for this chapter are closely related. First, we provide what might be termed an "origins story": a narrative about not only the origins and sponsors of the ADOHP but also the historical relationships that intertwine the University of Arkansas in Fayetteville, the "flagship" campus of the state's land grant institution; the people of Arkansas, particularly African Americans who live in the Delta; and the Brown Chair in English Literacy, an endowed chair at the university that assumed a mission of improving the quality of life throughout the state by involving citizens from all walks of life in reading and writing activities that they feel speak to their needs and goals, be they personal, professional, academic, or spiritual. Second, we describe in some detail how we "rolled out" the ADOHP: what we did right, what we did wrong, what we learned from our efforts, and what platforms we built for future projects. In short, this chapter tells a complicated, but we hope compelling and useful, story about what Deborah Brandt (1998, 166) refers to as literacy sponsorship, the process by which "any agents, local or distant, concrete or abstract, . . . enable, support, teach, or model, as well as recruit, regulate, suppress, or withhold literacy—and gain advantage by it in some way."

The origins story and the nuts and bolts narrative in this chapter set the stage for a central argument we develop throughout the remainder of the book: high school students from small, mostly poor rural communities can become central players in efforts to invigorate, revitalize, and generally improve the quality of life in their hometowns and regions. Developing this argument requires us to confront two related ideas that progressive thinking in the United States has promulgated about rural America: first, that it is a site of continual and continuing loss, and second, that it is, for successful citizens, a temporary way station in the path from rural to urban to suburban (and prosperous) living. The ADOHP tried to confront these prevailing ideologies head-on without condemning or condoning them. As leaders of a project situated in an economically declining region of the state, we could not encourage young people from the rural Delta to jump ship, abandon their home region, "get the hell out of Dodge." We could not blink at the concept of loss and the desire for movement that generally prevails in rural Arkansas—indeed, in rural America. Instead, we chose to confront the sense of loss by encouraging students to examine it directly. As a result, the students produced projects that might be characterized as nostalgic, but we tried consistently to emphasize that nostalgia serves not simply to glorify the past but also to point to ways that the future can be better. Therefore, we discovered that students, both from the participating high schools in the Delta and the University of Arkansas, primarily wrote epideictically, celebrating the narratives and the attendant values that shaped the past of the region as a means to argue that the region is worth revitalizing, saving, reinhabiting.

Two additional prefatory notes might be in order from the outset. First, about pronoun reference. When the text employs the first-person plural, the reference is generally to the personnel at the University of Arkansas who were centrally involved in designing and running the ADOHP: David Jolliffe, Christian Goering, and Krista Jones Oldham, three of the coauthors of this book; Anne Pearson Raines, Catherine Roth-Baker, and Laine Gates, who taught the ADOHP course described below with Jolliffe and Oldham; and James A. Anderson Jr., who conducted research on rural education that made its way into our manuscript. When the chapters use the first-person singular pronoun, as they do occasionally, the voice is that of David Jolliffe. We do our best to signal such shifts when they occur.

Second, about time. Readers might wonder why the ADOHP is characterized in the past tense—why, in other words, the project does not continue. All along, it was our intention to run the project for five years and then pause to reflect on it. This book is one of the manifestations of that reflection. But, as the final chapter makes clear, even though the ADOHP paused in its operation, the project continues to produce substantial community literacy projects in rural Arkansas, and a new iteration, this time named Students Involved in Sustaining Their Arkansas (SISTA), emerged as a pilot project in the spring of 2015, with a full-blown five-year version commencing in fall 2015.

The University of Arkansas, the Delta, the Brown Chair, and the ADOHP: Origins and Sponsorship

We began this chapter by positing that the University of Arkansas was literally five hours but figuratively a lifetime away from most of the high school students who participated in the ADOHP. As Shakespeare would say, therein hangs a tale. In this case, the tale involves a perplexing, and occasionally troubling, relationship that involves both institutions and the people represented by them: the University of Arkansas, the Brown Chair in English Literacy and its establishment and mission, the state of Arkansas, and the Arkansas Delta. Though it's embedded within the university, let's begin with the Brown Chair. (And, in this section, the voice is that of David Jolliffe.)

Since 2005, the Brown Chair has followed a mission of helping Arkansans of all ages and from all walks of life understand and take up the roles that careful, critical reading and effective writing play in their personal, educational, professional, psychological, and spiritual lives, and the chair has sponsored projects ranging from literacy workshops for parents and childcare providers to ACT test preparation sessions for high school students to oral communication modules for non-English-speaking clients of a community health center. The ADOHP was an early, major Brown Chair initiative.

The establishment of the Brown Chair at the University of Arkansas dates from 2003 when, as part of a large-scale capital campaign at the university spearheaded by Chancellor John White, the Brown Foundation of Houston, Texas—an organization with deep family connections to the state of Arkansas—donated $1.5 million toward the establishment of an endowed chair dedicated to addressing problems related to illiteracy in the state. The Brown donation was matched by another $1.5 million from the Walton Family Charitable Gift to the campaign, thus creating a $3 million permanent endowment. From the outset, the plan was to use part of the endowment's income to pay a portion of the chairperson's salary, but a substantial chunk of the proceeds was to be used for whatever programs and projects the chair would develop.

When I agreed to become the initial occupant of the Brown Chair in the spring of 2005, I really didn't have any idea what the job would entail. The English department, which houses the chair, had little history or experience in 2005 with graduate education in rhetoric, composition, and literacy. The department had one tenured faculty member who directed the composition program, taught one or two graduate courses a year, and led the only thing resembling a graduate concentration in the area, a secondary specialization in rhetoric and composition that, it was thought, would help PhD and MFA students in literature and creative writing get jobs.

Suffice it to say that I arrived at Arkansas with pretty much a blank slate for an agenda. The search committee knew something of my involvement with neighborhood school and family literacy programs in Chicago, which were partner organizations in the service-learning courses I taught under the aegis of the Steans Center for Community-Based Service Learning at DePaul University, where I worked from 1994 through 2005. Moreover, during the interview process I had garnered suggestions about the prospect of some kind of outreach program, and I had learned that an ill-defined (at least to me) area called "the Delta" was the region in the state that was the poorest, the most troubled economically, and the most populated by African Americans (except for Little Rock, which has a substantial urban black population). If I could do something in the Delta, it was suggested, the university, which constantly waged an uphill battle to diversify its student body, faculty, and staff, would be grateful.

So my first goal was to answer the obvious question: What is the Arkansas Delta?

The Delta: Former Economic Breadbasket Now in Decline

From a geographical standpoint, defining the Delta is apparently not a simple task. The Mississippi Delta Grassroots Caucus says the Arkansas Delta comprises forty-two counties, the watershed of which empties into the Mississippi River. To encompass this implausibly large definition of the region, one would essentially draw a line from the middle of the northern border of the state to the middle of the southern border, and everything east of that vertical line would be the Delta. No Arkansan would buy this definition. In contrast, the late Arkansas historian Willard Gatewood (1993) suggested a slightly refined characterization. Gatewood referred to the Delta as "a third of the state's counties," or twenty-five of the seventy-five counties (3). Presumably, Gatewood had in mind a triangle: Jefferson County (Pine Bluff is the county seat) its westernmost angle, the state's most northeastern point as the second angle, and its most southeastern point as the third. This view of the Delta is slightly more plausible—many Pine Bluffians would consider themselves residents of the Delta, and indeed the city is the home of the Delta Rivers Nature Center. Most Delta residents would argue, however, that the best definition of the Delta is the one promoted by the Arkansas Delta Byways Commission: the region comprises fifteen counties that either have a Mississippi River shoreline or sit between the river and an odd geological feature, Crowley's Ridge. This crescent-moon-shaped bump, the geological origins of which are disputed, stretches from just south of Cape Girardeau, Missouri, to Helena/West Helena, Arkansas, and is the only high ground in the otherwise flat alluvial plane of the region.

The most influential geological feature of the Delta is not so much the flat plane as it is the rivers: the Arkansas, the White, the Cache, the St. Francis, and, of course, the Mississippi. These rivers flood regularly, and receding flood waters always produce a superabundance of rich soil, so the Delta economy has always been agricultural. Cotton has consistently been a strong crop in the Delta, even though only two counties, Phillips and Chicot, had anything resembling the big plantation culture that one associates with the antebellum South (see Whayne 1996). Especially after the Civil War, when profit-minded lumber concerns deforested the region significantly, the newly cleared lands proved a fertile home for rice, soybean, and sorghum grain (or milo) crops. An old saying seems true about the Delta: the soil is so rich that you can toss out a pound of nails and harvest a bucket of crowbars.

There is nothing resembling a big city in the Delta. One might claim that Jonesboro, with a US Census Bureau 2010 population of 60,489, represents something of a population center in the north end of the region, while West Memphis, with a population of 26,245, provides a hub in the center, and Helena/West Helena, two municipalities merged into a single city in 2000, anchors the southern end with a combined population of 12,949. Most of the rest of the burghs are small farming, river, or railroad towns. There was a time, according to Gatewood, when many of these towns were bustling: they had main streets—often two of them, one for whites and one for blacks. They had shops and businesses. They had restaurants, movie theaters, even opera houses.

But a true triple whammy hit the Delta. First, as in many other sites in rural America, the Interstate came in the 1960s and whizzed past the small towns, moving commerce—generally franchises and big-box retailers rather than locally owned enterprises—either to larger cities or to malls on the bypass outside of town. Second, the agricultural economy that dominated the region was victimized by the twin forces of mechanization and globalization. The cotton plantation that used to take one hundred people to operate now employed three or four people. The Delta cotton that once upon a time was sold directly to the textile mills in the Carolinas now had to compete with cotton grown in South America and Asia. Third, the economy essentially converted from family agriculture to big agribusiness.

As a result of these three sets of forces, despite some rare bright spots in the Delta economy, the region is clearly troubled: businesses go under, industries shut down, populations dwindle, schools suffer. As Gatewood put it, one clearly notices "the deterioration of the human condition in the Delta. Virtually all the usual indices, from per capita income, unemployment, and housing to health, teenage pregnancies, and school dropouts, provide a statistical portrait of a people in distress" (23). Even a cursory look at demographic data confirms Gatewood's view. According to the University of Arkansas Division of Agriculture's *Rural Profile of Arkansas 2015*, between 2000 and 2013, when the population of the state grew by 9.5 percent, the Delta lost 11 percent of its population. The total number of jobs in the region dropped by 1,780 between 2007 and 2012. The average median household income between 2008 and 2012 was $31,153, and 26.6 percent of the Delta population lived in households under the scandalously low federal poverty level of $24,450 for a family of four. In the Delta, 76.5 percent of adults hold a high school diploma as the highest level of educational attainment, and only 11.3 percent have at least a bachelor's degree or higher.

Tropes reflective of decline sit at the center of public discourse about the Delta. For example, the homepage of an organization called Arkansas Delta Made, which promotes "goods and cultural offerings" produced in the region, refers directly to the area as "a region in a cycle of decline." The organization charged with economically rehabilitating West Memphis features this sentence on its homepage: "West Memphis, like much of the Arkansas Delta, is suffering from years of economic decline" ("Main Street West Memphis"). Perhaps nowhere in the Delta is this discourse of decline stronger than in Phillips County, of which Helena/West Helena is the county seat. According to census data, Phillips County lost 17.1 percent of its population between

2000 and 2010; in 2010, 32.4 percent of its population lived under the federal poverty level; and the county lost 22.8 percent of its private, nonfarm jobs between 2000 and 2009. Phillips County is the focus of the Delta Bridge Project, an initiative sponsored by Southern Bancorp and designed to revitalize the economy, education, and health care in the region. Notice the discursive predominance of decline in the most recent strategic plan (2010–20) of Delta Bridge:

> Many rural residents steeped in tradition are slow to embrace change, even in the face of positive impacts. The transition from labor intensive agriculture to mechanized agriculture has largely run its course, and the legacy of such an economic system is an under-educated and untrained workforce and an economy that has failed to diversify in compliance with the requirements of a 21st century global market place. Phillips County continues to suffer from political turmoil, the education system will take time to fix and the rate of job creation has failed to stem the tide of negative outmigration. Increased criminal activity threatens local perceptions about community improvement and casts a negative light over an otherwise successful development program. (Delta Bridge Project 2009, 8)

And yet the Delta keeps on trying. Communities institute civic improvement projects, school systems bring in new curricular programs, economic development commissions try to entice new businesses and industries to locate there. The Delta residents, and those who care about them, realize that here is a region with a storied past. They know the Delta as home to a rich ethnic mix of populations, both those who came to the region willingly to make a home and those who were brought there in servitude. They know the Delta as a place where the religious roots of southern American culture, particularly the Protestant ones, run deep and wide. They know the Delta as a region where the family traditions of cooking, putting up vegetables, sewing, hunting, and fishing get passed on from generation to generation. They know the Delta as the locale where, as Gatewood puts it, “people are likely to emphasize manners and exhibit ‘the small courtesies’” (25).

The Delta, the University's Diversity Initiatives, and "Your Work with Those Kids"

As I learned about the Delta and visited its communities, I quickly gathered that the students—indeed the residents in general—of the region were frequently portrayed as the sources of "diversity" in many of the initiatives under way in Arkansas designed to achieve this goal. I'm still not certain whether the establishment of the Brown Chair was connected to a particular University of Arkansas diversity scheme or whether I just thought that it should be and made it so. But it was clear to me from the day of my arrival that the university had worked very hard for a long time, with comparatively little success, on achieving more diversity—which generally translated to recruiting more African American students and faculty members.

From my reckoning, the university initiative regularly encountered four impediments to success. First of all, location: the University of Arkansas is located in the far northwest corner of the state. (From my home in Fayetteville, I can be in Oklahoma in 30 minutes and in Missouri in 45.) In a largely rural state with a substantial population that never went to college, families often don't want their children to go too far away from home to school, and the children generally accede to this desire. The county seats of the five counties in Arkansas holding an African American majority (Chicot, Lee, Phillips, St. Francis, and Crittenden) are located between four and five hours from Fayetteville, and it's simply difficult to get students to want to go to college that far away from home. Second, history: in Arkansas, there had been a version of state-sanctioned racial segregation within higher education that somehow residents could never quite forget. In 1875, just four years after the establishment of the Arkansas Industrial University (now the University of Arkansas in Fayetteville), the state legislature provided funding for a Branch Normal University in Pine Bluff, a city with a substantial African American population and an economic hub of south central Arkansas. Branch Normal was founded primarily to prepare African American teachers to work in the state's segregated schools. Over the years, Branch Normal underwent many transformations as a historically black university, most significantly being renamed Arkansas Agricultural, Mechanical, and Normal College in 1927, but even after joining the University of Arkansas system and being renamed the University of Arkansas at Pine Bluff in 1972, it maintained its reputation as the default higher education institution for African Americans in the state. There remains an unspoken tenet in Arkansas that the state founded what has eventually become the University of Arkansas at Pine Bluff so that African American students wouldn't want to attend the University of Arkansas at Fayetteville.

Third, the region's racist past, and perhaps its present: Northwest Arkansas itself had (and perhaps still has) a reputation for being an unsafe location for black folks. The region was the home of more than one community that people referred to as "sundown towns," meaning that residents—not the civic government, but private residents—would make it known that, if you were black, you shouldn't be in town after dark. As one neighborhood sign in a town near Fayetteville that I choose not to name said, "Don't let the sun set on your black ass around here." Fourth, the Nolan Richardson story: even with the university tucked away in the northwest corner of the state, folks throughout the state are rabid fans of University of Arkansas sports teams, especially football and basketball. In the latter, the university gained national renown in the 1990s under the guidance of Nolan Richardson, the first African American head coach of any major sport, both at the University of Arkansas and in the Southwest Conference. In 1990 Richardson's team made the Final Four in the NCAA basketball tournament, in 1994 it won the national championship, and in 1995 it was runner-up to the national champion, UCLA. In the second half of the decade, while his team continued annually to capture a spot in the sixty-four-team NCAA tournament, Richardson became increasingly uneasy with what he perceived to be an atmosphere of racism and racial discrimination at the university, and, at loggerheads with the administration, he openly dared the athletic director Frank Broyles to fire him. The university did indeed fire Richardson in 2002, claiming that his public commentary about his treatment signaled that he had "lost confidence" in the basketball program. Richardson quickly sued the university for racial discrimination, a suit that was dismissed in federal court in 2004. Lots of dirty linen was aired publicly in these legal proceedings, and especially in African American communities throughout the state, there was a feeling that the university had been at fault. When I was being recruited to come to the university, a dean told me this story: "I go to families of excellent African American students and tell them how much we'd like their son or daughter to come to the U of A. And they say to me, 'I appreciate your interest, but I couldn't dream of sending my child to your university, considering what you did to Nolan.'"

So it was in this milieu that the Brown Chair was launched. Here was a brand-new endowed chair, urged at least tacitly to reach out to the region of the state with a substantial African American population but housed at a university and in a region with lots of obstacles to overcome vis-à-vis interacting with that population, and created to do work in an academic area in which the chair's home department had little experience, no curricular program, and no explicitly stated expectations for the position.

Was the glass half empty or half full? The potential obstacles, the four impediments, were clear. But I could certainly shape the mission of the chair on my own and take its operations in any direction I wanted. Once I started showing some interest in working with communities in the Delta, I would frequently get pats on the back—literal and figurative—in which the patters would laud my "work in the Delta" and my "concern for those kids in the Delta." I saw these affirmations as a strong green light.

My Immersion in the Delta: Traveling the State from Day One

I began learning about the Delta from my earliest moments at the university because the dean who hired me excused me from teaching during the first year of my appointment. He and I agreed on this plan: I would spend the year traveling throughout the state, getting to know the lay of the land in terms of literacy. So I hopped in my car and, beginning in September 2005, traveled far and wide throughout

Arkansas. I met teachers, principals, and district superintendents. I met leaders in local economic development councils. I met philanthropists and foundation administrators. I met museum coordinators and education directors. I met directors and funders of job training programs. I met librarians. I met writers and owners of bookstores. I met musicians, actors, painters, and sculptors. I met medical professionals involved in health literacy. I met bankers involved in financial literacy. I met leaders of state and local literacy councils. I met parents. I met school kids.

It's impossible to explain, in short measure, what I learned on these trips. But for starters:

- I learned that, in terms of socioeconomic and educational geography, Arkansas comprises five relatively distinctive regions. In no particular order, they are: (1) Northwest Arkansas, a five- or six-county region where Walmart Home Headquarters, Tyson Foods, J. B. Hunt Trucking, and the University of Arkansas have created a high-employment, rich-quality-of-life environment with a Caucasian majority, a burgeoning Hispanic population, relatively few African Americans, good schools, and good arts. (2) Little Rock and its suburbs, the hub of state government with all the amenities one would expect in a metropolis of about six hundred thousand, but with a troubled racial history dominated by the famous 1957 Little Rock Central High School desegregation incident. (3) The piney woods of southwest Arkansas, with no substantial population center of gravity. (4) The great chunks of rural, sparsely populated areas in north-central Arkansas, where generations of mostly Scots-Irish immigrant families have farmed the land. (5) The Delta—home to a good bit of old, white landowner money, a relatively small (and shrinking) middle class, and a substantial African American population, many of whose families had settled there to work as slaves before the Civil War or as sharecroppers afterward.
- I learned that Arkansas really couldn't lay claim to a particular author or piece of literature that was emblematic of the state. To be sure, Maya Angelou had grown up in the small town of

Stamps, Arkansas, and depicted it in *I Know Why the Caged Bird Sings*, and John Grisham had been born in Jonesboro, Arkansas, and had drawn a vivid picture of Delta poverty in *The Painted House*. But Arkansas has no author who served as a metonym for the state as did, for example, William Faulkner for Mississippi, Mark Twain for Missouri, or Flannery O'Connor for Georgia.

- I learned that the state of Arkansas is a solid supporter of private-market literacy-improvement programs designed to raise students' scores on standardized tests, the results of which are generally treated as gospel throughout the state. So when education professionals in the state think "literacy," they think "adequate yearly progress" on tests and slickly marketed curricular and pedagogical packages for schools and students not making "AYP."
- I learned that, in the aftermath of school desegregation, which was not completely accomplished until the early 1970s in pockets of the state, an alternative private-academy movement emerged, producing schools in many towns in the Delta to which families, generally Caucasian, could send their children.
- I learned that, with the exception of the Agricultural Extension Service, the University of Arkansas has almost no intellectual or educational presence throughout the state, and particularly not in the Delta.
- I learned that opportunities for public engagement in activities that might enrich the literacy environment were rare outside Northwest Arkansas and the Little Rock region. There were public libraries, but I didn't get the sense that many towns supported, for example, public book clubs or public discussion forums. Movie theaters were open only in towns larger than ten thousand or so, and those theaters generally only showed first-run, big-studio pictures. Museums were rare, and what museums there were generally showcased the founding frontier culture of the towns and regions that housed them. As far as I could tell, local theater groups or touring theater companies were very rare.

- In the high schools, I perceived what I have come to call the demise of the literacy co-curriculum. Once upon a time, most schools would have some collection of these five things: student newspapers, literacy magazines, speech and forensics teams, yearbooks, and drama programs. As populations decreased and standardized testing increased, many—in some cases, nearly all—of these activities disappeared from the schools. Generally, the only one of the five entities one could count on finding was the yearbook, but that was often undertaken by a faculty member rather than students. As a result of this demise, students lived in what I could only characterize as an impoverished literacy environment. They learned to encounter consciously "the world of the word" only in English classes, where the curriculums were generally dominated by teach-to-the-test pedagogies that emphasized the barest rudiments of reading comprehension of text excerpts, not whole texts, and extremely formulaic writing that called for little deep thought and no challenging argumentation. This is not to say that the young people I encountered were not called on to take up tasks that required extensive reading and writing. In twenty-first-century culture, it's impossible for adolescents who are making their way toward educated, responsible adulthood to avoid situations that are dominated by what I call "languaging problems"—situations that call for them to use their reading, writing, and speaking abilities to frame problems that need solving and develop solutions for them. As I got to know the state, I was regularly impressed by young people's attempts—and relatively often their successes—to use a range of literate abilities to understand issues, propose solutions, and develop plans of action in such venues as 4-H competitions, Future Farmers of America and Future Business Leaders of America activities, and particularly in Arkansas schools projects sponsored by Environmental and Spatial Technologies (EAST) classes.

All of these points swirled through my thinking during the first year and a half of my time at Arkansas, when the contours of the ADOHP began to emerge. Both my own personal predilections and the urging of folks in the University of Arkansas convinced that me I needed to do something in the Delta first and fast. As I have repeatedly explained to people who wonder why I initially focused (and have continued to focus) on Delta communities, it's not that there aren't lots of places in Arkansas where the intersection of economic decline and literacy is exigent and troubling, but there's no place in the state where this intersection is *more* exigent and troubling than it is in the Delta. I knew I wanted to do something that would empower young writers to begin *creating* texts, artistic and "ordinary," about their hometowns, home regions, and home state. I wanted to generate a project that would enrich the students' intellectual lives but that wouldn't rely on some reductive test to tell lawmakers how much the kids had learned. I wanted to lead an initiative that would benefit students in mainstream public schools. (If you want to know who are the children left behind that No Child Left Behind was meant to help, I'd urge you to visit a community where either a private school or a corporately funded public charter has harvested the very best students and heaped ample resources on their teaching and learning. Those left behind are the kids in the mainstream public schools.) I wanted to signal an intellectual, humanistic University of Arkansas presence in the Delta communities, a presence that wasn't connected either to athletics or to agriculture—both noble enterprises in their own right, but certainly not representing a full picture of what the land grant university in a rural state ought to be providing. And, most important, I wanted to bring the world of the word alive for these students in ways that traditional high school English classes, with their emphasis on excerpts of American and English literature from the standard canon or on undemanding young adult literature didn't seem to be accomplishing. In short, there were lots of issues sticking in my craw as I dreamed up the ADOHP.

Jump-Starting the ADOHP: Staff, Students, and Sites

With the resources of my endowed chair, for which I remain constantly grateful, I was able to hire a wonderful staff to help me get the ADOHP under way. Given her extensive knowledge of life in the Delta—she had been born in McGehee and had lived, at various times, in Helena, Pine Bluff, and Forrest City—and her interest in innovative teaching and learning experiences, Anne Pearson Raines, director of tutorial services for the Enhanced Learning Center at the University of Arkansas, became a codirector of the project. Through Anne, I met Krista Jones (now Krista Oldham, one of the coauthors of this book). Krista was a graduate student in the Department of History at the time, specializing in southern US history generally and Arkansas history in particular. She became another codirector of the project. I was fortunate to find such colleagues. I would joke that Anne had lived at one time or another in every town in the Delta and that Krista had read every book and article about the Delta. With Anne and Krista in the fold, we added a third codirector, Catherine Roth-Baker, a wonderful creative writer in my department's famous MFA program.

We had to accomplish two major tasks in the fall of 2006 in order to launch the ADOHP in spring 2007. First, we had to find participants in the Delta. Largely through people I had met in my travels the previous year and Anne's personal acquaintances, we made contact with folks we knew at five high schools in the Delta: Forrest City, where the superintendent, Lee Vent, had made me feel so comfortable and where Anne Raines had lived while teaching at the local community college; Lee County, located in the small town of Marianna, where I had gotten to know the economic development council members; Marvell, the high school closest to the tiny burgh of Elaine, Arkansas, site of a famous post–World War I race riot; McGehee, a small farming town in the very southern tip of the Delta and Anne's hometown; and Pine Bluff, still something of an economic hub in the center of the Delta and home to the largest of the participating high schools in the first year. To the leadership—the principals and the superintendents—of those schools we offered this proposal: We could not work with the entire school, but we could work with one teacher and one or two of the teacher's classes. We didn't want teachers to be required to develop any new lessons, texts, or materials for the ADOHP, unless they wanted to. We simply wanted teachers to use oral history as a teaching method. We envisioned teachers looking at their readings for the second semester and, in consultation with us, identifying topics in the texts that are still vibrant and viable in our century. Then we hoped that they would guide students to conduct oral history projects about those topics. For example, suppose a text being assigned was Chinua Achebe's *Things Fall Apart*, in which a central character had gained his political status as an adult in large measure because he had been a successful athlete in the village. Students could then, we proposed, investigate via oral history the extent to which leaders in their own towns and regions had gained their renown at least in part from their fame as athletes. (It didn't quite work out that way, but that's what we had in mind.)

The superintendents and principals in these five districts were happy to become part of the project, and they readily assigned teachers at each school to be our contacts: Steve Murray and Ima Fleming-Foster at Forrest City, Ruth Mitchell at Lee County, Yogi Denton at McGehee, Delores Smith at Marvell, and Brenda Doucey at Pine Bluff. To help these teachers prepare to build the project into their second-semester course, we convened them for a daylong getting-to-know-you session in Little Rock. We all—the teachers and the University of Arkansas teaching team—stayed in the same hotel, took our meals together, and talked at great length about what the project would entail.

In addition to recruiting and helping the teachers prepare, we also had to bring the participating communities into the conversation about the project before it launched. After all, in five communities, high school students would be engaging in a type of behavior rarely seen these days: they would be going into communities, identifying citizens from all walks of life who had informed perspectives on their topics, and interviewing them. With the help of our participating teachers, we had public open houses in all five communities, inviting folks not only from the schools but also from churches, service clubs, not-for-profit organizations, and local government. In McGehee, for example, the open house was held at the local museum, a converted railway station, and drew a substantial crowd of local history buffs. In Pine Bluff, the open house at the school was visited by the mayor, who offered the assistance of his administration in getting the project off the ground. In no community did we experience anything but warm enthusiasm from the local constituencies.

Finally, we needed to recruit a group of University of Arkansas students who would be the initial cadre of mentors. Our first source for such students was the university's Honors College where the new dean, Bob McMath, openly encouraged honors students to participate in community-outreach and service opportunities whenever they could. Anne and Krista were also well positioned to recruit students. Anne was associate director of the Writing Center and had met a wide range of excellent students there, and Krista was actively involved in the undergraduate history organization. We had no problem recruiting an initial group of seventeen students, mostly English, history, and anthropology majors.

And We're Off! Courses in Motion at the University of Arkansas and in the Delta Schools

While the ADOHP can be perceived as a regional literacy project or as an ambitious high-school-to-college articulation initiative (on the latter, see Jolliffe 2010a), at its most basic level the ADOHP was a course, actually a set of courses, one taught as an undergraduate colloquium at the University of Arkansas and others in range of content areas at the participating high schools.

As we suspect is true with most experiential-learning courses, the ADOHP course at the University of Arkansas looked good on paper: it had a solid syllabus, serviceable readings, and an array of challenging assignments. Similarly, as we at the University of Arkansas described the ADOHP to teachers (and their principals) who agreed to bring their students into the project as participants, it seemed a big venture but not an insurmountable one. We wanted the teachers to help their students, collaborating with University of Arkansas mentors, to propose and carry out oral history and literacy projects of the students' own design. We told the participating teachers what we planned to do *for* and *with* them, and we explained what we expected they could do to make the project a success. (Appendix A contains our introductory communication with teachers and principals.)

Despite our good intentions, we quickly realized a truism that other scholars of "public-turn" experiential courses in composition and literacy (Mathieu 2005, Flower 2008) have described: once you begin incorporating human beings as active shapers of the curriculum and pedagogy—that is, once a class becomes something more than a teacher and students with traditional texts and assignments—all sorts of intricate strains, involving changing minds, changing lives, changing communities, and changing power relationships come into play. Most of the tensions involved social, economic, educational, and political differences between the University of Arkansas mentors and the Delta high school students, and between Northwest Arkansas and the Arkansas Delta, tensions that often proved difficult to dissipate but that ultimately taught everyone in the project more than they had imagined they would learn. We persevered and developed a couple of aspects of the program, which we describe below, that helped to stabilize a good bit of the helter-skelter occasioned by these strains.

Nuts and Bolts: How the ADOHP Worked

The logistics of the project were relatively straightforward. We invited schools that participated in the first two years, but after that word of mouth began to generate interest among other teachers and principals in Delta high schools. The project was never hyperselective. If a teacher or principal wanted his or her school to participate, we were happy to extend an invitation. After the first year, schools were invited into the project for a two-year cycle: during the first year they would be "novice schools" and during the second "mentor schools."

We couldn't accommodate working with an entire school's student body, so each participating high school agreed that in one class, the teacher would use oral history as a teaching method. The teacher did not need to alter what he or she was planning to teach for a semester. That is, no matter the content of the course, the students:

- identified a topic that in some way involved local history, legend, or lore;
- did some background research on the topic;

- identified someone with a unique perspective on the topic whom they could interview;
- planned, practiced, conducted, and transcribed the interview verbatim; and then
- wrote a final project of their own design—an essay, a story, a series of poems, a play or video script, a brochure, and so on—that grew out of the interview.

The steps in the first four bullet points are, of course, standard operating procedure in oral history projects, and the ADOHP relied on clear descriptions of the steps in Glenn Whitman's *Dialogue with the Past: Engaging Students and Meeting Standards through Oral History* (2004), published by the American Association for State and Local History, and in Pamela Dean, Toby Daspit, and Petra Munro's *Talking Gumbo: A Teacher's Guide to Using Oral History in the Classroom* (1998), produced by the T. Harry Williams Center for Oral History at Louisiana State University. The final step converted the oral history enterprise into a full-fledged literacy experience, pulling together all the students' readings, interviews, drafts, collaborations, and rewriting experiences in a substantial final project. Many oral historians simply produce transcripts. The ADOHP called for the transcripts *plus* the students' substantial written work that grew out of them.

A central concept underlying the students' final project was *choice*. As we explain further in chapter 2, we wanted students to choose to produce whatever genre seemed appropriate for their project, embracing a pedagogical component that scholars argue contributes to identity formation and student engagement.

Though the University of Arkansas course didn't begin until January of each year, the ADOHP staff met with the participating high school teachers in the fall and provided them with a student manual—essentially a brief textbook—to help them build the project into their ongoing courses. (We reprint the text of the manual in Appendix B.) It substantially addressed eleven questions:

1. What is oral history?
2. How do you focus on potential topics and interview candidates?
3. How do you arrange for the oral history interview?

4. How do you do background research?
5. How do you plan the interview?
6. How do you develop effective questioning techniques?
7. How do you role-play a mock interview before the real interview?
8. How do you conduct the actual interview?
9. How do you record the interview?
10. What should you do immediately after the interview?
11. How do you create a transcript of the interview?

Although the ADOHP staff presumed that the entire manual would be helpful for the students, we thought that the sections answering questions 2, 6, and 9 were most congruent with the project's emphases on youth cultural studies, critical pedagogy of place, and authentic intellectual work, concepts that we unpack in chapter 2. The question-2 section led students to focus on the history of the region, the chronology of their potential interviewee within this history, a "decision tree" for that person or his or her organization showing the person's or organization's vital life turning points, significant events in the region, stories they had heard mentioned but that had never been fleshed out for them. The question-6 section, in addition to introducing students to the "big-six" questions (who, what, when, where, why, and how) that are the journalist's key prompts, also taught students important differences among four other types of probes:

- An evocation question, which asks the interviewee to tell you "how it felt" or "what was it like" to be in a situation.
- An influence question, which asks, "Why was X such an influential presence in your life?"
- A meaning question, which asks the interviewee specifically to describe the meaning he or she attaches to an experience.
- A "who else" question, which seeks to discover who else could have been there to corroborate the story.

The question-9 section emphasized the importance of fleshing out fragmentary notes as quickly as possible after the interview and of drafting a "what did I learn" composition, even a brief one, while the interview was fresh in memory. In short, the manual urged the students to think: What issues simmer in the lifeblood of this region?

How does the region itself affect these issues? How can I construct knowledge about these issues, not simply reproduce knowledge?

The high school courses were as diverse as the teachers who taught them and the communities that housed the schools. At some locations, for example in Cindy Gutridge's course at Augusta High School, which joined the ADOHP in year two, the project got embedded in a relatively traditional eleventh-grade American literature class, and the students' projects represented their major work in composition during the first half of the second semester. Brenda Doucey at Pine Bluff High School incorporated the project into an elective creative writing class taken by juniors and seniors. She helped the students focus during year one on the history of the desegregation of their school, a common theme for many of the participating schools, as we explain in chapter 5. In year two, the Pine Bluff students examined the disintegration of businesses in downtown Pine Bluff. Brenda's primary concerns, teaching the techniques of writing fiction, poetry, and drama in this class, are evident in the student work. Yogi Denton at McGehee High School made the project an integral part of the work students did in an eleventh-grade Advanced Placement English language and composition course, requiring students to settle on topics during the fall semester and then coaching them through their writing of short fiction, poetry, and essays about their topics during the spring. Mary Meacham at Brinkley High School, which joined the project in year three, built the ADOHP into an Environmental and Spatial Technologies (EAST) course, one that required community service and service learning and was thus a happy home for the ADOHP. Perhaps the most unusual home base for the project was at Marvell High School, where Delores Smith taught the ADOHP as part of a family and consumer science (formerly known as "home ec") course. As chapter 4 will show, the Marvell students capitalized on their curricular home base by doing fascinating oral histories of regular and fancy meals in the 1950s.

At the same time that the high school students were taking their courses, the English, history, and anthropology departments at the University of Arkansas at Fayetteville offered a cross-listed undergraduate colloquium designed to help students meet these learning goals:

- To understand how oral history complements more traditional historical methods and provides a rich portrayal of local history and culture;
- To comprehend how the history, politics, economics, and demographics of the Arkansas Delta shape the region's current status;
- To develop their own in-depth perspective on a selected aspect of the history and culture of the Arkansas Delta; and
- To learn about adolescent literacy by interacting both in person and via the Internet with groups of students from high schools in the Arkansas Delta.

The University of Arkansas course was taught by a team consisting initially of David Jolliffe, Anne Pearson Raines, Krista Jones, and Catherine Roth-Baker. Beginning in year two, the teaching team included Laine Gates, who was an undergraduate participant in year one and then matriculated as a graduate student in cultural anthropology.

The University of Arkansas students read Jeannie Whayne and Willard Gatewood's edited collection *The Arkansas Delta: Land of Paradox* (1993), an anthology of ten substantial essays by a distinguished group of Arkansas historians, and Margaret Bolsterli's memoir, *Born in the Delta: Reflections on the Making of White Southern Sensibility* (2000). They relied on *Dialogue with the Past* and *Talking Gumbo* to develop their individual projects, following the same steps as the high school students, who had been introduced to the project's stages and placed into their writing groups at the semester-opening meeting in Helena described below.

The major assignments in the University of Arkansas course fell into two categories, the mentoring and outreach activities and the response papers. The requirement for the latter was robust. First, for every reading assignment, each student posted two discussion questions on the course web-based discussion board at least twenty-four hours in advance to allow time to incorporate the questions into class discussions. Second, selected students for each class session wrote and posted two-page responses to the reading assigned for that day. Third, selected students for each day wrote and posted one-paragraph responses to a designated discussion question.

Similarly, the mentoring and outreach activities were multilayered. There were only three times during the semester-long course when the University of Arkansas mentors and the Delta high school students met face-to-face. At the first encounter, at the beginning of the second semester, the university students and their Delta counterparts all traveled to the University of Arkansas Community College at Phillips County (UACCPC) in Helena. The meeting, which we describe in more detail below, was designed to establish rapport and lay the groundwork for a good working relationship between the university mentors and their Delta charges. At the second encounter, the early March "Fayetteville weekend" described below, the Delta students traveled to the university and the writing groups met for in-progress work on their projects. At the last encounter, in late April, having traveled back to Helena, the university students and the Delta high schoolers gathered to perform and celebrate the work they had done during the entire semester.

Supplementing the face-to-face interactions was the operation of the online writing groups. Each university mentor was assigned to work with four or five students from the Delta high schools—the groups generally comprised students from different schools so they could learn about how their counterparts in different towns were dealing with the project. The groups were expected to "meet" asynchronously once a week; that is, the Delta students were expected to log in to the university's Blackboard site at least once a week and respond to a prompt, following a schedule provided by the university mentor, who was expected not only to monitor and orchestrate the discussion but also to serve as a resource to the high school students as they finished their projects. Each university student ultimately wrote a substantial final reflective essay that synthesized their insights gleaned from reading the course materials and from working with the high school students.

Meetings, Topics, and Tasks

The kickoff event at the UACCPC was a big deal. Helena, Arkansas, is five hours from the University of Arkansas, so the university students and their faculty mentors would ride in vans across the state the night before and stay at one of only two motels in Helena, the Best Western. The high school students and their teachers would get up early and board school buses to travel to Helena, which was, for some participating institutions, four or five hours away from their home base. Once everyone got to the UACCPC, the meeting consisted of four hourlong workshops that introduced the participants to the defining characteristics of an oral history project, to best practices of planning and conducting an oral history interview, to options for converting an interview transcript into a creative final project, and to the logistics of participating in online discussions about one's ongoing project.

Lots of ice-breaking had to happen at this initial meeting. The participating students were assigned to four- or five-person writing and working groups, mostly made up of folks from different schools. A University of Arkansas mentor was assigned to chair each group. Here was an initial tension: high school students, many of whom had never traveled out of their hometowns or counties, encountering students from other schools and meeting their new mentor, who in many groups was from a very different socioeconomic and ethnic background. The ice would break slowly over the course of this opening day, but it eventually did break.

After getting to know one another a bit, each group was given an agenda for the project, detailing when participants should have selected a topic, finished their background research, selected an interviewee, drafted interview questions, practiced the interview, conducted it, transcribed it, and started working on their final projects. Here, for example, is a sample agenda:

DATES AND SUGGESTED DEADLINES FOR THE PROJECT

Week One	Opening workshop at Phillips County Community College in Helena: Please have a topic for oral history project selected by this date.
Week Two	Deadline to select an interviewee.
Week Three	Deadline to have first draft of questions.
Week Four	Deadline to have practice interview completed.
Week Five	Deadline to have actual interviews completed.

Week Seven	Working trip to University of Arkansas, Fayetteville.
Week Eight	Deadline to have follow-up activities ("What did I learn?" text and Thank-you letter to interviewee) completed.
Week Ten	Deadline to have transcription of interview completed.
Week Twelve	Deadline to have first draft of final project completed.
Week Fourteen	Closing celebration and performance, University of Arkansas Community College at Phillips County.

At the end of this opening day, the students would return to their respective institutions with the agreement that each student would, at least once a week, log on to Blackboard, the University of Arkansas's electronic discussion platform, and share drafts, ask questions, participate in discussions—in general, work together on the project. To motivate these discussions, we provided a list of starter prompts. Here is a typical list:

WEEK OF:

January 28	Introduction: Who are we? What are our first thoughts about the project?
February 4	What person are we thinking of interviewing and why?
February 11	Whom did we select to interview? What are our impressions and concerns about our interview questions?
February 18	What are we nervous, anxious, excited about concerning the interview?
February 25	How did the practice mock interview go? What will we need to do differently in the actual interview?
March 3	U of A students report on their interviews or progress. Delta students provide feedback.
March 10	Delta students report on their interviews or progress. U of A students provide feedback.
March 24	Open topic: whatever needs to be discussed. Remind students to send thank-you letters to interviewees.
March 31	What kinds of concerns do we have about our transcriptions?
April 7, 14, 21	Conversations about developing drafts of final projects.

The "Fayetteville Weekend"

As is evident from the agenda of deadlines and the list of discussion-starter prompts, after about six weeks of this kind of group activity on the project—everyone in his or her home school, ideally following the project agenda, logging on to the discussion forum regularly, and sharing ideas and drafts—all participants traveled to the second encounter, "the Fayetteville weekend," an intensive two days of face-to-face group work, campus activities, and fun.

On Friday, the visiting students from the high schools arrived in Fayetteville by early afternoon—having traveled up to five hours by school bus—to tour the campus and meet with university admissions and academic officers. At the end of Friday afternoon, the visitors checked in at their home base for the weekend, Mount Sequoyah, a residential conference center near the university campus run by the United Methodist Church but open for business to any visiting groups. After dinner at Mount Sequoyah, the high school students always wanted to see Fayetteville, so an evening excursion to the Northwest Arkansas Mall would be in order. (Some students lived up to four hours away from the nearest mall and were fascinated to spend time in one.) On Saturday morning, the writing groups convened to work on their emerging projects—only the second time the groups had met face to face—sharing stories of finding interviewees, conducting and transcribing the interviews, and so on. On Saturday afternoon, as we detail below, the weekend's conceptual center of gravity would emerge in a three-hour workshop called "From Page to Stage," conducted by the local playwright and director Bob Ford. On Saturday night, the whole group would take in some aspect of the cultural scene in Fayetteville. In the first year, for example, the students saw a superb university theater production of Nzotake Shange's *For colored girls who have considered suicide/When the rainbow is enuf*; in the second year, they participated in a slam poetry and dance workshop; in the third year, they attended a theatrical showcase of the "greatest hits" of African American theater; in the fourth year, they saw a professional production of *Underneath the Lintel* at TheatreSquared, the local professional theater company.

The magic, the enchantment of live theater—which regular theatergoers too often take for granted—was usually palpable among the visitors from the Delta, many of whom had never seen a play performed. A wonderful moment, for example, transpired at the end of *Underneath the Lintel*, a quirky one-person play in which a librarian solves a riddle related to a book that was returned 113 years after it was due and to a laundry ticket found in the book. After the curtain call ended and the house lights came up, a very robust student named Austin, who played defensive tackle for the Augusta High football team, sat there, tears in his eyes. He turned to his teacher, sitting beside him, and said, "I never want to go home." We trust he was inspired by the magic of live theater rather than moved to reject his hometown roots.

On Sunday morning, everyone would return to his or her home school invigorated and ready to bring the project to a conclusion. Working in their online writing groups again, the students moved from interview transcripts to creative stories, essays, poems, plays, and so on.

The Concluding Celebration

In late April, the whole group reassembled for a final face-to-face encounter, again in Helena, for a day of celebration and performance of the final projects. It was a beautiful, glorious day on the banks of the Mississippi. In three venues—the Miller Hotel on Cherry Street, the Delta Cultural Center's outdoor stage, and the Delta Eagle Room in the train station—sixteen presentations from high school students, some individually and some in groups, and twelve solo presentations from University of Arkansas participants unpacked the projects. In plays, videos, essays, poems, and stories, they told tales of farming, floods, tornadoes, hunting, music, medicine and home remedies, food and foodways, integration and school desegregation, voting and civil rights, and the lives of military veterans in the Delta.

Many of the topics students chose to focus on in year one—farming and the land, desegregation and civil rights, natural events and disasters, food customs, social rituals, and music, for example—returned as continuing favorites in the following years. Moreover, the range and quality of ADOHP student work expanded in subsequent years. Later, groups of students ushered in projects on the origins and growth of African American churches in the Delta, the rediscovery of "vanished" municipalities, little-known legends about historic structures in small towns, and the duck-hunting and fishing traditions, to name just a handful of topics.

Potholes: Tensions We Should Have Anticipated but We Eventually Learned From

We approached every aspect of the ADOHP with unbridled and, in retrospect, naïve enthusiasm. We anticipated that both groups of students would light up at the prospect of proposing, designing, and developing their individual projects; that they would turn on to the idea of communicating about their emerging projects not only within their school boundaries but also across those boundaries, connecting with the participants from the other institutions; that, being digital natives, they would enjoy the chance to go online and engage in lively conversations about their communities, the oral history project, and their evolving work with the other members of their writing group. We got some of what we expected, but we also encountered considerable obstacles that we somehow had to smooth out or drive around.

First of all, we need not downplay the infectious enthusiasm that the project bred among both the University of Arkansas students and their Delta counterparts. The university students' reflective papers generally resonate with this positive buzz. For example, James Ardis, who had previously been an ADOHP high school participant before matriculating at the university, wrote, "I don't think I've ever been this engaged with fellow classmates at any level of school." Similarly, Lori Neuemeier offered this reflection: "For me, this project has been invaluable. It has been a lot of work (and writing the transcription was probably one of the most tedious experiences of my life), but I have loved having so much agency in my own work. I have never taken a class quite so interactive, or one that depends so much on my own initiative."

Erin Robertson's reflection eloquently captured the gusto she sensed at both outposts of the project, the university and the Delta: "This project is tender and tentative, and yet means more to these students than we all probably realize. . . . More and more, I am humbled by the opportunity to work on such a great project—and more and more I realize that these kids are teaching me more than I could hope to impart to them."

She was aglow about the verve and focus of the participants in her group: "Our students were completely tuned in to what was going on at our table [during the Fayetteville weekend group meeting] and proved this by crafting intelligent and intentional questions about their respective projects. They surprised me with their deep interest in doing the project and doing the project well."

Without specifically using the phrase, Robertson focused on the aspect of mentoring that takes the form of what James Paul Gee calls "shape-shifting" (2002, 52), a concept we unpack in some detail in chapter 2:

> I have found that these students are approaching their projects with diligence: not only are they interested in their subjects, but I believe they feel some positive pressure from us as college students, almost as if we are holding them accountable to succeed. In conjunction, they seem to thrive on the smallest bit of independence and freedom allotted to them, even in the most seemingly mundane details of when and where to conduct an interview. I have been impressed with the students' display of responsibility in these projects, and I can tell that they regard their current and future work with seriousness and gravity.

In short, the University of Arkansas students found themselves mentoring their high school charges not only about their evolving ADOHP projects but also about more general topics—academic success, the prospect of going to college, the nature of daily life on the University of Arkansas campus.

High school participants were similarly affirmative in their evaluation of the project. Lori Browning, who attended Augusta High School, lauded the project because it led to her "meeting new people and delving into the state's history." Anna Paige Frein, a participant from Brinkley High School, affirmed that "the opportunity to interact with college students allowed me to have a glimpse into the life of college students and made me even more excited to attend the University of Arkansas." She noted that, from the very first meeting in Helena, she realized that "this experience with the Arkansas Delta Oral History Project was the first time that many of the students had been exposed to the idea that they could go to college." She added, finally, that "from this project, I learned that I was actually proud of being a Delta native."

Despite this level of enthusiasm and commitment, however, we frequently experienced "traction" problems in forging good communication about the project between the University of Arkansas mentors and their Delta charges. In short, often it was just plain difficult to get the high school students to log on to the discussion platform and talk about their work, and if they did so, they frequently wanted to comment only to the University of Arkansas student group leader, not to their peers. The course leaders hypothesized—correctly, we believe—that despite our efforts to encourage an environment of peer inquiry and community, the Delta high school students were seeing the university mentor as an ersatz teacher and, therefore, felt compelled to report in only to this "authority" figure.

Many of the University of Arkansas students, not long out of high school themselves, sensed discontent among some of their Delta charges, manifest as a tendency not to meet project deadlines and a blatant hesitancy to participate fully and willingly in the Blackboard discussions. One university mentor offered this assessment of the situation:

> Judging by the overwhelming lack of turnout in the chatroom, I feel that these high school students are either overworked, lazy, or intimidated by the project. I understand, because I would have been anxious at the prospect of doing an entire project by myself, even if it was spaced out over a semester. However, with a mentor, I would have been just fine. I also wasn't very analytical, only giving regurgitated information and the most basic of reasoning. I and all my

> classmates really only did the minimum work necessary. I can see that these students aren't any different.

Another University of Arkansas mentor attributed the malaise about the project and school in general to the environment of the Delta public schools, of which he was a veteran:

> Even with a load of what are supposed to be our best and brightest teachers, with Teach for America, students still look apathetic. Many of the students seem continually zoned out and glassy eyed. I can only guess that this has come about due to years of teachers passing them ahead without addressing the problems they had in those grades. When I talked to students in my high school group about college, none of them had ever considered really going.

Yet another University of Arkansas mentor saw the roots of the problem not solely in the Arkansas Delta but also in the essential isolationism of American education:

> It seems that everyone is very independent in regard to their own projects. . . . I think this is because throughout our years in school, we've all been taught to work on things by ourselves and not rely much on the help of others. Personally, I think this is a travesty on behalf of the education system in America. People should learn how to work together. It is an important skill in the workplace and life in general. And, sadly, one we're not trained in enough by most teachers. I think it is great that the Arkansas Delta Oral History Project is stressing the value of teamwork and idea-sharing. We college students are in need of this just as much as the high school students are.

In a retrospective interview at the end of the project, Mary Meacham, the teacher at Brinkley High School, summed up the interaction problem this way: "The project was just so new to the students. They'd had very little experience with collaborative work, and they were a little shy about sharing their work with college students. They considered the U of A students the 'experts'—they didn't know that the U of A students were learning along the way, just like they were."

We found a helpful perspective on the tensions and communication roadblocks that emerged between the university mentors and the high school students in the work of Richard A. Settersten Jr. and Barbara Ray (2010), who review the ways demographic shifts, psychosocial concepts, and a handful of misconceptions affect educators' perceptions of young adults' access to higher education. Without falling victim to stereotyping that might lead to self-fulfilling prophesies, let us posit that, as a group, the University of Arkansas mentors were generally successful students who had already figured out how to navigate college. Many were enrolled in the Honors College, and many came from middle- and upper-middle-class families. Even to be admitted to the University of Arkansas requires a composite score of twenty or higher on the ACT examination. In contrast, the students from the participating high schools frequently came from poverty—only one school with whom the project worked over the five years of its existence did not qualify for the 90 percent free-and-reduced lunch allowance—and they hailed from communities where a substantial proportion of adults do not hold college degrees. The high school students ranged in academic abilities, but time and again we encountered students who ranked in the top 10 percent of their classes but whose ACT composite scores were in the upper teens. Considering these two groups in light of Settersten and Ray's work sheds some light on the potential mismatches we had to overcome.

Settersten and Ray unpack four major demographic shifts occurring over the past half century that affect young adults' access to higher education. First, they interrogate the "independent living" assumption—the idea that "youth leave home early and never return"—showing how we have entered an era in which more and more young adults continue to live with their parents and families (115). The University of Arkansas mentors were living the myth—they had left their family homes, established their lives in Northwest Arkansas, and were looking forward to their next domestic moves after graduation. The Delta high school students were still living in their home environments, and we found out from their online questions that independent living was a real mystery to them. Often the high school students queried their mentors with such questions as, "What kind of parties do you go to?" and "What is your dorm room like?" Second, Settersten and Ray examine the phenomenon of "widespread aspirations" for college. They note that whereas two-thirds of all high school students expect to earn a degree from a four-year college and a quarter expect to earn a two-year degree, students' perceptions about their own readiness for college, the directions their college education might take, and the costs of attending college are not fully fleshed out. The University of Arkansas mentors had generally either come to college ready for its rigors or developed the requisite readiness, they had by and large made decisions about their major and minor courses of study, they were dealing with the costs. All of these elements were mysterious for the high school students (116–17). Third, Settersten and Ray focus on the scarcity of family financial resources. Noting that parents and guardians of young adults, no matter their economic status, tend to devote about 10 percent of their income to their young adult offspring, Settersten and Ray point out that 10 percent of a family income of $40,000 is considerably less than 10 percent of a family income of $200,000 (120–21). We would hazard that the University of Arkansas mentors generally could expect a figure more resembling the latter than the former. Fourth, Settersten and Ray display what might be termed "disconnection" data: the percentage of adults aged eighteen to twenty-four who are "not in school or the military, not employed full time, and have only a high school diploma": 24 percent of African Americans in this age range are in this category, as are 29 percent of Native Americans and 20 percent of Latinos. Twelve percent of Caucasians are "disconnected," and only 7 percent of Asians are (12–22). Given the typical demographics of the ADOHP, we can guess that the students from the Delta high schools probably knew lots more people in this "disconnection" pool than the University of Arkansas mentors did.

Settersten and Ray unpack a pair of psychological concepts, and again we profit from contrasting our two groups in light of these tenets. First, Settersten and Ray label "the need to manage uncertainty" as a "hallmark" of young adulthood. The willingness of the University of Arkansas mentors to sign on to a service-learning course requiring them to interact with students whom they didn't know in a region with which they were not familiar signaled to us the mentors' openness to the unknown. We feared that a similar prospect of the uncertain and unknown was not so comfortable for the Delta high school students. Then Settersten and Ray describe young adults' "need for interdependence": the development of "wide and strong relationships with other adults, supportive ties that can be activated as needed to access opportunities" (123). The mentors had professors and advisers at the university, many of whom helped them land part-time and summer jobs and get internships; they had circles of largely successful friends; they usually had supportive parents and families. The Delta high school students too often lacked these resources.

Settersten and Ray see two frequently invoked tropes about higher education and young adults as misconceptions that impede access to higher education: the notion that the college years are the ideal years of "exploration and growth"—they may be for financially secure students, but not so much for working- or middle-class folks—and the assumption that "the middle of the last century" was "normal" in terms of going to college (124–26). For many students today who struggle to go to college, let alone to persist and graduate, the "normal" may be far removed from the myth of the student who matriculates at eighteen, lives at school, graduates at twenty-two, and enters the workforce.

The new "normal" may be the status quo we saw so frequently among the Delta high school students: they saw both independence and interdependence as unfamiliar territories, they struggled with getting ready for college in terms of both academics and finance, they tended to shy away from exploring the unknown. In this state of affairs, it's small wonder they often shut down in the face of needing to interact with generally ambitious, well-heeled, well-spoken mentors from the flagship university, located hours away from them in a part of Arkansas that is very different from their home region.

In hindsight, we should have seen these tensions coming since several of these themes resonate with observations from seasoned professionals in community literacy. From the earliest moments of scholarship about service learning—for example, in Bruce Herzberg's (1994) cautionary tale about his students' proclivity to see social problems they encounter as strictly personal rather than systemic—the literature redounds with narratives and explanations of mismatches between the providers and the recipients of literacy-outreach service courses such as the ADOHP. Linda Flower's (2008) consideration of these dynamics in her community literacy project in Pittsburgh is particularly germane. Flower's take on the interface between university participants and community participants illuminates the problems that result when dominant ideologies embedded in traditional schooling interact with the sudden presence of university "experts" who descend into the site of literacy work. Flower points to the "stultifying, limited literacies demanded in urban schools [and, we could argue, in rural schools as well], workplace training, and many workplaces (focused only on learning and playing by the rules)" that portray the writer as only "meeting institutional expectations . . . with little hope of making a difference in either a personal or a public arena" (20). She perceives the difficulties that arise when "the 'university' arrive(s) with its vanload of white, middle-class, educated outsiders, short on savvy, long on good intentions, and comfortably invested in their own set of elite, academic, literate practices" (23). When these two cultural groups interact, Flower maintains, "community members typically exist as *participants* in social projects, not as *partners* with expertise who must be respected as agents in their own right" (28, emphasis in original). As a result, when university community literacy missions aim to mesh with constituencies separated from the university by distance, resources, and ideologies, the "university students seem perplexed about their role in a public sphere or rhetorical community," and the community participants might "consider the notion meaningless if not patently absurd. The notion that adults [or older college students] would listen, much less that these teens' own ideas and writing might matter and might even provoke serious thought or change, fit little in their experience" (43). The sociocultural forces that Flower explicates certainly seem to us a plausible explanation for the communication difficulties we encountered.

As an antidote to the unidirectional communication (or communication breakdown) that can result from such a dynamic, Flower calls for "intercultural inquiry and collaborative problem solving." A successful community literacy project, she argues, "calls for a hybrid discourse and for rhetorical competencies that are rarely developed in public schools, college composition classes, public debates, or community organizing" (40).

The community literacy scholar and practitioner Paula Mathieu (2005) offers a perspective similar to Flower's in an attempt to "come clean" about service learning. "The people we work with in the streets don't live or think in terms of semesters or quarters or finals or spring breaks," she writes (99). Too seldom, according to Mathieu, do community outreach projects "consider the community as a source of expertise, and acknowledge and seek to work rhetorically with the specificity and limitations of space and time" (106). As the ADOHP proceeded, we worked consciously to see, and treat, the participating high school students as partners in the project rather than simply as participants offering opportunities for the service part of our service-learning venture.

Three Retooling Strategies: Ruby Payne, Page to Stage, and Direct Instruction Prompts

As the ADOHP developed in the years following its exciting but often tension-riddled initial years, we knew we needed to retool the entire enterprise—the course, the web interactions, the face-to-face meetings—to mitigate these roadblocks we kept encountering. We added or emphasized three elements that helped to open channels of communication: to teach the University of Arkansas students a bit more about the effects of the myriad differences between them and their high school mentees, to enfranchise more fully the voices of the high school students from the Delta, and to put all participants on a more even teaching and learning ground, one not so completely definable as "teacher" and "student." Reading Ruby Payne's (2005) work on poverty brought to the surface a range of relatively helpful, but ultimately limited, perspectives about the ways intergenerational poverty affect student success. Bob Ford's "page-to-stage" workshop provided a live, real-time bonding experience. Anne Raines's direct instruction prompts offered pathways to better talk in the online writing groups.

Reading Ruby Payne: A Preliminary, Marginally Helpful, Step

Given our assumption—one supported by Settersten and Ray's work—that at least some of the communicative tensions we encountered stemmed from socioeconomic differences between the university mentors and the high school students, we began in year three to ask the University of Arkansas class to read Ruby Payne's best-selling book *A Framework for Understanding Poverty* (originally published in 2001, now in its fourth edition). Payne, a former public school teacher and administrator, takes a taxonomic view of her subject, enumerating and unpacking the characteristics of poverty in a way made popular by Stephen Covey's (1989) explication of "the seven habits of highly effective people." (Payne herself quotes Covey twice in *A Framework for Understanding Poverty*.)

Payne begins by defining poverty as "the extent to which an individual does without resources" and then proceeds immediately to subdivide "resources" into eight categories: "financial, emotional, mental, spiritual, physical, support systems, relationships/role models," and "knowledge of hidden rules" (8). She returns regularly to this list of resources later in the book.

Payne's next move is to explain "the role of language and story" in understanding poverty (27). Citing a linguistic theory popularized by Martin Joos (1962) in his book *The Five Clocks*, Payne notes that "every language in the world has five registers"—"frozen," or "language that is always the same," such as "the Lord's Prayer" or "wedding vows"; "formal," or "the standard syntax and word choice of work and school," characterized by "complete sentences and specific word choice"; "consultative," a "formal register . . . used in conversation" with a "discourse pattern not quite as direct as formal register"; "casual," or "language between friends . . . characterized by a 400- to 800-word vocabulary," in which the "word choice [is] general and not specific" and the "sentence syntax is often incomplete"; and "intimate," or the "language between lovers or twins" and the "language of sexual harassment" (27). Payne argues, citing contrastive rhetoric research, that "the majority of minority students and poor students do not have access to formal register at home" and indeed that "these students cannot use formal register" (28). These students, Payne suggests, default to casual register not only in word choice and syntax but also in "discourse patterns"—Payne defines a "casual-register discourse pattern" as one in which the "writer or speaker goes around the issue before finally coming to the point" (30)—and in "story structure"—Payne characterizes a "casual-register story structure" as one that "begins with the end of the story first or the part with the greatest emotional intensity," is interrupted by "audience participation," and "ends with a comment about the character and his or her value" (31).

Payne also offers an extended definition of "generational poverty," the state of "having been in poverty for more than two generations" (47). Many of the defining features of generational poverty are the same as those explained under "poverty" in the "hidden rules" taxonomy. For example, in both the hidden rules of poverty and the generational poverty definition, "personality" is seen as "the ability to entertain, tell stories, and have a sense of humor" (51) rather than the propensity to value achievement, as it is in the middle-class hidden rules, or to value "financial, political, and social connections," as in the hidden rules of wealth (43).

Payne proceeds with her excursus on resources by arguing that "emotional resources" come from "role models" that lead a child from "dependence" to "independence" and eventually to "interdependence" (64–65); by explaining that "support systems" fall into "seven general categories," ranging from "coping strategies" and "options during problem-solving" to "positive self-talk" and "procedural self-talk" (70–71); and by focusing on the "cognitive strategy" of "mediation," in which the person tapping into this resource learns three steps: "identification of the stimulus," "assignment of meaning" to the stimulus, and "identification of a strategy" to deal with the stimulus (90).

Several critics of Payne's work have surfaced over the past few years (Gorski 2006; Ng and Rury 2006; Osei-Kofi 2005), the most vocal of whom is a group led by Randy Bomer, professor of education at the University of Texas, Austin. In a 2008 *Teachers College Record* article, "Miseducating Teachers about the Poor: A Critical Analysis of Ruby Payne's Claims about Poverty," Bomer, Joel Dworin, Laura May, and Peggy Seingson criticize Payne both for the ideas presented in *A Framework for Understanding Poverty* and for the impact she has allegedly had on teachers and the broader educational community. Chief among their criticisms of Payne is that she purveys an unsubstantiated deficit-thinking model in dealing with the poor. The authors further hold that, given the huge popularity of her book (over eight hundred thousand copies sold) and professional development seminars and lectures for teachers (she has appeared before teachers in thirty-eight states), Payne is misinforming teachers about the nature of poverty and poor students. Bomer and his colleagues analyzed the discourse of Payne's text, seeking to determine "what patterns are detectable in Ruby Payne's truth claims about children's lives in poverty" and "to what extent are those truth claims supported by existing research" (2). Examining each sentence for truth claims—those that made specific claims about reality—they created four superordinate headings under which to categorize Payne's tenets: social structures, daily life, language, and characteristics of individuals.

In each category, the central problem they found with Payne's formulations was the same: deficit thinking. The authors explain: Deficit thinking "holds that students that struggle or fail in school do so because of their own internal deficits or deficiencies" (2523). In deficit thinking, when a pedestrian is hit on campus, it is his or her fault for not looking before walking in front of traffic. A deficit thinker does not consider that the pedestrian might be deaf, at a crosswalk, or that the driver could have been impaired by text messaging and speeding when the accident happened. Rather, a deficit thinker moves toward blaming the victim instead of investigating the conditions of the accident. In *Rural Literacies*, Kim Donehower, Charlotte Hogg, and Eileen

Schell explain the deficit model too frequently held out as a means of understanding people in rural situations is a stereotype: "Life in rural America is seen as 'lacking': lacking education, lacking economic opportunities, lacking cultural opportunities" (14).

Bomer and his colleagues suggest some of the most damaging potential effects of Payne's work are in the perceptions that poor people need to be "fixed." "She pathologizes the 'culture' or 'rules' of the poor and valorizes the 'culture' or 'rules' of the middle class" (6). They argue that at a school level, "teachers are called upon, then, to narrativize and envision the lives of poor children in the way that Payne suggests, so that they can have certain kinds of ideas about those children and use particular language in speaking to them and their parents" (6). Leveling a summative claim, they assert: "Teachers may be misinformed by Payne's claims. Poverty in Payne's work is marked only as negative, only as a divergence from a middle-class norm, and students who are 'of poverty' need to be fixed" (13).

The Payne-Bomer tension represents the backdrop against which we asked the University of Arkansas mentors to write about their perceptions of how poverty and class influenced the lives of the Arkansas Delta high school students whom they were mentoring. We hoped our students would begin to interrogate the complex relationships involving social, political, and economic forces that influence high school students' educational practices and goals in rural Arkansas. As we explain elsewhere (Goering et al. 2011), our students' reflections seemed to provide them a deeper level of understanding, one that made communication with their high school mentees more productive. After one year of asking our students to read only Payne, we added Bomer et al. to the course reading list.

Bob Ford's Page-to-Stage Workshop: "Everyone on Your Feet!"

Ford's three-hour workshop was held on Saturday afternoon of the yearly "Fayetteville weekend." Ford is a true polymath: a playwright, novelist, and musician who serves as artistic director of TheatreSquared, the award-winning professional theater company based in Fayetteville. It would be an understatement to assert that Bob is an excellent teacher and an even greater understatement to characterize the page-to-stage workshop as transformative. In three hours of contact with all the ADOHP students, both from the high schools and the university, Ford managed to bring the writing groups into focus, ratchet up the quality and quantity of their interactions, and help many of the students envision a productive path from their interview transcripts to their final projects, whatever form they might take.

During the Fayetteville weekend, Saturday was a relatively nonstop working day. In the morning, the writing groups met again—face-to-face for only the second time during the semester. This meeting gave participants the chance to catch up with their colleagues on their progress and to fill in some of the gaps caused by their hesitation or neglect to post to the group online. There was also ample time during the morning for students to do some additional writing about their projects on the spot and to share and discuss their work immediately afterward. A quick lunch served as the prelude to Ford's workshop.

At first blush, the workshop resembled pandemonium: all the high school students and their University of Arkansas mentors convened in a large assembly hall on Mount Sequoyah, gathering in a huge circle, usually of around sixty people. Ford began with some elementary theater games using volunteers from the circle: simple improvisation exercises, basic collaboration tasks (for example, "I'd like you three to get this chair moved from one side of the room to the other without saying anything or touching it yourself"), some vocal warm-ups.

Once everyone was focused and ready, Ford divided the entire crowd into writing groups. To these collectives, Bob explained the basic template for creating compelling narratives: "Somebody wants . . . but . . . so." In other words, there is a central character with a goal, a desire, a motivation to act; there is an obstacle, someone or something getting in the way of that goal; the character, either alone or in collaboration with other characters, devises some course of action that supersedes this obstacle so that the main character—and perhaps his or her collaborators—can achieve the desired goal. Ford gave each group a chunk of time to work together—not much, perhaps 15 or 20 minutes. The group's objective was to take one person's work on the project so far—the background research and the interview—and create a five-minute play that finds and puts "on stage" the project's dramatic potential. Then the groups would start performing, with Ford stopping along the way to affirm and praise, shape action, suggest revisions, and allow the participants whose project was not selected to talk with the group about what they might do themselves to find the dramatic potential in their work.

The workshop ran for nearly three hours, with only minimal breaks for bathrooms and beverages. Amazingly, the focus, the purpose, and the students' diligence never flagged. They stuck with it from the beginning to the end. And equally amazingly, a great many students discovered in the process embodied in page-to-stage the initiative and motivation to move their projects from inchoate stories, often buried deep in their interview transcripts, to texts, verbal and visual, that examine and celebrate the Delta.

In a retrospective interview, Ford reflected on why this workshop got so many students off the dime—why it pushed so many of them to work more collaboratively with their writing groups and to move their individual projects toward completion. "The moment you start inhabiting this world, saying those words through the mouth of a character," he explained, "something starts happening in a part of your brain that rarely gets used within the four walls of a traditional classroom." He connected what the students accomplished in the workshop to what kids always do when they play—they make up stories. "To take a story and move it into the world of drama is something that you can do quickly. We don't have to use such terms as protagonist and antagonist, although we eventually do. We simply ask the students, 'Who are you? What do you want? What do you need? Who or what is getting in the way?' Just these three things—a character, a need, and an obstacle—and now you've got a play."

Ford's assessment of the "magic" of the workshop pointed to why it was so successful in moving students' projects toward completion: "Everyone has a character when we get in that big circle. And here's the first magic moment: you walk up to a kid and say, 'Who are you?' Some of them get it right away. And the others, when they do, the magic clicks. All that need to be cool, all that 'oh, this is silly' is gone. When everyone is with it, when something's on the line, when someone they know is engaged, then the whole process is alive."

A veteran teacher of acting, directing, and playwriting, Bob realized that for a great majority of the participating high school students, the workshop is completely new pedagogy, but he was adamant in his praise of the students' work: "The magic of it is the kids themselves—that's what I wasn't expecting. The talent that emerged was stunning, especially the proportion of it. If you take any group of a hundred or so kids, you might find six or seven with a real penchant for drama. But with these kids, I was flabbergasted—everyone wanted to do it, and especially the ones who were initially so reluctant. I've never seen a kid who didn't throw himself into the process, or at least show up honestly and diligently."

Ford particularly noted the intensity and focus the students brought to projects that touched on issues of race in some way: "Some of the stories are so full of passion, and some of the civil-rights-era stories that come out, and the level of acting—the level of dropping everything and becoming totally invested in the stakes of the moment—it's all so unusual. I mean, I struggle to get this with my acting classes here."

Curiously, Ford's surprise at the creativity of the students' work with these issues was not always shared by their teachers. He related this anecdote: "I remember going up to one of the teachers and saying, 'This is phenomenal—this connection to the stakes of the moment—I never see that.' And he replied, 'Well, they know that. They've seen that. They've seen the struggle.'" Ford added: "I don't mean to generalize, but they're living on the edge."

Ford readily conceded that what he did with the ADOHP students in three hours on a spring day on Mount Sequoyah is not out of the ordinary for students from larger, more affluent schools that have full-fledged drama programs. Indeed, the page-to-stage workshop brings into focus what might be characterized as the demise of the literacy co-curriculum brought about by high-stakes, No-Child-Left-Behind testing. As districts and schools have come under increasing pressure for their students to perform well on tests of reading comprehension and basic, expository writing, co-curricular activities such as drama, speech and forensics, literary magazines, and student newspapers have taken a back seat to students-in-their-seats classroom instruction, with a heavy dose of test preparation served up. Ford eloquently assessed the ill effects of eliminating drama as an integral part of literacy education:

> It's crushingly tragic that schools don't at least use drama as an outlet, if not as the major medium for breathing life into literature. Look at what we do in just three hours. If you could stretch that out over a year, look at the lens you're putting on yourself, your heart, your community, your world. It's shocking that educators don't recognize the value of what happens with drama. If we can't bridge between, say, a multiple-choice test on vocabulary and how society is using the same words as are on the test, then we're doing the kids a great disservice. What happens in that room is the absolute heart of education. You see someone take on a character—take a point of view. Everyone is looking at the world through some other person's eyes and starting to understand. If education isn't about taking on the perspective of others—what was life like for our ancestors? What is life like in Papua New Guinea—then what is it about? What better way to get at these questions than to say, "I'm going to utter the words of that person and see what that feels like, saying them out loud."

ADOHP was fortunate to have Ford's leadership of the page-to-stage workshop for the project's entire five-year run. If he could bottle and sell his "magic" to other literacy-outreach initiatives, we maintain, he would have lots of takers.

Direct Instruction Prompts: Paths to Better Writing Group Talk

In addition to the page-to-stage workshop, we thought that the ADOHP participants, both University of Arkansas students and the Delta participants, needed something more ongoing and heuristic to keep the peer inquiry going strong. Therefore, we retooled the emerging ADOHP by providing explicit instruction to the university tutors on how to get the Delta high schoolers to communicate and collaborate with one another. As we noted above, the writing-group problems were twofold: not only were students hesitant to sign on to Blackboard once a week, as directed, but even when they did, they were wont to communicate only with the University of Arkansas student leading the discussion. Of course, this communication pattern contradicted directly our goals for the project, namely, for the students from the different high schools to learn from one another about their towns, their issues, their concerns, and their progress. We were probably naïve to assume that our students, both from the university and from the Delta, would just naturally slip into productive conversations, as if they were fast friends and regularly cooperating classmates. Clearly, our students needed some guidance.

One of the ADOHP codirectors, Anne Raines, served as director of tutorial services at the Enhanced Learning Center (ELC), a center on the University of Arkansas campus that offers academic assistance and support for courses throughout the undergraduate curriculum. About the same time that we began to experience our communication problems, the ELC had adopted a pedagogical method called direct instruction, also called explicit instruction, for use in one-on-one and group tutorials. As the direct instruction expert Douglas Carnine (2000) puts it, "Instruction is explicit when the teacher clearly, overtly, and thoroughly communicates to students how to do something" (np).

In the spirit of explicit instruction, Anne designed a guide to help the University of Arkansas mentors get the Delta students talking to one another, not just to the authority figure of the mentor. She began the guide with eight "things to remember" when leading writing-group interactions:

1. Get students talking to one another about the project.
2. The type of questions you ask affects the feedback/answers. Ask higher order/open ended questions. (See below.)
3. Avoid the role of "teacher" or "authority."
4. Remind the students you are completing the same steps of the project as they are.

5. Refer to the timeline for completion of the project.
6. Understand that this project may be the first major project the students have managed.
7. Share your expertise in school and project management.
8. Be aware of language use. Discuss the different levels of language and how to know when to use which level.

Anne then provided a list of question prompts that the university mentors could use specifically to redirect the conversation away from student-to-mentor only and toward students-to-students. Taken from the direct instruction literature, these prompts led the writing-group participants to address specific questions rather than simply being invited to share their thoughts generally.

- Can anybody help Mary answer that question?
- What do you think about that?
- How would you say that in a different way?
- What are we trying to find out?
- What do you need to do next?
- How did you do that?
- What do you mean by . . . ?
- Tell us more. . . .
- What else did they do?
- Anything else?
- Can you be more specific?
- In what way?
- What are you assuming?
- Why would that be so?
- How can that be?
- How would you do that?
- Are you sure?
- Give an example of that.
- How is that related to . . . ?
- Can you summarize the discussion up to this point?
- How does your response tie into . . . ?
- If that is true, then what would happen if . . . ?
- What would ______ say about that?

- Let's see if we can figure out how to answer it together.
- Can you think of another way to think about this?
- Would any of you like to add something to this answer?
- How is your answer (point of view) different from ______?

With explicit attention paid to these protocols of open communication, the correspondence between the university mentors and the Delta high school students improved noticeably over the life of the ADOHP.

Conclusion

What came to fruition in the ADOHP and what is detailed in the forthcoming chapters is not magic, the flawless concoction to cure all of our country's educational woes, nor is it something, as we've suggested in this chapter, refined and perfect in its approach. What came to fruition was messy and full of room to invent, shift, and redo, and we argue that is how endeavors like this must behave. A set educational program prepared in a neat booklet to handout to participating teachers and students at either level would and should be wholeheartedly rejected. This isn't to say we didn't know what we were doing; it is only to say that by knowing what we were doing, we knew that the ADOHP would be just as iterative for us as it was for our participants. And isn't it by-the-books projects like this that have almost reached the extinction status of dinosaurs in the drill and kill, test and punish, accountability crazed American schools? The ADOHP grew from the autonomy of the Brown Chair and simultaneously created autonomy for the university teachers and students, the high school teachers, and the high school students, all of whom created meaning and forged new knowledge through their authority to do exactly that. Moreover, as we explain in chapter 2, ADOHP allowed us to look beyond our comfort zones to name and explain our dynamic theoretical positioning that mirrored our practice.

2

Theories

Consulted, Combined, Expected, Unexpected

WE SURMISED from the outset that the ADOHP would be a theoretically robust project, leading us into corners of literacy, rhetoric, composition, and pedagogy where we hoped we could converse with the existing literature and add insights that grew out of our work. We think our conjecture came true. But just as the project's design—its curriculum and pedagogy—took us into terrain we didn't expect to encounter, so did our theoretical grounding shift in ways we hadn't planned from the beginning. And, we must admit, we like the new turf we discovered.

We knew from the beginning that the project provided us an entrée into four conceptual arenas that are relevant to teaching and learning in general and community literacy in particular: ADOHP connected to cultural studies. It related to studies of student choice and engagement. It exemplified the principles of authentic intellectual achievement, a field in which one of us (Jolliffe, see Sisserson et al. 2002) has been engaged since the middle 1990s. And it resonated with the tenets of an interdisciplinary field called critical pedagogy of place. As the project proceeded, we were led in new directions. We found the work of the students, both from the University of Arkansas and the Delta high schools, pointing us to a conceptual nexus of rurality, loss, nostalgia, and epideictic rhetoric, an ideological node that we hope (modestly) put the project on a leading edge in community literacy projects.

Cultural Studies: The "Garden Variety" and Then Youth Cultural Studies

One aspect of the ADOHP that brought us great joy—an emotion we think we shared with both sets of students and the high school teachers—was its nontraditional, noncanonical bent. Here were students engaged in a project that did not disdain traditional pedagogy but that certainly didn't require them to read standard texts of literature, history, and social studies or take tests that forced them to reproduce what they were supposed to have learned. Here were students proposing and developing their own topics, focusing on discrete corners of local legend and lore, recording real human beings' voices, representing their work in genres of their own choosing. Here were students engaged in cultural studies.

Since it embodies several principles that we think were manifest in the ADOHP, Simon During's (1993) magisterial definition of "engaged cultural studies" is worth quoting at length. Engaged cultural studies, he writes,

> is academic work (teaching, research, dissemination, etc.) on contemporary culture from a non-elite or counter-hegemonic perspective ("from below") with an openness to the culture's reception and projection in everyday life, or, more generally, its impact on life trajectories. Engaged cultural studies encourages and takes notice of culture's capacity to express and invoke less restricted (more "other," counter-normative ways of being) . . . it aims to produce knowledge from perspectives lost to and in dominant cultures and to listen to far-off and marginalized voices. (25)

Indeed, we acknowledge that it might have been the nonelite, counterhegemonic nature of the inquiry and investigation in the ADOHP that flummoxed some of the students, contributing to the traction problem outlined in chapter 1. As Henry Giroux (1994) explains: "The university has long been linked to a notion of national identity that is largely defined by and committed to transmitting traditional Western culture. Traditionally this has been a culture of exclusion, one that has ignored the multiple narratives, histories and voices of ethnically and politically subordinated groups" (299).

During's and Giroux's perspectives led us to ponder whether students from poor, working-class families in the Arkansas Delta might have found it hard to believe initially that students and faculty members from the flagship university were actually interested in the history they were creating. Of course, we were—intensely so.

Time and time again we heard from students that ADOHP was offering them the first opportunity they had ever had to propose, investigate, and develop their own topic. It was the first project that many of them had ever taken up in which they didn't have to read whatever textbooks the teacher assigned and to write in genres that would report this knowledge back to the teacher. As the following chapters make clear, ADOHP urged the students to find out about and create knowledge concerning what *their* culture understood, for example, about religion, food, and race. They were studiers of culture.

Given the relatively homogenous age range of participants, moreover, ADOHP also connected theoretically to a subfield of cultural studies: *youth* cultural studies, a burgeoning research area that examines in particular what young people *do* with reading-, writing-, and research-intensive cultural studies projects. Our connection to youth cultural studies, of course, raises the question of whether the two groups of students in the project, the University of Arkansas students and the Delta high school participants, can both be classified as "youth" cultures. To be sure, the two groups differed somewhat in age and socioeconomic background, but they generally had in common membership in a population that the psychologist Jeffrey Jensen Arnett (2000) refers to as "emerging adulthood," a time span from the late teens through the early twenties. Arnett describes emerging adulthood as "a period characterized by change and exploration for most people, as they examine the life possibilities open to them and gradually arrive at more enduring choices in love, work, and worldviews" (479). Though he expresses concerns about labeling emerging adults as "youths," Arnett's perspective aligns with that offered by Kenneth Kenniston (1971), who sees "conceptualized 'youth' as a period of continued role experimentation between adolescence and young adulthood" (Arnett 2000, 470). We had no problems with thinking about the two populations as having enough in common to be considered not only youths but also participants in youth culture studies.

As we detailed in chapter 1, the articulation between the two groups was complicated, occasionally tense, but ultimately quite productive. The University of Arkansas students, many of whom were enrolled in their college's honors program, were very much "down with" the twenty-first-century university experience: generally, they were enthusiastic about the experiential, interdisciplinary nature of the ADOHP course, they felt comfortable with classes that required online discussions and collaboration, they loved the latitude they had to design and develop their own projects, and they thoroughly embraced the opportunity to experiment with electronic, graphic, and visual modes in their final presentations. The high school students, by contrast, although bright and academically promising, were generally still in the midst of traditional secondary schooling: they had not had much, if any, experience with interdisciplinary or experiential education; though they were adept at texting and e-mail, they usually had not experienced academic work that involved online collaboration; they had had relatively few opportunities to design and develop their own projects; and their academic "performances" were still predominantly tests and essays. The University of Arkansas students therefore mentored their Delta counterparts not only in how to carry out their oral history projects but also in how to understand and become adept at the new literacies embedded in a twenty-first-century college education—literacies that link strongly to the principles of youth cultural studies.

Especially as it relates to schooling, youth culture studies owes allegiance to the groundbreaking work of the anthropologist Shirley Brice Heath and her frequent collaborator, Milbrey McLaughlin, whose investigations of youths participating in voluntary community-based organizations make clear "that these kinds of environments recognize young people as resources by engaging them with sustained projects and performances released to real audiences" (Maira and Soep 2004,

257), projects and performances very much like the ones generated by ADOHP. One of the principal investigators of youth culture studies, Elizabeth Birr Moje (2002), defines the field in this way: "Youth culture studies focus on the resources (including literacy practices and textual resources), contexts and spaces to which youth have access as they live their everyday school and social lives" (216); the field "focuses on how youth use literacy to navigate, synthesize, and hybridize multiple spaces" and examines "how literate practice gets complicated and changed by the social and political practices demanded in a globalized, technologized, and hybridized world" (217). In other words, youth culture studies examines the choices youths make involving literacy—choices about reading, writing, texts, and media—to navigate the complicated byways of twenty-first-century youthful living.

A key theorist in youth culture studies, the linguist James Paul Gee, argues that young people who thrive in this complex, contingent sociopolitical space do so because they learn to become "shape-shifting portfolio people," or

> people who see themselves in entrepreneurial terms. That is, they see themselves as free agents in charge of their own selves as if those selves were projects or businesses. They believe they must manage their own risky trajectories through the building up of skills, experiences, and achievements in terms of which they can define themselves as successful now and worthy of success later. Their set of skills, experiences, and achievements, at any one time, constitutes their portfolio. However, they must also stand ready and able to rearrange these skills, experiences, and achievements creatively (that is, to shape-shift into different identities) in order to define themselves anew (as competent and worthy) for changed circumstances. (2002, 105)

As the ADOHP projects evolved, the University of Arkansas mentoring frequently took on the feel of instruction in choice-making, identity-formation, and shape-shifting. What on the surface seemed a simple process—the high school students wrote and submitted their work to a college web platform for formative peer commentary—became quite complex: high school students, often from limited social and educational backgrounds, worked with their mentors, many of whom were in the midst of their own heady, emerging-adult intellectual ferment, and learned by doing so what kinds of choices involving literacy they would need to consider making in order to position themselves as successful, now and in the future. Moje puts it this way: "As youths engage in these texts, practices, and experiences, they read, write, and speak themselves into the texts, and they construct new texts of experience for themselves" (222). Kris Gutierrez et al. (1995) describe a similar phenomenon that they label the creation of a "third space" in innovative instructional programs. Summarizing Gutierrez's work, Sunaina Maira and Elisabeth Soep (2004) explain, "The aim in . . . third space is not for students to achieve fluency in the teacher's privileged academic discourse, but for all participants in a learning encounter to rescript (or unscript) their interactions within a 'responsive' and 'collaborative' environment where youth culture is recognized itself as a site and a resource for knowledge production" (257). Time and again during the ADOHP, we observed students, both from the University of Arkansas and from the high schools, developing a discourse—slam poetry, dramatic monologues, radio essays, to mention just a few examples—that would allow them to bring their own literate resources as engaged youths to the social scripts that embodied the issues they took up in their projects.

Youths Making Choices, Shaping Identities

The linchpin of ADOHP's incorporation of youth cultural studies was the complementary, dialectical operation of student choice and identity formation. In short, ADOHP students had broad license to choose topics, strategies of questioning, use of evidence, and production of genre, and these choices strongly affected their emerging identities as students and writers.

Student choice, of course, is a commonplace in discussions of student engagement. The school reformer Phillip Schlechty (2004), for example, makes student choice one of the key "design features" of engaged teaching and learning. The literacy scholars Michael Smith and Jeffrey Wilhelm (2002) maintain: "We believe that we need to work harder to provide options and choices regarding curricular content and the way that content is pursued. We need to work harder to help students see what their options are so they can make meaningful choices" (197). Though their teachers, mentors, and peers might have suggested some potentially fruitful focuses, by and large the students had free rein to choose and investigate any topic related to legend or lore in the Delta. Moreover, the students, working individually or in groups, chose for themselves the questions they asked the interviewees, and the students selected the portions of the interviews that would actually make their way into their final projects. Finally, the students could choose any genre for their final project.

All of these choices—of topic, of question, of evidence, and of genre—are, of course, literate practices, and ADOHP students' deployments of them offered instances of the interplay between youth cultural studies and identity formation. In a comprehensive review of the literacy-identity formation connection, Moje and coauthor Allan Luke (2009) foreground the concept's basic principles: "People's identities mediate and are mediated by the texts they read, write, and talk about; . . . texts and the literate practices that accompany them not only reflect but may also produce the self; . . . texts can be used as tools for enacting identities in social settings" (416). Reflecting on these principles, we came to realize early on that full, purposeful participation in the ADOHP invited—even required—students to craft what were radically different new identities for themselves. In this project, they couldn't simply be readers, test takers, and academic paper writers; to succeed, they needed to be inquisitive historians, diligent interviewers, and authors—in the true etymological sense of that word, "creators" and "promoters"—of real texts that identified and upheld traditions and values of their home culture that were worth endorsing and saving.

Given the extensive scholarship on genre as a tool for accomplishing knowledge work discourse communities (for a review, see Russell 1994), we were particularly interested in the ways the students' choice of genre for their final project helped to shape their identities, and we found a theoretical touchstone in the work of Anis Bawarshi (2000). In his influential article "The Genre Function," Bawarshi develops a concept parallel to Michel Foucault's term the "author function," which "refers to the author's name, [but] which, in addition to being a proper name, is also a literary name, a name that exists only in relation to the work associated with it" (337). As Bawarshi explains, the author function endows both the work and the idea of "'author' with a certain cultural status and value": "the author-function not only constitutes the work, but it also constitutes the author of that work, the 'rational being' we call 'author,' as opposed to the real writer with 'just a proper name like all the rest'" (337). Bawarshi's counterpart term "the genre function" "constitutes all discourses and writers' modes of existence, circulation, and functioning within a society, whether the writer is William Shakespeare or a student in a first-year writing course, and whether the text is a sonnet or a first-year student theme" (338). In short, as Bawarshi puts it, "Genre . . . is largely constitutive of the identities we assume within and in relation to discourse, whether we are characters in a novel or presidents delivering states of the union addresses" (343). In other words, a writer assumes a different literate identity when he or she decides to write, say, a play, than when he or she chooses to write a poem or short story or an essay. We found it fascinating to observe ADOHP students selecting and crafting the genres—not only academic essays but also plays, brochures, websites, short stories, illustrated poems, to name a few—that they thought most effectively reflected their emerging identities, conveyed their ideas, and helped them accomplish their purposes.

The ADOHP and Authentic Student Work

The ADOHP elicited strong, positive reviews from students and teachers alike. Mallory Day, who participated as a high school senior at McGehee High School in year one of the project, wrote: "When I started this project, I thought it was just another assignment that I would get a grade for, but I was completely wrong. I did get a grade and do all of the work, but I was very surprised when I actually made the project a part of my daily life at school and at home." Jean Jones, who was a senior English major and African American studies minor at the University of Arkansas when she participated, offered this perspective: "Throughout school, we are often called on to research and make arguments about issues and ideas with which we have no direct experience. Participation in the ADOHP made our work directly relevant to our lives. The best thing about the project was that it was student-centered—we were able to choose topics of concern to us and therefore had an immediate sense of motivation." The student-centered nature of the project was also cited as a major benefit by one of the teachers, Brenda Doucey from Pine Bluff High School: "My first step in the project was to allow the students to brainstorm and come up with ideas that they wanted to work on, not what I wanted, because I felt that if it was their choice, they could be more interested in completing the project."

Testimony like this prompts us to make two additional, and related, claims about the ADOHP. First, it led to much more strongly *authentic* and *engaged* learning than students generally experience in most high schools, colleges, and universities. Second, in large measure because of the level of authentic engagement that students experienced, they ultimately understood, at least subconsciously but often explicitly, a dual-edged definition of literacy that could serve them well as students and citizens: (a) the ability to see the problems they face and the potentialities that lie before them as deeply connected to—or *imbricated* with, as the late James Berlin (1988) put it—reading and writing, and (b) the ability to use reading and writing in their own lives to address problems and capitalize on potentialities.

Authenticity, of course, is an often-quoted buzzword in education these days, and teachers are regularly being urged to set students to work on "authentic" projects. Most scholars who call for authenticity (see, for example, Wiggins 1999 and Jerald 2009) argue that, for an assignment, project, or task to count as authentic, it must meet at least the first if not both of two sequentially related criteria. First, they maintain that the assignment must at least mimic, if not represent, the kind of task that a real person in the real world would do. The second criterion tops the first: the task must require students to interact with the real world in some way, generally by submitting their world to some audience beyond the teacher-as-examiner and classmates. We don't want to downplay the importance of real-world relevance and activity, but the concept of "authenticity" that we incorporate with the Arkansas Delta Oral History Project goes beyond these two criteria.

Our notion of "authenticity" derives from the ideas of Fred Newmann and his associates (1996) that Carmen Manning, Kendra Sisserson, Annie Knepler, and David Jolliffe have been working to extend for the past two decades. Newmann and his coauthors from the Wisconsin Center for Educational Research held that a project, task, or assignment is authentic when it accomplishes three things: (1) it predominantly calls for *construction of knowledge*—interpretation, analysis, synthesis, and/or interpretation of the material students read, observe, or experience—in contrast to *reproduction of knowledge*, merely parroting back and reporting directly whatever they read, observe, or experience; (2) it engages students in *disciplined inquiry*, a way of knowing and representing knowledge that is employed and respected by an academic discipline; and (3) it is connected to students' lives in some way and is not simply a rote routine valued only within the classroom walls.

We believe the work that teachers assigned and students completed in the Arkansas Delta Oral History Project exemplifies the concept of "authentic" intellectual achievement at its best. First of all, to complete their projects, the students were required to do some reproduction of knowledge—they had to report back, verbatim, exactly what their interview subjects said in the interviews—but in order to produce their final product, they had to interpret, analyze, synthesize, and evaluate the information they discovered. In other words, the dominant expectation for each student's project was that he or she would *do something* with what was learned from the interview. Second, because they were working at the boundaries of three academic content areas—English/language arts, history, and anthropology—students were earning solid exposure to the disciplinary ways of knowing in both of those fields. They were learning how oral historians carry out their projects and acquire extensive knowledge about their research topics. They were learning how good writers create prose that makes solid points and then support those points with specific details, illustrations, anecdotes, and reasons. They were learning how cultural anthropologists define cultures and then ferret out evidence that instantiates their definition. Third, they were engaging in projects that were relevant in their own lives—they had to interview people who knew something about their topic, and they ultimately performed their projects in a public venue—as well as relevant in more than one academic content area. The Newmann-based definition of "authenticity" helped us see the concept as intellectual as well as experiential.

Critical, Place-Based Pedagogy: Decolonization and Reinhabitation in the Arkansas Delta

One of the Delta high school teachers whose students were early participants in ADOHP, Yogi Denton from McGehee, without specifically referencing youth culture studies, nonetheless recognized many of its hallmarks in the mentor-mentee articulation process at the end of her school's two-year stint in the project. The collaborative experience "is more than just a working relationship," Denton wrote.

> It allowed students to share more than their writing and research. It gave them the opportunity to share ideas and culture with people they might never have known otherwise. The Fayetteville students, usually a much more culturally diverse group than my high school students, have been a constant reminder that there is a world outside of the Delta. The Fayetteville students' interest in the stories and culture of the Delta has made my students realize that there is a rich heritage in their hometowns that must not go untold.

Denton's comments not only tacitly referenced ADOHP's connection to youth culture studies, but her words also hinted at the project's significance as a critical pedagogy of place. While the high school-college articulation in the ADOHP fostered identity-forming, shape-shifting change in its participants, it also strove to promote change in the Delta: by teaching the students to recapture and revere some aspect of the past, the project consciously tried to hold up the image of the Delta as a region *worth* reclaiming and within which Arkansans can build a future.

The chief proponent of "place-based pedagogies," David Gruenewald (2003), argues that teaching projects emphasizing place "are needed so that the education of citizens might have some direct bearing on the well-being of the social and ecological places people actually inhabit" (3). Sounding a theme that we introduced in chapter 1, Gruenewald explains further:

> Current educational discourses seek to standardize the experiences of students from diverse geographical and cultural places so that they may compete in the global economy. Such a goal essentially dismisses the idea of place as a primary experiential or educational context, displaces it with traditional disciplinary content and technological skills, and abandons places to the workings of the global market. Place-based educators do not dismiss the importance of content and skills, but argue that the study of places can help increase student engagement and understanding through multidisciplinary, experiential, and intergenerational learning that is not only relevant but potentially contributes to the well-being of community life. (7)

Rather than reverting constantly to generic curriculum and pedagogy—in literacy instruction, the general-skills reading and writing approach—students and teachers, according to Gruenewald, should "actually experience and interrogate the places outside of school—as part of the school curriculum—that are the local context of shared politics" (9).

Two key concepts embodied in Gruenewald's explanation of place-based pedagogy seemed particularly germane to the work of the ADOHP: decolonization and reinhabitation. Gruenewald describes these two concepts not as sequential but instead as complementary back-and-forth processes. Citing the work of the "bioregionalist pioneers [Peter] Berg and [Raymond] Dasmann" Gruenewald defines reinhabitation as "learning to live-in-place in an area that has been disrupted and injured through past exploitation" (9). Almost as if he were peering into the forces that have led to the economic decline of the Delta, Gruenewald explains how the two processes work in tandem: "If reinhabitation involves learning to live well socially and ecologically in places that have been disrupted and injured, decolonization involves learning to recognize disruption and injury and to address their causes. From an educational perspective, it means unlearning much of what dominant culture and school teaches, and learning more socially just and ecologically sustainable ways of being in the world" (9). A substantial portion of the ADOHP course taught at the University of Arkansas examined the political and economic forces that have shaped the Delta, trying to identify the causes of the "disruption and injury" the region has experienced. A major emphasis in the conversations, both online and face-to-face, between university mentors and Delta high school students was consistently how both the students and their communities could take steps toward revitalization and sustainability. Gruenewald thus supports the position underlying the ADOHP, namely, that recovering and revering the past can support reinhabitation in the present and future:

> Decolonization as an act of resistance must not be limited to rejecting and transforming dominant ideas; it also depends on recovering and renewing traditional, non-commodified cultural patterns such as mentoring and intergenerational relationships. In other words, reinhabitation and decolonization depend on each other. A critical pedagogy of place aims to (a) identify, recover, and create material spaces and places that teach us how to live well in our total environments (reinhabitation); and (b) identify and change ways of thinking that injure and exploit other people and places (decolonization). (9)

We certainly hope the ADOHP achieved both of these sets of goals.

Place-based pedagogy seems to hold special relevance for rural students, helping them to connect to reading and writing in ways that more traditional approaches cannot. Amy Azano (2011), for example, sees the pedagogy as being valuable to rural students "who may feel a 'disconnect' from the mandated curriculum" (8). And because it is perceived as more relevant, place-based instruction can in turn increase engagement. As Matthew Irvin et al. (2011) explain, relevant and engaging coursework can lead to a positive academic self-concept, which has been strongly related to academic achievement and postsecondary aspirations. Place-based pedagogy offers students an opportunity to engage in relevant and rigorous academic coursework that can give them a sense of belonging and introduce them to new perspectives that contextualize their "place" in the matrix of education and literacy.

Blending Cultural Studies, Authenticity, and Place-Based Pedagogy: The Foxfire Project

One visible outgrowth of the ADOHP's allegiance to youth cultural studies, authentic intellectual work, and critical pedagogy of place emerged in the project's extension of literacy practices beyond the walls of the school. Students in the ADOHP courses, both in the high schools and the university, learned not only to read and think critically and write effectively in a genre of their choice, but they also let folks in their communities know that they were doing so. By requiring students to identify someone with a unique perspective on their topic and then plan, practice, conduct, and transcribe the interview, the project put students in touch with a data source that academia seldom taps into—people with lived experiences that speak to the students' topics. In so doing, the ADOHP valorized not only the narratives and observations of the interviewees but also the project's process as a whole. An ADOHP student having a purposeful and informed conversation with, say, a minister in Brinkley, a business executive in Pine Bluff, or a famous restaurateur in Marianna allowed that person to reflect, "Gee, that young person thinks I have something important to say," and to conclude, "That local school of ours has its students doing a very interesting and valuable project."

An intellectual progenitor standing behind oral history education in general and this aspect of the ADOHP in particular needs to be acknowledged: Eliot Wigginton, the founder of the Foxfire Project. As he explains in the introduction to *Moments: The Foxfire Experience*, the project began in 1966 when Wigginton, fresh out of his Master of Arts in Teaching Program at Cornell, took a job teaching ninth- and tenth-grade English and geography at Rabun Gap-Nacoochee School in rural Georgia. Wigginton says he began to realize he wasn't connecting with his students when one of them tried to set his lectern on fire—during class. After some soul-searching, Wigginton "walked into class and said, 'How would you like to throw away the text and start a magazine?' And that's how *Foxfire* began" (113). What would be the content of the *Foxfire* magazine? Again, Wigginton's own words in the introduction of *Moments* tell the tale:

> There were lots of possibilities. Many older people in this area, for example, still plant today by the signs of the zodiac and stages of the moon. I had heard them mention it, but I didn't know what it meant. Rather than interrupt a conversation to find out, I figured I'd get my students to tell me. They'd probably know since it was mostly their parents and grandparents who were doing it. But my kids didn't really know what it was either, and soon they were curious as I was. Why not find out and turn the information into an article? (114)

So Wiggington worked to place each of his students in what he called "an interview situation with a charismatic contact" (19). From the earliest days of *Foxfire*, the students "went home and talked—really talked—to their own relatives, some for the first time. From those conversations came superstitions, old home remedies, weather signs, a story about a hog hunt, a taped interview with the retired sheriff about the time the local bank was robbed—and directions for planting by the signs" (114).

From this auspicious beginning in 1966, *Foxfire* has continued to publish a magazine of students' essays, stories, poems, and artwork generated from their work as oral historians. *Foxfire* subscribers now receive two issues a year, and twelve volumes of the *Foxfire* books, collections of the best pieces from the magazine, have been published.

For someone who has been involved with oral history education for nearly four decades (David Jolliffe conducted his first large-scale oral history project in 1976, well before the coauthors of this book were born), it is a bit difficult to talk about Wigginton's influence and the successful fruition of his vision for *Foxfire*. In 1992, Wigginton was convicted of a single count of sexual abuse of a minor; subsequently, he resigned his teaching position, served a term in prison, and moved to Florida, where he is required to register as a sex offender. The *Foxfire* operation was taken over by a collective of educators at Rabun County High School; an organization called the Foxfire Fund keeps the project alive.

But without apologizing for or condoning his criminal behavior, we nonetheless admire Wigginton's original vision for *Foxfire*, and its spirit is imbued in the ADOHP. Alluding to the importance of capturing in writing the culture's lore that had previously been passed along orally—"the magnificent hunting tales, the ghost stories that kept a thousand children sleepless, the intricate tricks of self-sufficiency acquired through years of trial and error, the eloquent and haunting stories of suffering and sharing and building and healing and planning and harvesting"—Wigginton turns the task over to students:

> If this information is to be saved at all, for whatever reason, it must be saved now; and the logical researchers are the grandchildren, not university researchers from the outside. In the process, these grandchildren (and we) gain an invaluable, unique knowledge about their own roots, heritage, and culture. Suddenly they discover their families . . . as pre-television, pre-automobile, pre-flight individuals who endured and survived the incredible task of self-sufficiency, and came out of it all with a perspective on ourselves as a country that we are not likely to see again. They have something to tell us about self-reliance, human interdependence, and the human spirit that we would do well to listen to. (116)

Although the ADOHP does not limit interviewees to the participating students' families, we adhere to Wigginton's central premises: that getting students to talk to informed, interested adults is a vital but frequently overlooked element of effective teaching and learning; and that only the dedicated work of oral historians will keep the legends and lore alive that undergird the culture of a town or a region.

We also maintain that the curricular and pedagogical dimensions of the ADOHP resonated thoroughly with core principles that reside at the center of the Foxfire method to this day:

1. The work that teachers and learners do together is infused from the beginning with learner choice, design, and revision.
2. The academic integrity of the work teachers and learners do together is clear. Mandated skills and learning experiences are identified to the class.
3. The role of the teacher is that of facilitator and collaborator.
4. The work is characterized by active learning.
5. Peer teaching, small group work, and teamwork are all consistent features of classroom activities.
6. There is an audience beyond the teacher for learner work.
7. New activities spiral gracefully out of the old, incorporating lessons learned from past experiences, building on skills and understandings that can now be amplified.
8. Reflection is an essential activity that takes place at key points throughout the work.
9. Connections between the classroom work, the surrounding communities, and the world beyond the community are clear.
10. Imagination and creativity are encouraged in the completion of learning activities. (11–12)

Though their work circulates in different academic milieus, the scholars of youth cultural studies and critical pedagogy of place promote principles completely consonant with Foxfire's. Educators in all of these realms embrace the notion of youths crafting social texts that help them make sense of their complex worlds and that could lead to the reinhabitation of their hometowns and regions. And, as the next section makes clear, the Foxfire project also resonates thoroughly with the notion of "authenticity" at the center of the ADOHP.

Situating Our Theoretical Touchstones in a Rural Context: The Key Nexus Forms

Although we initiated the ADOHP with an inclination toward contributing to scholarly conversations about cultural studies, choice and engagement, authentic intellectual work, and critical pedagogy of place, it wasn't until we were actually involved in running the project that we discovered an intriguing theoretical nexus that we ultimately concluded existed as our conceptual center of gravity—the confluence of theory that really focused our gaze on the student work. We knew, of course, that siting ADOHP in the Delta made it, de facto, a rural community literacy project. What we discovered was how the concepts of rurality, nostalgia and a sense of loss, and the students' epideictic rhetorical work converged in such an interesting way.

When we assert that ADOHP was a rural community literacy project, operating with schools and students from eastern and central Arkansas, we realize we might be accused of begging the question on a key term: What do we mean by "rural?" The term is, by all accounts, difficult to define quantitatively. As Bill Green and Michael Corbett (2013) put it, "Rurality itself is a contested and problematic concept that is caught up in . . . an oppressive biopolitics" (4). One definition of rurality, embraced by the US Census Bureau, the Office of Management and Budget, and the US Department of Education, holds that a rural area is one that exists "on a fringe, distant or remote" from an urbanized area of fifty thousand residents or more (qtd. in Vernon-Feagans et al. 2010, 164). A simpler definition comes from the US Department of Agriculture: "According to official US Census Bureau definitions, rural areas comprise open country and settlements with fewer than 2,500 residents" (Cromartie and Bucholtz 2008, 31). The University of Arkansas's Division of Agriculture (2015) adheres to the latter, defining rural residents as "people living in places with less than 2,500 residents or outside an urbanized area or urban cluster" (9). No matter which of these definitions is operant, all of the high schools whose students participated in the ADOHP were rural.

Our students' experiences were readily apparent in the qualitative features of rural life in contemporary America, which are easier to grasp than its quantitative definition. A 2002 Kellogg Foundation study discovered that a majority of the American public holds "highly positive images" of rural America: "settings that are distinct from urban areas with agriculture dominating the economy," that are "family oriented with strong religious grounding and self reliance," that feature "a bucolic environment with beautiful vistas," and that are "generally a better place to raise families in a friendly and relaxed atmosphere" (University of Arkansas Division of Agriculture 2015, 9). Introducing their edited collection, *Reclaiming the Rural*, Kim Donehower, Charlotte Hogg, and Eileen Schell rehearse these "morning-in-rural America" images but add a crucial caveat: "Many Americans think of rural areas as geographically 'nowhere,' and rural people as quaint, hardworking, and useful as long as they don't require federal resources like urban and suburban Americans do" (2).

These rosy public perceptions notwithstanding, rural America in the past several decades has also frequently conjured up images of loss and decay—what Donehower, Hogg, and Schell characterize as images of "lack and lag . . . 'backwardness,' 'inefficiency,' 'lack of progress'" (4). In a comprehensive review article, Lynn Vernon-Feagans, Kathleen C. Gallagher, and Kirstin Kainz (2010) describe some material sources of these images. For the past four decades, they explain, rural America has experienced its share of troubles, all related to economic shifts: the mechanization of agriculture leading to a decline of farm jobs, the outmigration of "talented young adults," the concomitant swing toward an elderly population, and the availability of better educational opportunities in urban areas (165). As these authors point out, "Rural areas did not gain from the economic boom of the 1990s because most rural areas did not participate in the technology revolution that centered on more urban areas, leaving them more vulnerable to economic losses in the 21st century" (165). But, as the rural theorist Paul Theobald (2005) notes, even urban America has not escaped the deleterious effects of economic change. "Given the so-called shift to a service economy, the trend in overseas job exportation via 'free-trade' initiatives, and rising poverty levels," he writes, both urban and rural areas are suffering. He concludes bluntly, "Prosperity has moved to the suburbs" (122).

As might be expected, schools and students in rural America have resonated to the effects of these economic changes. For example, Vernon-Feagans and her colleagues list several features reflective of down-turning conditions:

- Rural schools generally have less access to financial resources than more urbanized school districts; administrators often note their communities' lack of not only funding but also "community capital" (167).
- Rural schools are often less able to attract highly qualified teachers; teachers in rural schools have less access to professional development than urban teachers and are paid on the average about 80 percent of what their urban counterparts make.
- Rural schools are frequently less able to offer challenging college-preparatory courses or co-curricular programs.
- Rural students often have to spend a longer time on school buses getting to and from school; as a consequence, they get to devote less time with their families, and they often spend considerable time interacting with a student population of disparate ages with almost no adult supervision (166–67).

On the other hand, Vernon-Feagans and her colleagues cite a handful of benefits that rural schools and students enjoy:

- The schools are generally located in a small town or village, in "an environment that has roots in an agrarian culture" (164).
- The schools are often more ready to address and meet their community's needs than are more urban schools. Teachers and administrators in rural schools frequently call attention to their schools' access to nature and play areas, to the relative scarcity of violent crime, to the support they receive from "community connectedness" (167)
- The students and their families are often "grounded in a sense of place" (164).

Our experience with the ADOHP leads us to quibble a bit with Vernon-Feagans, Gallagher, and Kainz's second purported advantage of urban schools. Both the lower salaries generally offered by rural districts and the No-Child-Left-Behind requirement that teachers be "highly qualified" have led to teacher shortages in rural America, prompting districts to hire teachers from more urbanized areas who then must commute to the rural sites daily. Time and again in our work, we met teachers employed in the Delta who commuted to their jobs up to two hours daily from Little Rock, Memphis, or Jonesboro. It's tough for these teachers to feel connected to the community or for the community to feel connected to them.

This conundrum of the glass being half empty or half full regarding rural education is reflected in rural students' aspirations for further education. Between 2007 and 2009, the National Research Center on Rural Education Support surveyed 8,764 students and about 1,500 parents, teachers, and administrators from small-town and rural high schools. They found that over 50 percent of the students wanted to continue their education beyond high school; 36 percent wanted a four-year degree, and 35 percent wanted an advanced degree. Over 50 percent wanted a career that requires a four-year or advanced degree. But 72 percent of the students reported they had not talked to a school counselor in the past year, and few students reported participating in such school-to-work transition programs as job shadowing, mentoring, or internships. The rural aspirations study showed a direct correlation between the size of a school and its tendency to offer college-preparatory courses and activities: "A majority of rural youth are aspiring to continue their education beyond high school. They are also choosing jobs and occupations that will require a college education. Furthermore, a majority of the (rural) youth (surveyed) planned to live in a small town or rural community as adults. From the perspective of community development, the results indicate that schools continue to play a critical role in building sustainable rural and small town communities. However, it appears that rural youth have limited access to the advanced coursework, college and career counseling, and other postsecondary preparation programs to prepare for the transition to postsecondary education or adult work" (National Research Center on Rural Education Support 2011).

Decline, Loss, Nostalgia, and the Epideictic

As we noted in chapter 1, tropes of decline pervade the discourse about the Delta. Given the prevalence of this discourse, what might be an effective path of action for educators—indeed, for citizens in general—who hope to address the decline and help to revitalize the region? Literacy educators need to realize a central tenet of critical discourse analysis: discourse, such as that which characterizes the decay of the economy, the population, and the quality of life in the Delta, not only reflects social, political, and economic conditions but also helps to constitute them. As Norman Fairclough (1993) has made clear in his extensive work in critical discourse analysis, discourse is reciprocal in its relation to social practice: it provides citizens with subject positions and roles that allow them to act in certain ways in relation to economic and political realities and, concurrently, that deny them other options. A simple question follows: How does the discourse encourage and allow us to act? Clearly, one of the options for action that the discourse about the Delta might foster is benign (or even malicious) neglect—but no one in the region thinks it right that citizens simply should give in to despair and allow Delta towns to die.

The possibility of crafting a more productive discourse about the Delta was central to the ADOHP from the outset. We never thought, however, that we could simply remake the thinking about the Delta by starting from scratch in the present moment. Particularly in a region where the heritage has been so tied to agriculture—to the land, the soil, the rivers, and the ways of work and life they have sponsored—we felt it imperative that we focus our revitalization project initially on what the Delta has been and that we urge our participants to think about what from the Delta's past has produced a region and a culture worth saving.

We found a valuable perspective that supports our efforts in the work of the Canadian educational theorist Ursula Kelly (2009). In her article "Learning to Lose: Rurality, Transience, and Belonging," Kelly lays out a conceptual background that coheres hand-in-glove with the educational philosophy that guided the ADOHP. Kelly begins her argument with a claim that could be referring to the Arkansas Delta: "Rural places," she writes, "now more than at any other point in history, are places of great loss—of people, natural resources, and often, as a result, any vision of long-term viability" (2). Yet, she adds, this sense of loss need not necessarily lead to "an acceptance of disadvantage"; often it can lead to "an intricate and, on many fronts, satisfying negotiation of abiding attachments, longings, and hopes set against a background of ecological and economic uncertainty"—in other words, to a consideration to what is worth saving in regions in decline.

Directly confronting this sense of loss, rather than denying it, Kelly asserts, can "create a space in which one might plan and preserve, turning a love of place into an ethic of responsibility and sustainability" (2). However, acknowledging and articulating this sense of loss, she allows, is difficult: "Indeed, within the cultural contexts where prohibitions limit expressions of loss and mourning, loss is rarely articulated in productive ways" (2). One avenue for confronting loss, Kelly suggests, is embracing nostalgia, a discursive move at which some scholars in literacy education look askance. Donehower, Hogg, and Schell, for example, warn that "scholars must be vigilant about not falling into celebratory rhetorics of rural life that rely too much on nostalgia for their power. Doing so risks placing rural areas in the paradigm of mere longing for 'days gone by' where life is 'simpler' and less affected by social and economic changes" (5). Kelly takes a different view of the power of nostalgia: "Despite its register of dissatisfaction with the present through the idealization of the past, [nostalgia] is often dismissed and misunderstood as lacking agency. But the dissatisfaction that fuels nostalgia is an expression of the alienation and conveys in muted ways a nonetheless strongly felt desire for a better world. For this reason, nostalgia should command our critical attention so that we might understand its inclinations and consider how best to tap into its potential in order to promote change" (2).

In the ADOHP, we saw nostalgia as playing a vital role in our curriculum, one that we hope Kelly would agree is ethical. As she puts it, "An education that encourages an investigation into the nature of our affinities and attachments—rather than one that romanticizes or zealously mobilizes them—is an ethical project" (3). Kelly finds an ideal source for ethical "education for rurality" in a concept promoted by Allan Luke and Victoria Carrington, a concept that again resonates with the educational philosophy underlying the ADOHP. As Kelly puts it, "for times of transience and change," Luke and Carrington suggest teaching literacy "for a critical engagement with glocalized economies: a literacy to build cosmopolitan views and identities through a shunting between 'historical memories and contemporary understandings' of the material, economic, and political conditions in a region" (qtd. in Kelly 2009, 3). This dialectic between the history of the Delta, as portrayed in the interviews provided by hundreds of the project's informants, and the contemporary circumstances of Delta life, was a central engine driving the ADOHP.

For rural students, Kelly calls for a pedagogy very close to that of the ADOHP's, which we unpack in detail in chapter 1. As she writes, "Education must create the conditions for students to leave their home places, to travel intellectually and emotionally—within and across the borders of their own communities and elsewhere, and within *themselves*, in search of the forces that constitute them, socially, culturally, and emotionally" (3). The ADOHP, we believe, instantiated Kelly's call for a pedagogy that will "see loss as an opportunity to reexamine old certainties, to provoke new knowledge, and to forge new relations" (3). Within this pedagogy, "sustainability should be the centerpiece of an education" that involves "ethics, politics, and effect—a complex call to care in which transience is feature of life, a way of thinking, a mode of identification, a form a belonging, and a mark of loss as possibility and hope—of reparation, for people and their places" (3).

As the chapters that follow make clear, the multistage assignments that students participating in the ADOHP completed produced final products that differ considerably from those produced by participants in other community literacy projects. The default move in most of these projects—for example, the Community Literacy Center in Pittsburgh and the Open Doors Collaborative in Philadelphia (for a review, see Long 2008)—is for participants eventually to write what rhetorical theorists would call "deliberative" prose: texts that consciously focus on the future and generally even propose specific courses of action. In the ADOHP, on the other hand, in order to embody the desired dialectic involving the Delta's past, present, and potential future, participants created documents that rhetoricians would classify as "epideictic."

In classical rhetorical theory, the epideictic is one of three types (or *eide*) of discourses described by Aristotle in *The Art of Rhetoric*, the other two being the judicial or forensic and the deliberative or political. In contrast to judicial texts, which focus on what happened in the past, or deliberative texts, which promote action in the future, epideictic texts concentrate on the present. Often called ceremonial, epideictic discourses, according to Aristotle, were designed to offer praise or censure for some aspect of a situation at hand. Indeed, throughout the classical period, the archetype of epideictic discourse was the funeral oration, a ceremonial speech praising the deceased.

In modern rhetorical theory, several theorists have proposed broadening the definition of the epideictic so that it can refer to discourses beyond the ceremonial. George Kennedy (1994), for example, proposes that the epideictic refer to "any discourse that does not aim at a specific action but is intended to influence the values and beliefs of an audience" (4). Chaim Perelman and Lucie Olbrechts-Tyteca (1991) see the epideictic rhetor as "an educator . . . promoting values that are shared in the community" (52). Brian Vickers (1988) urges an expanded definition so that epideictic encompasses any discourse "affecting internal decisions—opinions and attitudes" (56). Lawrence Rosenfield (1980) explains: "Epideictic's understanding calls upon us to join with our community in giving thought to what we witness, and such thoughtful beholding in commemoration constitutes memorializing" (133). Cynthia Miecznikowski Sheard (1996) synthesizes these perspectives in her article "The Public Value of Epideicitic Rhetoric." Sheard maintains that the function of epideictic discourse is "to confirm and promote adherence to commonly held values of a community with the goal of sustaining that community" (766). She sees the epideictic as discourse that can address "private and public 'disease,' discomfort with the status quo" (766) and "a vehicle through which communities can imagine and bring about change" (771). She defines the epideictic, therefore, as "a rhetorical gesture that moves its audience toward a process of critical reflection that goes beyond evaluation toward envisioning and *actualizing* alternative realities, possible worlds" (787, emphasis in the original). Both the University of Arkansas course and the projects produced by both sets of students were frequently imbued with the discomfort with the status quo that Sheard unpacks; the readings and projects focused on critical reflection toward a different and better future for the Delta.

Youth Culture, Critical Pedagogy of Place, Authentic Work in the Students' Projects

As chapters 3 through 5 make clear, the scores of students who have been involved with the ADOHP fleshed out the skeletons of three pedagogical theories in remarkably diverse, creative, and engaging ways.

From the standpoint of youth culture studies, the students' projects must be seen in a broader perspective than simply the one that their final product—be it an academic essay, a play, a piece of historical fiction, a series of poems, or website—offers. The students' projects were a unified whole consisting of the questions they generated for the interview—questions that grew out of the background research they did on their topics—plus the verbatim transcript of the interview *and then* the final product. Therefore, to examine how the students wrote themselves into a social text of the issues they are investigating—be it religion or food or race—one must look as closely at the *questions* the students asked as at the *answers* their informants provided and the *literate artifacts* the students produced. As these youths were making sense of their environments and connecting their projects to their own lives, it's vital to examine what they thought *they* needed to know.

From the standpoint of a critical pedagogy of place, the students' projects can be seen as manifestations of their choice to backburner the discourse of decline about the Delta that surrounded them in the media, in scholarship, and in daily life. As they interviewed folks from the Delta who instilled value in stories from the past and pointed with hope toward a revitalized future for the region, the students were taking countercultural strides, clear steps toward decolonizing what had been a colonized past for the Delta and reinhabiting it.

From the standpoint of authentic intellectual work, the students' projects can be viewed as evidence that, for the first time in many of these students' lives, they were experiencing a transformative power of literacy. They devoted a substantial chunk of their time, as sophomores, juniors, or seniors in high school, or undergraduate university students, to developing and putting into their own words a story that captured, enhanced, and made permanent an ephemeral tale from their family's or their town's past. They realized that their work was part of a larger project to save a region that many people saw as being unredeemable. They knew their work would be archived both at the University of Arkansas and in their school library. They hoped—and their teachers encouraged this hope—that future generations of residents of their town and students in their school would consult their projects as evidence of the will to thrive, to honor the past, and to face a promising future of their region.

Part Two
Representations

Introduction

The ADOHP Student Work

THE NEXT THREE CHAPTERS present a modest sample of the very best aspect of the ADOHP: the student work it produced. In either electronically scanned or hard-copy form, we now have an archive of about two hundred projects—the students' interview questions, tapes, transcripts, and final projects—in storage. The range of topics is impressive, large enough to make taxonomizing a challenging task.

A great many projects take up issues related simply to the land: the fields, the farms, the weather, in the projects "A Day in the Field," "The Levees and River Flooding," "Trials, Tractors, and Tribulations," and "The 1974 Forrest City Tornado." One of the most engaging projects in this category captures the story of one Lily Peter of Phillips County, the first woman ever to own and run her own farm in the Delta.

Music was perennially a favorite topic. "An Interview with Sonny Payne" unpacked the history of the long-running King Biscuit Time blues radio show, broadcast since 1951 on KFFA in Helena, from the perspective of the program's host, "Sunshine" Sonny Payne. Johnny Cash's roots in the Dyess Colony, a New Deal settlement founded in 1934 in Mississippi County, captured the attention of one oral historian. "The Gospel Truth: A History of Gospel Music in Ashley County" was brought to life by another.

Small-town life received ample treatment. "Dating and Etiquette in the Delta" brought out stories about debutantes and debutante balls. "Fishing in the Delta" and "Hunting in the Delta" connected these recreational pursuits to issues of subsistence and food security. "Friday Nights: High School Football in the Delta" allowed one oral historian to write a series of wonderfully evocative poems and then accompany them with her own charcoal and ink sketches. Projects like "Duke's Grocery," "Dr. J. B. Dilberry's Veterinary Practice," and "The Historical Significance of the Black Barber Shop" demonstrated the importance of small-town businesses, while an array of projects provided studies of people who gained a modicum of fame—as artists, architects, teachers, and musicians, for example—after coming from modest roots in Delta towns.

Projects about different ethnic populations in the Delta were abundant. One year produced projects on "A History of Polish Immigration to the Delta," "Italians in the Delta," and "Jewish Immigration." The effect of the Second World War on ethnicity in the Delta also seemed to fascinate students. A project called "Japanese Internment Camp" detailed the history of one of two such camps in Arkansas, the one at Rohrer in Desha County, and the project "POW Camps" examined the history of the facility that housed German prisoners in Dermott in Chicot County.

The taxonomy could continue, describing projects that focused on education, medical care, crime, military service, philanthropy. Given the richness of the data, we were hard pressed to select the topical areas we use in the following chapters to demonstrate how the student projects evolved. But select we did, focusing on projects about religion, food, and race in chapters 3, 4, and 5, respectively.

Why did we select these three topics? Three reasons came into play. First, while nearly all the topics students chose to write about were imbricated in the history and future of the Delta, these three seemed particularly exigent to both sets of students. Religion, particularly fundamental Christianity, seems to envelope citizens in all corners of Arkansas, and religion's influence in political and social life has historically been strong and appears to be growing even stronger. Food forms the basis for a perplexing love-hate relationship for many Arkansans: they love the varieties of Southern food that seem totemic in the region, but they also get bombarded with warnings about the ill effects of consuming too much of it. And race—well, despite the claims of some commentators that we live in a postracial society, the divide between black or brown and white in Arkansas schools, communities, churches, and workplaces still remains quite visible. Second, we discovered that students rarely have the opportunity to talk and write about these topics. As we note in chapter 3, talking and writing about religion in schools constitutes skating on dangerous ice. Talking and writing about food seems relegated solely to consumer economics courses, and the discourse about it rarely has a cultural-studies dimension. And, surprisingly, although folks from Arkansas hail from a state where the desegregation of schools in the late 1950s made the national news, the students in the ADOHP apparently had had scarce opportunities to think or write reflectively about race. Third, the projects that emerged in these topical areas were just downright interesting.

A final prefatory note: in each of the following three chapters, we have included a modicum of historical background material that, we trust, contextualizes each of the projects. We do so not to diminish the importance and vitality of the students' work but quite the opposite—to enrich and vivify their efforts. We trust that the student work, some from Delta high schoolers and some from University of Arkansas students, faithfully shows the participants' studying their culture, effecting literate strategies to position themselves as thinkers and writers within it, making choices of topic and genre that give shape to their emerging identities, engaging in authentic intellectual work, contributing to the reinhabitation of their locale, and producing epideictic pieces that celebrate the values they think are worth preserving in the Delta.

3

The Church and Religion

Forces for Reinhabitation in the Delta

WE IMAGINE that most participants in the ADOHP would not have understood an analogy that equated any aspect of their work with the third rail, the electrified beam in city subway train and bus systems. The third rail not only powers the trains and buses but also kills people who come into contact with it. But we think there's no more apt figure to describe talking and writing about religion in public schools generally and Arkansan schools particularly.

Arkansas is a profoundly religious state. The Pew Research Center's 2013 religious landscape survey found that 84 percent of Arkansans held an "absolutely certain" belief in God; 74 percent reported that religion was "very important" in their lives. Sixty-eight percent reported that they prayed at least once a day, and 51 percent adhered to the belief that the Bible is the word of God and is literally true. Fifty-three percent of Arkansas respondents belonged to a category of churches grouped under the rubric of "Evangelical Protestant," whereas 16 percent affiliated with denominations within the "Mainline Protestant" tradition. Exactly 50 percent of the respondents from Arkansas reported attending church at least once a week.

The impact of this religious fervor rarely remains private in the state. To the contrary, in Arkansas issues touching on religious belief, dogma, tolerance, and intolerance surround the populace and influence both legislation and daily life. The state's constitution prohibits avowed atheists from holding state office or testifying as witnesses in court. In 2008 the state's voters overwhelmingly passed Arkansas Proposed Initiative 1, which prohibited adults living in the same house but not united in a "traditional marriage" from adopting a child. (The act was later declared unconstitutional.) The state has some of the strictest abortion laws in the nation, mandating that a woman receive counseling that advises her not to have the abortion and then wait at least one day before having the procedure. Thirty-seven of the state's seventy-five counties prohibit the sale of alcohol, and a statewide referendum to unify the counties' liquor laws and make them all "wet" was defeated 57 to 43 percent in a 2014 election. In 2015, the state legislature passed acts that would permit people not to comply with laws that interfered with their "sincerely held religious beliefs," that would prohibit municipalities from passing local ordinances outlawing discrimination based on sexual preference or identity, and that would authorize the construction of a Ten Commandments monument on the capitol's grounds.

Yet despite the apparent ubiquity of religious thought and discourse, young people in Arkansas schools apparently don't study religion critically or read, write, or talk about it in their classes. Indeed, talking and writing about religion in schools can be the proverbial third rail—it can derail instruction, lead to friction between students, and cause disputes with teachers and parents.

Given the free choice students enjoyed in ADOHP, religion was a popular topic. Why so? As we hope the projects in this chapter show, writing about religion allowed the participants represented here—a team of writers from a high school and two students from the University of Arkansas class—to show how they tapped into religious faith to negotiate and establish an identity for themselves and their home region, to shed some light on the role their religion might play in the reinhabitation of the Delta, and to engage in the authentic intellectual work of constructing knowledge rather than simply reporting it. The student projects in this chapter, we maintain, are lovely epideictic texts, celebrating values worth reviving, maintaining, and promoting in the Delta.

Religion in the Lives of American, Southern, Arkansan Youth

No one can doubt that the periods of youth and emerging adulthood—the late teen and early twenties years—are dynamic moments in people's religious lives. To begin with, religion seems to be a very important aspect of life for young folks in general. In the early 1990s a Gallup poll found that 76 percent of adolescents (aged thirteen to seventeen) in the United States believed in a personal God and that 74 percent prayed at least occasionally (Gallup and Bezilla 1992, qtd. in Regnerus, Smith, and Fritsch 2003, 9). And although attendance at religious services tends to decline over the high school years for US teenagers, young people's participation in other religious activities—fellowship organizations, prayer groups, service projects, and so on—actually rises over the same period (Regnerus, Smith, and Fritsch 2003, 9). Christian Smith, the principal investigator for the National Study of Youth and Religion based at the University of North Carolina at Chapel Hill, offers a compelling explanation of the draw of religion for young people. Smith argues that "religion may exert positive, constructive influences in the lives of American youth through nine distinct but connected and mutually reinforcing factors." Through "moral directives, spiritual experiences," and "role models," Smith maintains, adolescents gain a sense of "moral order." In addition, their religious experiences provide them "community and leadership skills," "coping skills," and "cultural capital," the latter coming usually from the experiences with different cultures young people can gain from service trips and exchange programs. Finally, they earn "social capital" in terms of leadership skills, participate in "relatively dense networks of relational ties," and forge "extra-community links and skills" (Regnerus, Smith, and Fritsch 2003, 19–27).

If religion is a salient feature among US adolescents in general, it seems even more so in the American South. Smith and his fellow researchers in the National Study of Youth and Religion analyzed data drawn from the 1995 National Longitudinal Study of Adolescent

Health and found that "only 8.4 percent of southern youth (in grades 7 through 12) report having no religion," in contrast to 12.1 percent of northeastern youth, 15.2 percent of midwestern youth, and 17 percent of youth living in western states (Smith et al. 2002, 607). And, in terms of religiosity, Arkansas is thoroughly southern: a 2008 Gallup poll of 350,000 United States residents found that Arkansas was tied for fifth in a ranking of the "top ten most religious states" (Newport 2009).

These quantitative characterizations of religion's prominence in Arkansas are supported by more qualitative descriptions. Nancy Britton, for example, writes in *The Encyclopedia of Arkansas History and Culture* that "the number of people in Arkansas who believe in and practice a religious faith has always been high, with the greatest percentage identifying themselves as Christian and Protestant. Numerically, the largest denomination in the state is now Baptist, including its Southern, Missionary, Free Will, Primitive, and other branches" (n.p.). Not only is religion strong in Arkansas, but it also is generally quite conservative. As Orville Taylor (1984) notes in his profile of religion in the state: "Ministers and members of most Arkansas churches have tended to be theologically conservative, although there has been a small liberal minority. This is illustrated by the controversy over teaching of the theory of evolution, which has periodically appeared in the state since the 1920s." Taylor adds: "Arkansas churches and their leaders also have tended to be conservative on social issues. Generally they have favored prohibition or restriction of the sale of alcoholic beverages and have opposed gambling, commercial activities on Sunday, liberal divorce laws, abortion, and the Equal Rights Amendment" (54–55).

Given that most of the ADOHP University of Arkansas students were from the state and that many of the home communities of the high school students could be perceived as sites of religious conservatism, one might suspect the storm clouds, that is, clashes over the relevance and appropriateness of religious faith in academic writing that generally accompany student writing about religion in school, to appear. As the project descriptions below attest, the storm clouds never materialized.

Religious Emphases in Student Writing—Inviting a Problem?

Teachers frequently preach this mantra to novice writers: "Write about what you know." Moreover, a common directive in many writing assignments in both high school and college is for the students to support their points with examples, details, or reasons drawn from their reading, observations, or experiences. Both pieces of advice can invite students into a quagmire. For many adolescents, their religious faith is what they know, and the examples, details, or reasons they might draw from their religious life seem to them appropriate to the academic writing task at hand. Problems can arise when students refer to their religion, however, because what they know about their faith is generally not the kind of "knowing" that their teachers expect them to demonstrate in their compositions. A substantial array of scholars in composition studies (see Vander Lei and Kyburz 2005, for example) direct attention to what Shannon Carter (2007) calls an "intolerable gap" (574) between teachers and their students who profess their faith in response to writing assignments. As Lizabeth Rand (2001) points out: "Religious discourse in the classroom frequently seems to offend, or in its more benign state it merely suggests a quaint naivete. Compositionists have swapped stories of the Christian student who writes a testimonial about the saving power of Jesus Christ. Reactions include embarrassment, anger, and a refusal to even consider an essay based on what is termed 'dogmatic,' dualistic thought" (357).

Bronwyn Williams (2005) echoes and amplifies the point: "Some teachers feel a more pronounced discomfort, sometimes bordering on implicit hostility, to any mention of religion in student writing. This is particularly the case in dealing with students from evangelical Christian traditions" (515). Juanita Smart (2005) ultimately characterizes the problem in the starkest terms: "Within the academic community . . . the student's profession of faith is perceived as a kind of ill-informed, if not illegitimate, monster—a rhetoric that offends and threatens rather than instructs or enlightens other members of the composing community" (14).

Why did these kinds of issues not emerge in the ADOHP project about religion? Let us offer three hypotheses based on the conceptual groundwork laid out in chapter 2. First, the student writers were given leeway to interrogate the roles that religion plays in the fabric of life in the region and in the pattern of their own lives. This interrogatory attitude stands in stark contrast to the determinedly assured stance that often dominates students' work when they choose to write about religion in traditional composition classes. Second, the student projects generally look at issues of religion that are embedded in a specific place and time. Religion for these students is not some floating abstraction, some set of generalizations that can be plugged into academic discourses almost at random. Religion for the creators of these three projects is a particular social practice that can be seen as contributing to the decolonization and reinhabitation of the Delta. Third, the creators of these projects were engaged in a consummately authentic intellectual project, one that required them to synthesize and interpret the myriad roles that religion plays in the context and to elaborate their ideas in an appropriate genre of their choice, a text type that most vividly embodies their constructed knowledge about their topic.

All Eyes on Zion: Over One Hundred Years of Worship

In the third year of ADOHP, three students from Brinkley High School—Michael Devine, Keona Jackson, and Destinie Shelton—undertook a project that allowed them to reflect on a vital part of their culture, assess its value to their town and region, and engage in authentic intellectual work. *All Eyes on Zion* represented an opportunity for Michael, Keona, and Destinie to contribute to the celebration that their home church, Mount Zion Missionary Baptist, was holding to commemorate its hundredth year of worship at the site of the current church building. These students, all juniors, interviewed Rev. Eddie Harvey, the current pastor of Mount Zion, and their final project was a three-scene play depicting the history of the church. The first scene concentrates on the founding of the church in Brinkley in 1886. Scene two focuses on the building of the current church structure, and the final scene describes the ebb and flow of the congregation's membership over the years and the authors' hope for the church to prosper for another hundred years.

Brinkley is a town of approximately three thousand people, located some 70 miles east of Little Rock, which has had a colorful history and experienced a close brush with near fame in the recent past. Settled as a railroad town in 1852 to facilitate the construction of the Memphis and Little Rock Railroad, Brinkley was known for the first seventeen years of its existence as "Lick Skillet"—so named because the railroad construction crews, mostly from neighboring towns, would cook their suppers over an open fire and return home when the last skillet was licked. It was only after 1869 that the settlement was named for the railroad president, Robert C. Brinkley, a prominent banker from Memphis. The town was incorporated as Brinkley in 1872.

Railroads continued to be the centerpiece of the town. The Memphis and Little Rock was eventually sold to the Rock Island Railroad, and Brinkley was located at the junction of that company's tracks and those of the Cotton Belt Railroad. During the height of the agricultural economy in the Delta, tons of cotton, rice, soybeans, and milo would have been loaded and shipped through Brinkley. To this day the town boasts the Lick Skillet Work Station Historic District, comprising the Central Delta Depot Museum and the former Rusher Hotel, a grand old Southern railroad hotel that now houses a bridal gown shop (Dennis 2011).

Like many small Delta towns, Brinkley has faced some times of struggle, both early in its history and more recently. In 1909, a tornado—which many residents still refer to as "the cyclone"—swept through the town, killing sixty-five people and destroying many homes, businesses, and churches. In the early twenty-first century, Brinkley faced the consequences as family agriculture turned into agribusiness. Monroe County, in which Brinkley is the only municipality of any size, lost 7 percent of its population between 2010 and 2014; the median household income in the county was $27,263, as compared with $40,768 for the state of Arkansas. The 2010 census found 28.8 percent of all citizens of the county living below the federal poverty level, as compared with 19.2 percent throughout the state (US Census Bureau 2000–).

Brinkley's fortunes nearly changed radically in the summer of 2004 when naturalists in the Cache River National Wildlife Refuge thought they sighted an ivory-billed woodpecker, a supposedly extinct species often referred to as the "Lord God Bird" because of its lavish coloring. For several months after the purported sighting, both avid, enthusiastic ornithologists and the national media flocked to Brinkley, the former to catch sight of the rare bird and the latter to cover the story. Tourism began to flourish in Brinkley, and one business owner even worried during a National Public Radio interview whether the infrastructure of the town could support the onslaught of visitors. Alas, the sighting of the bird could not be confirmed—many bird experts later concluded that what had been spotted was a relatively common pileated woodpecker—and the tourism business faded (National Public Radio 2005).

But just as it has faced hardships, like many small towns in the Delta, Brinkley has experienced many joys. The burgh enjoys its fame as the hometown of the famous rhythm-and-blues singer Louis Jordan. And the church as an institution has clearly brought stability and spirit to the town. Brinkley, in fact, was the home of the Consolidated White River Academy, an institution founded in 1893, and operating until 1950, to offer "African American students the opportunity for a full high school education, rather than the mere tenth-grade education available to them in the area." As Amanda Manatt and Louise Mitchell (2009) point out: "The goal was to provide a top-notch Christian education in a boarding school environment following a modified version of Alabama's Tuskegee Institute. The educational opportunities and convenient residential facilities attracted students from across the state and nation for over fifty years." Prior to the construction of the actual school—one building housing classrooms and the boys' dormitory and another for the president's home and the girls' dormitory—the sessions of the Consolidated White River Academy were held in the Mount Zion Missionary Baptist Church (Manatt and Mitchell 2009), the history of which is the subject of *All Eyes on Zion*.

The founding of Mount Zion in 1886 preceded the formal establishment of the national Baptist organization with which most Missionary Baptist churches are loosely affiliated, the National Baptist Convention, U.S.A., Inc. The Southern religion scholar Leroy Fitts (1993) notes that the NBC, which was founded on September 24, 1895, "is the largest body of organized African American Christians in the world," with about 7.5 million members in the early 1990s, "and the fourth largest denomination in the United States." Fitts points out that the "constitution and program development" of the organization "reflected the determination of the leadership to develop a denomination uniquely relevant to the needs of African American Baptists"; he adds that "freedom and self-determination were creative factors" in the establishment of the church (537).

Hearing from the Students: Michael, Keona, and Destinie at Work

The three oral historians, all members of Mount Zion, immersed themselves deeply in the project. Their questions ranged from church music, to the doctrine concerning baptism, to Reverend Harvey's views on his leadership. Central to the interview, however, are questions about the history of the church, its role in the African American community in Brinkley, and the church's stability. Their project positioned Michael, Keona, and Destinie both as interrogators of a religious tradition they had grown up in and as authors of a play, a new genre to them that would celebrate Mount Zion as a steadfast institution in a town and region struggling to remain viable.

Here are the nineteen questions that Michael, Keona, and Destinie posed:

1. What are your views on the styles of the church music?
2. What are your views on baptism by water?
3. What is your position like in the church now?
4. Who was the pastor before you took over the church?
5. Do you know how many people had attended the church back when you first started compared with now?

6. How would you describe your church?
7. As the years passed, what were interior changes to the church?
8. Were there any special members who came to this church?
9. Were there any churches competing with Mount Zion?
10. Did the church attendance increase or decrease at an alarming rate?
11. Can you give a brief description of the history of the church?
12. What was the most valuable aspect of the church back then?
13. How would you describe a successful church pastor?
14. What is your reason for taking over the church?
15. Is this church the oldest black church in Brinkley?
16. Before this church was built where did African Americans gather for service?
17. Do you know anyone who witnessed the Brinkley cyclone?
18. Were there any conflicts or problems between members of the church?
19. Describe your leadership style in the church, along with what have been some of your weaknesses and strengths.

Certainly, this list might strike a reader as an eclectic collection. Its various foci probably result from its having been created by a committee of three students, each with his or her own special interests, but we maintain that the center-of-gravity questions on the list are those evoking the students' concerns about the history of the church, its prominence in Brinkley, and its stabilizing force.

When we asked Destinie to select a handful of excerpts from the transcript that she thought were most important to the project, she chose the following four. Notice the confluence of concerns: Destinie's initial focus is on religious doctrine, but her center-of-gravity interest lies in questions about the steady attendance figures, the connection of the church to the history of the cyclone, and, in particular, the role of Mount Zion as a spiritual home for African Americans in Brinkley:

DESTINIE SHELTON: What are your views on baptism by water?

REVEREND HARVEY: Well, baptism by water symbolizes the birth, death, burial, and resurrection of Christ and I think that baptism by water being that it was started in the Bible that we should do so. And I feel that by doing that we are being obedient to what is written in the word of God.

DS: Do you know how many people had attended the church back when you first started compared with now?

RH: Through looking over some old records I think that highest attendance of this church was back in the early 1900s at about 136. If I am not mistaken, I believe that we are somewhere around that number now . . . so attendance now is probably about the same as it was at its best back in the early 1900s.

DS: Can you give a brief description of the history of the church that you know of?

RH: Well, this church was organized, it was actually organized in 1886 and later on it was destroyed by the cyclone that came through in the early 1900s and this church was rebuilt and reconstructed in 1909. That would make this particular building about one hundred years old now.

DS: Before the church was built, where did the African Americans gather for service?

RH: I believe that before the church was built there were other churches that were on the outskirts of the city of Brinkley. Since that time those churches have been torn down, but I believe that there were other churches in other places of worship before this church was built, to my understanding.

The Script and the Performance

It's always difficult for a written version to do justice to the power of a play. *All Eyes on Zion* was performed with singing, with call and response, and with scene changes as suggested by the dialogue. The entire gathering of ADOHP participants—University of Arkansas students, high school students, and teachers—witnessed the performance in April 2008.

All Eyes on Zion: Over One Hundred Years of Worship

CAST MEMBERS

J. D. Humphrey . . . Michael Devine
Deacon Walker . . . Larry Walker
Appointee Chunn . . . Wesley Chunn Jr.
Sister Julie Swanigan . . . Keona Jackson
Sister Emma Harvey . . . Destinie Shelton
Sister Patsy Arnett . . . Kathleen Meacham
Historical Reader . . . Anna Paige Frein

HISTORICAL READER: This is the story of Mt. Zion Missionary Baptist Church where it all began in Brinkley, Arkansas. In 1886, a group of Christians led by Rev. J. D. Humphrey came to worship the Lord together, but they did not have a sanctuary. That didn't stop them. They met under a shade tree to have their services.

Scene 1

J. D. HUMPHREY: Let us stand for prayer and then we will begin with a song led by Deacon Walker and joining the congregation.

DEACON WALKER: Pass me not, O gentle Savior,
Hear my humble cry,
While on others Thou art calling,
Do not pass me by.

CONGREGATION: Savior, Savior,
Hear my humble cry,
While on other Thou art calling,
Do not pass me by.

Let me at a throne of mercy
Find a sweet relief,
Kneeling there in deep contrition,
Help my unbelief.

Savior, Savior,
Hear my humble cry,

While on other Thou art calling,
Do not pass me by.

J. D. HUMPHREY: Psalms 125: They that trust in the Lord shall be as a Mount Zion, which cannot be removed, but abideth forever. As the mountains are round about Jerusalem, so the Lord is round about his people from henceforth even forever.

HISTORICAL READER: The congregation eventually built a church, but the cyclone of March 8, 1909, destroyed it. Services were held under a tent at the south end of New Orleans and Lynn Street. Before the year was past, the brick church that now stands was erected on land donated by Major William Black, one of the earliest settlers of Brinkley. The church has gothic architecture, and was listed on the National Register of Historic Places on November 4, 1986.

Scene 2

J. D. HUMPHREY: Our topic for today will be obedience. If you obey the will of God merciful blessings will come your way.

CONGREGATION: Amen, Amen (*claps*).

J. D. HUMPHREY: Soon enough, we will have equal rights, this civil rights movement won't last forever, God's people will be free and as Martin Luther King said, we will not be judged by the color of our skin but by the content of our character.

CONGREGATION: Amen.

J. D. HUMPHREY: God will never let his people down because he has that what we call unconditional love. All we have to do is to live a holy life and obey his word. Now, let us have the benediction. Leading this will be Brotha Chunn.

APPOINTEE CHUNN: Let us bow our heads. Dear Heavenly Father we ask that you protect us from hurt, harm, death, evil, and accidents. Lead us in the path of righteousness and we just thank you Lord for the many blessings you have stored upon us and the many more we will receive. Amen.

HISTORICAL READER: By 2006, the membership of the church dwindled to 3 members. Led by Pastor Eddie Harvey, there are now over 136 members. The church has Wednesday night services and choir practice for all ages, led by the pastor's wife, Mrs. Cassandra Harvey. The church also has Sunday morning worship and services, and occasional programs. We are sure that the anointing of Mount Zion Missionary Baptist Church will continue for the next hundred years.

Scene 3

(Song: "Let's Have a Little Church")

J. D. HUMPHREY: At this time we ask—is there anything that need to be said . . . testimonies or anything.

SISTER PATSY ARNETT: Yes, Reverend, I have something to say.

J. D. HUMPHREY: At this time I grant you the floor.

SISTER PATSY ARNETT: Well, the storm from the past week blew a tree down four steps from my son's house. Thank God there was no one home Lord Jesus, because it could have hit right in the living room of his house. Thank you Jesus.

(Song: "Excellent")

SISTER JULIE SWANIGAN: I'll tell you what. That storm left a lot of debris everywhere. After the storm, there was a tree knocked over across my driveway blocking me in. I could not go anywhere that day. That is, until they came and got the tree. I am very grateful to be here today. Lord knows where I would be right now if it wasn't for him.

J. D. HUMPHREY: At this time I ask that we prepare ourselves for the announcements by Sister Emma.

SISTER EMMA HARVEY: Good Morning, Saints!

CONGREGATION: Good Morning!

SISTER EMMA HARVEY: Sunday March 8, 2009, we will have pastor and wife's anniversary. That is all we have for today. Thank you and have a blessed week!

(Song: "Battle Field")

All Eyes on Zion: Youth, In Place, Celebrating the Epideictic, Doing Intellectual Work

All Eyes on Zion evinces a seemingly strange mélange of interests—issues about music in the church, beliefs about baptism, the number of people who attended Mount Zion in the past and do so now. We believe the most salient of the interview questions, however, are two near the end of the list, about "our reasons for taking over the church" and whether Mount Zion is "the oldest black church" in Brinkley. We surmise that the young Brinkley oral historians, all of whom were African American, found a symbol of strength and stability in the history of Mount Zion. Their interrogation of Reverend Harvey looks for sources of these characteristics in the church's history: Were there conflicts between people or factions? How were they worked out? The church population had dwindled considerably—how did Reverend Harvey and the congregation bring the church back to life? These are questions that no course these students had taken in American history, or even Arkansas history, had allowed them to ask. These are questions that invite the students to perceive local forces that might be conducive to reinhabitation. The brief play unobtrusively but clearly answers these questions: Mount Zion Baptist Church has survived in Brinkley since 1886 by its members' praying, praising in song, and taking care of one another's needs.

The project, culminating in the play, provided the students the opportunity to write themselves into the narrative that Mount Zion Baptist Church has written in Brinkley since 1886. *All Eyes on Zion*, with its mixture of preaching, dialogue, call and response, music, and scripture, emerges as a hybrid text, allowing its young creators—citizens of a town facing facts of declining population and economic prospects—to find roots and stability. Like the students who produced the first *Foxfire* magazine, the Brinkley trio captured stories of perseverance and self-sufficiency from the church elders. The play is pure epideictic, celebrating the values of the church as a pillar of the community. Moreover, the play offers clear instances of its creators' examining the church's history, analyzing its methods, evaluating its past and its present—all hallmarks of the construction of knowledge one expects to see in authentic intellectual work.

The Whole Church Sings: The Story of Crossett's Westside Church of Christ

For her project during year two of the Arkansas Delta Oral History Project, Lauren Wilson, then a first-year student at the University of Arkansas, decided to interrogate a thorny bit of church history in her hometown of Crossett, Arkansas. Crossett, a town of about 5,400 people in the southeast corner of the state, is known as the lumber capital of the South. Founded in the late 1890s by a businessmen from Davenport, Iowa, and incorporated in 1903, Crossett's lifeblood has always been the Crossett Lumber Company, established in 1899. The town is solidly working class, about 55 percent white and 40 percent African American. As the lumber industry began to shrink in the early 2000s, so did Crossett: it lost 11.3 percent of its population between 2000 and 2009 and another 2.5 percent between 2010 and 2013 (US Census Bureau 2000–).

Wilson wanted to learn about the founding of her home church, the Westside Church of Christ, and in particular about the relationship between her church and the all-white Pine Street Church of Christ that was already established in Crossett before the founding of the Westside Church. Although the two churches shared a religious philosophy, the members of the black Westside Church of Christ were allowed to use the Pine Street Church of Christ for baptisms only after all the white churchgoers had left for the evening. In a retrospective interview, Wilson explained what sparked her inquiry. "I just wanted to find out why there were two Churches of Christ, a white one and a black one. I mean, in the Bible it says there's only one church, and yet in Crossett and lots of other little towns there are often two churches for the different races."

What Wilson learned disturbed her: "I discovered that instead of inviting black people into their church, the folks in the white church would go into a black community and help them start their own church. They would let the black folks use their church for a while, but only after hours, when the white congregation wasn't using it. They let the black folks use their baptism. But it wouldn't surprise me if they changed the water afterward." Although the Pine Street congregation provided financial support for the Westside Church's founding, they were, as Wilson puts it, playing with "the most essential ingredient in one's total soul salvation."

Though she was interested in the church's past, Wilson was equally concerned with ensuring that her church continues to thrive in Crossett, or at least survive. She interviewed two leaders of the Westside Church of Christ congregation, Nathaniel and Velma Kidd, asking them about the founding and current status of the church.

The Church of Christ and African American Congregations

The Church of Christ is a mainstream Protestant denomination that formed in the early nineteenth century as an outgrowth of the efforts of several religious reformers: James O'Kelly in Baltimore, Abner Jones and Elias Smith in New England, Barton Stone in Kentucky, and Thomas and Alexander Campbell in what is now West Virginia. Each broke away from established churches to form new congregations that were devoted to reproducing what each reformer perceived to be the Christian Church that had originally been established on the Day of Pentecost in 30 AD. Each Church of Christ congregation is autonomous—there are no national or regional governing bodies or officials. The theology of the Church of Christ is firmly rooted in the New Testament.

Two notable features about the Church of Christ make their way into Wilson's project. The first is the custom that communion be served every Sunday, following Paul's model as set out in the Acts of the Apostles. The second is the proscription against the use of musical instruments in services. The Church of Christ historian Batsell Barrett Baxter (1995) explains the latter regulation in this way:

> As a result of the distinctive plea of the church—a return to New Testament Faith and practice—a cappella singing is the only music used in

> the worship. This singing, unaccompanied by mechanical instruments of music, conforms to the music used in the apostolic church and for several centuries thereafter (Ephesians 5:19). It is felt that there is no authority for engaging in acts of worship not found in the New Testament. This principle eliminates the use of instrumental music, along with the use of candles, incense, and other similar elements.

Although most people associate the African American Church with such denominations as the African Methodist Episcopal (AME) Church, the Church of God in Christ (COGIC), and Missionary Baptist churches, the Church of Christ has historically had significant African American congregations in large cities, small towns, and rural areas, and there is ample evidence of African American and white Church of Christ congregations coming together to worship, especially as a result of the civil rights movement in the 1960s.

Hearing from Lauren: A Conversation about Race and Religion in Crossett

Lauren's interview with the Kidds had a substantial thirty-seven questions. Reproducing the vernacular she used to talk with the Kidds, the interview is more akin to a conversation than to an actual oral history transcription. Lauren prompts her interviewees to talk about the history of race relations in Crossett and to relate stories about the founding of African American churches in the region, the founding of Westside Church and its relation to Pine Street Church, the roles that gospel preachers in general play in small towns in the South, Westside's relation to other African American churches in neighboring communities, and the particular practices of Church of Christ worship that Westside adheres to. Though it's difficult to find the best place to drop into Lauren's conversation, listen to the way she shapes the conversation in the last eight or so questions:

30. Does Westside have any relationship with those churches at all, or is it just kind of to itself . . . ?
31. What about its relationship with Westside, even though, I mean Pine Street, even though Pine Street helped with

building, was there racial tension in between the members of both congregations?

32. So what is that relationship like today?
33. When y'all worshipped there, were y'all the only blacks to worship there or were there others?
34. Do y'all have anything else that y'all would like to say about the founding of Westside in general or about its effect on the Crossett community as a whole?
35. So, what do y'all think? I know there's somewhat of a split in the Church of Christ, because of that issue. People not really wanting to go to Church of Christ. Some churches are conforming. They're bringing instruments in. They take the "of Christ" off, and just have the "Church." So what do y'all think about people who do it like that to try to bring more members in?
36. So, the membership, whenever y'all first came in, was it growing? Was the church growing when y'all first got here, like Westside?
37. When did it stop or decline?

Moreover, Lauren's questions make better sense as an interrogation of the culture she grew up in, as a contribution to critical pedagogy of place, and as an authentic construction of knowledge if one considers them in the context of the interview excerpts that Lauren designated as most important to her project.

LAUREN WILSON: So what were race relations like between blacks and whites here in Crossett?

VELMA KIDD: The race relationship here in Crossett was basically like it was all over the South. It was, we were segregated, and when we moved to Crossett, I had never heard of the term "black town" and "white town," and it still is today, you know, and I think Crossett is the most prejudiced town in the South (*VK and LW laugh*).

LW: Do you have anything to add to that, Brother Kidd?

NATHANIEL KIDD: Well, she's right about that. Yeah, it's like all over, you couldn't do this, you couldn't do that, and you had a special place that you didn't go to it, the special place and you got in trouble 'bout it, so it's the same all over.

LW: You just traveled to that congregation, for like gospel meetings? Could you talk about gospel meetings, for those who don't really know what they are?

NK: Well, gospel meetings is when preachers, when we get established good, then we go out and try to teach other people of the lost souls and bring them to Christ, and that's mainly what a gospel meeting is for. Preachers come to, we preachers come from different parts of the country, to come in and conduct the meeting, and we all try to talk it up and bring in what we can, so that they can find salvation for their souls.

LW: What about its relationship to Westside? I mean, even though Pine Street helped with the building, was there still racial tension between the members of both congregations?

VK: Because a lot of the older Christians, and I'm, and I know that you have to be taught to, taught against racism, so a lot of the older people didn't accept it, and they don't really accept it today, but they, they go along with it.

NK: What we would have to do, when we baptized someone, we were welcome, wasn't really welcome, but we could go to Pine Street and baptize them, but that would have to be at night after they had gone from the service, and we would go in and baptize.

LW: So, what do y'all think? I know there's somewhat of a split in the Church of Christ because of that issue. People not really wanting to go to Church of Christ. Some churches are conforming. They're bringing instruments in. They take the "of Christ" off, and just have the "Church." So what do y'all think about people who do it like that to try to bring more members in?

NK: Well, what we should to, we should go to work on stuff like that immediately, and when we have our gospel meetings and things, let those people speak, let those people speak their mind, and then we'll know what's hurting them and where and how to heal.

VK: Now, I know the Church is not for entertainment, and a lot of people like the music, and we do have music in the Church. Christ

> commanded us to sing with our voice, we can just, our music is vocal, and those that are, who want to have the music, like I say, they like the entertainment, but when we go to church, we go to worship the Lord, and if we want to be entertained, we have to leave the church to be entertained. But I don't, I know, like back in Christ's day, they were dissatisfied with His teaching, so when some of them obeyed the gospel, they left, they left because they did not agree with what Christ was teaching. So that's how it is today, you know, like those who were among and they went out from among us and established their own doctrine. So Christ is true, and like you said, like Peter said, "Let Christ be true in every man alive," so if we don't follow what Christ is, we don't follow the pattern, then that's going to be bad, you know spiritually in the last day. And some people are just dying to go to hell because Christ said, "Broad is the way to destruction and Narrow is the way to righteousness." And a lot of us don't, we're following those that were among us what . . . they're following the broad way, and the majority does not rule in the Church.

Lauren's Final Project: A Poetry Performance

As we noted in chapter 1, a great many students' final projects ended up being plays, influenced by Bob Ford's magnificent page-to-stage workshop. The inspiration for Lauren's choice of genre came from a different source. She was already familiar with the concept of "performance" poetry prior to her work in ADOHP, and one of the workshops in which ADOHP students participated in year two, led by Fayetteville's "poet laureate" Clayton Scott and the dance therapist Rebecca Hahn, focused on slam poetry. Some definitions might be in order for the uninitiated. As Lindsey Ellis, Anne Ruggles Gere, and L. Jill Lamberton (2003) explain, "Performance poetry is a broad term that describes poetry performed in a variety of contexts. A poet slams (performs) a poem at a slam (a performance poetry competition). In other words, slam poetry is performance poetry written specifically for competition, usually adhering to rules about length and use of props. Performance poems are presented to an audience with the whole body:

in word, in voice, and in gesture" (44–45). In her performance at the closing event for ADOHP in year two, Wilson thoroughly slammed "The Whole Church Sings."

As with the play in *All Eyes on Zion*, it is difficult to do justice to the vigor and spectacle—in word, voice, and gesture—of Wilson's performance of her project. Here is her script:

Matthew 16:18 "Upon this rock I will build my church; and the gates of hell shall not prevail against it."

And with these words, Jesus spoke the Church of Christ into existence.

It has undergone very few changes, remaining today through unyielding persistence.

"Holiness, Fundamentalist. . . ." No, just true to THIS text [*hold up Bible*]

Wit the same ultimate purpose
As the Church that Christ built,
Because it is Christ's Church, the Church of Christ.
Yet still, you ask, "What is it?"

The following was taken from a bulletin of the Westside Church of Christ in Crossett, Arkansas, whose founding I centered my project around:

"We would like you to make a careful comparison of this church with the one described in detailing your Bible. We believe that you will find that this church is not similar to, but is identical in everyway to the church you read about in the New Testament. This isn't an exclusive or wealthy church; everything about it is very simple, and it is not its purpose to feed vanity or pride with a display of vain things.

It is not its aim to amuse or entertain those who attend services. It exists here as a simple New Testament body, pointing those of its community to the Christ and God of the Bible. Its doors are open to those who from the quiet depths of their hearts would reach out to God in simple worship and by obedient living.

If you like to worship God in spirit and in truth, if you enjoy thinking and meditating on God's word; if you enjoy the work of God, if you appreciate warm, intimate, genuine brotherliness, you will enjoy attending the services of the Church of Christ."

Romans 16:16, Matthew 16:18

And now I will present to you a poetic and somewhat theatrical interpretation of Westside Church of Christ's founding from four points of view.

Iciphine Penn

Hi, my name is Iciphine Penn.
I just moved to Crossett from Ralston.
Yes, right over there by Camden!
Well anyway, I just thought I'd inquire
If Crossett has a black Church of Christ?
No, you say?! But it's 1958!
Oh, I suppose I'll just have to get one up here some way.
Do you know of anyone who could help me out?
Al Hunter, hm.
Ok, I'll give him a shout. Thank ya kindly, see ya around!

Velma Kidd

Crossett is just the most racist little town!
I'll be SO glad when we get this church building off the
ground.
Yeah, the white church is contributing financially
Toward the building and minister's salary
And actually,
They call themselves being "kind";
We can use their baptismal pool when they've left for the
night.
Are you kidding me?
I mean, sure, I'm appreciative
But how can you play with baptism?
The most essential ingredient
In one's total soul salvation?
Anything could happen from the time someone repents,

Confesses to Christ as the Son of God and prepares to be dipped
In the water, not sprinkled, but full immersion.
A murder could happen before the conversion!
You would risk a soul being lost
Because of your paranoia of skin that you think is too dark?
God doesn't like mess, but Lord willing we'll soon fix this.
We need to hurry up and get this building! I'll talk to you after the service.

Nathaniel Kidd

Yes, we're over at 109 North Georgia Street.
Church starts at 11, hope to see you next week!
Man, I gotta get ready for this gospel meeting.
I sure hope Brother Foster makes it up for the singing.
I need to make sure Velma has the sisters prepared;
The meal tomorrow needs to be a huge affair!
We got brothers and sisters coming from all over the state,
And even some from Louisiana and Mississippi are making their way.
Nah, I haven't been trained; didn't even graduate.
But yes, I am the minister, and I'll preach on Sunday
Morning, Foster can teach Sunday school;
Then after lunch and fellowship, he'll put us in a spiritual mood
With some spiritual food,
Dessert, if you will, to the delicious meal
That I hope will be revealed
After morning service; that's how it's supposed to go.
I wonder if any of those "others" will come in and ruin the show.
It gets old, them coming in and challenging what we teach.
How many times must we tell them?
Read your Bible, and there'd be no reason to disagree.
They call us intimidating, the Church of Christ!

Say we divide the black community; ha!
OPEN YOUR EYES!
Christ built one church, not one hundred.
At least, that's what my Bible says;
Theirs may not be the same. . . .

Me, Lauren Wilson

Fifty years ago, a church was begun
With faith and a home, a small victory was won.
Then two souls came in with a zeal so strong,
Got the church a building,
Spent eight years there preaching,
And in Fountain Hill, got a church coming along.
Westside has had its share of struggles,
From part-time preachers,
Full-time hustlers
Conflict with others
From whom they are still separated
To this day. Even relations
With its sister congregation
Aren't that great; yet Westside survives
On North Georgia, 109.
Continually passing the test of time.
Maybe you all should visit sometime.
Be prepared to sing, you'll find no choir
Nor piano, drums, guitar; the whole church sings
To God's desire.
Every Sunday, you'll take communion,
According to verses 23–29 in first Corinthians.
And when you hear the sermon,
It is solely for your learning,
So that you may hear, believe, repent, confess, and be
    baptized
For your sins' remission.
This would be your finding,

If you stepped into Westside
Church of Christ.
I hope you enjoyed your tiny glimpse inside.

"The Whole Church Sings": Past, Present, and Future in Crossett, Authentically Done

Wilson pulls no punches in her final product. She is adamant in her castigation of the Pine Street congregation and in her adherence to the practices of the Church of Christ that she sees as rooted in New Testament theology. But Wilson's project is more than a simple "this I believe" story, more than just an instance of the kind of bald assertions about religious faith that cause discomfort. Drawing liberally from the interview transcript, the performance poetry script represents Wilson's interrogation not only into the history of Westside Church but also into its prominence in the African American community in Crossett and its potential to keep the community vital and growing. With "The Whole Church Sings," Wilson contributes her part to the ongoing discourse about how to keep Crossett, and towns throughout Arkansas like Crossett, viable and sustainable. Conversing with the Kidds at a level that most students don't get the opportunity to, Wilson speaks to a question central to critical pedagogy of place: What do we need to know about this institution to assist in decolonization and reinhabitation? The script clearly bears the hallmarks of authentic intellectual work: interpretation and evaluation of knowledge embodied in a new genre, one appropriate to the purpose Wilson wanted to achieve and the audience she was addressing.

A Matter of Respect: African American Women and Hats

People refer to Sunday mornings as the most segregated hour of the week in the South, and there is more than a grain of truth in the statement. Sunday mornings in the Arkansas Delta are a time when many people attend worship services and choose to do so at a church attended by people of their own race and culture. Certainly African American and white churches offer different styles of worship to attendees. But the preaching and singing are not the only differences.

The clothing the worshipers wear and, in particular, the hats worn by many African American women draw another distinction between the groups of worshipers.

In year three of the ADOHP, the University of Arkansas junior Estrellita (Estee) Goss tapped into the connections between clothing and church cultures in her project. Estee interviewed Thelma Bailey Thomason, who was born in Arkansas City, Arkansas, a small community in Southeast Arkansas located on the banks of the Mississippi River. Throughout her youth, Thomason attended the First Baptist Church in her hometown and was baptized there. After graduating from Arkansas city schools, she attended Arkansas Baptist College in Little Rock, Arkansas, and then the University of Wisconsin in Madison, where she earned a degree in elementary education. Thomason worked as an elementary teacher one year in Augusta, Arkansas, prior to taking a position in Fayetteville, Arkansas, where she taught elementary school for over forty years. At the time of the interview, she was an active member of the congregation at St. James Missionary Baptist Church in Fayetteville, where she attended each Sunday, as she said, "proudly wearing a hat."

Goss wrote three original poems based on the interview with Thomason. She entitled the group of poems *Respect*, and certainly the theme runs through each of the poems. "Hat Hunt" tells the story of the search for the right hat for the project—a hat that fit both Goss's desire for a hat she could use again for "racing day" and a hat that would hold its own "amid the black queens' best." In the second poem of the trio, "On the Black Woman in Her Hat," Goss pays homage to the spirit of the black woman, alluding to the pride and dignity connected to wearing the Sunday hat. "Don't be Fooled" juxtaposes the outward appearance of the black woman—polished in dress, pearls, and shoes—with the actions she has taken in order to survive the life she has lived. Only the hat of the black woman's outfit is truly what it seems—her crown.

Goss gave a riveting performance of the poems at the culminating event of the 2008 Arkansas Delta Oral History Project. Rising from where she sat demurely in the audience dressed in her Sunday best and newly purchased "crown," Goss approached the podium to denounce the fashions she sees in church and then gave a dramatic reading of "Hat Hunt" and "On the Black Woman in Her Hat." Goss then sang "Wade in the Water," a traditional African American spiritual, and finished her performance with "Don't Be Fooled."

African American Women and Church Hats

In a great many African American Protestant churches, the custom of women wearing hats to Sunday service reflects not only a tradition passed down from grandmothers and mothers to daughters and granddaughters but also the strong influence of the apostle Paul's theology on the church.

The documentary *The Tradition of Hats in the African American Church*, which aired on PBS on February 13, 2004, captures the traditional aspect strongly. The reporter, Bob Faw, a regular on *NBC Nightly News* at the time, interviewed the Rev. A. Knighton Stanley, pastor of the People's Congregational Church in Washington, DC, several of Rev. Stanley's parishioners, and Craig Marberry, the coauthor (with Michael Cunningham) of *Crowns*, a book about the wearing of hats in African American churches that was later adapted for the stage by Regina Taylor. As Faw points out early in the program, "Hats are so prominent, so vital here because it's the heritage: the African tradition of adorning the head for worship. Slave women, for example, would cover their heads with bandanas, giving them that special touch by decorating them with wildflowers." Later in the program, Marberry noted that the custom became stronger after emancipation. "Hats became an instant symbol that you have arrived, that you are on your feet. . . . The hats became more and more flamboyant because the more trinkets and adornments that you could add to your hat, you were saying, 'Look how God has blessed me.'" Rev. Stanley added a humorous aside, noting how seriously the older women especially in his congregation took the responsibility of wearing hats: "I'm of that generation when African American women wore hats, they meant business! So there's a kind of moral authority in hats. So when I look out and see those hats, it's frightening."

The injunction that African American women should wear hats to church comes ultimately from Paul's letter to the church at Corinth, but the foundation of this theological dictum, as experienced in the African American Church, is stronger than a simple "thou shalt" from the apostle. Indeed, the groundwork for the apostle's belief underlying the pronouncement has resonated through African American culture and politics from the days of slavery to the present. The specific reference to hat wearing comes in 1 Corinthians 11:5: "every woman who prays or prophesies with her head unveiled disgraces her head." Certainly for any person who looks to scripture for specific advice on how to comport herself in church, that sentence would be enough to mandate the wearing of hats. But Paul's letters have always held a particularly revered prominence for African Americans, so it's appropriate to consider his general influence as well for this particular injunction.

Though Paul's attitudes toward slavery have occupied volumes of scholarship (see, for example, Harrill 1995), the early African American Church found in the apostle an antislavery crusader, a clear position articulated in two passages of scripture. The first is in Galatians 3:28, where Paul writes, "There is neither Jew nor Greek, slave nor free, male nor female, for you are all one in Christ Jesus." The second comes in the rather elaborate story of Onesimus, a runaway slave. Colossians 4:9 tells the backstory: Onesimus had fled his master, Philemon, and gone to Rome where the imprisoned Paul had converted him to Christianity. Paul's later letter to Philemon tells the story of Paul's sending Onesimus *back* to his master, but it gives special instructions on how Onesimus is to be received. Paul directs Philemon to receive him "no longer as a slave, but more than a slave, a beloved brother, especially to me, but how much rather to you, both in the flesh and in the Lord" (Philemon 1:16). Since Onesimus is now "no longer a slave" but instead "a beloved brother," Paul urges Philemon that "if you now count me as a partner, receive him as you would receive me" (1:17).[1] Careful attention to scripture, therefore, directs devout African

1. The contemporary biblical scholar John Dominic Crossan sees this story of the return and "unslaving" of Onesimus as an example of "the radical and historical

American believers to not only do what Paul says must be done in proper worship—for example, women must cover their heads—but to also revere him as cultural leader and role model.

The emphasis in the African American Church on attending to Paul's theology in African American religion and politics, moreover, goes beyond his New Testament letters. To African American religious leaders, particularly to Martin Luther King Jr., Paul has been a key figure in a theory of biblical interpretation called *typology*. Malinda Snow (1985) explains how typology works: "In traditional biblical exegesis, one searches for (or discovers) *types*: people or events in sacred history, usually in the Old Testament, that anticipate or foreshadow people or events, usually in the New Testament. For example, Moses may be seen as a type of Christ, the tree of Eden as a type of the "tree" of Calvary, and so on (the second item in these and similar pairs is the *antitype*)" (319). Prior to the Protestant Reformation, Snow maintains, typological interpretation was limited to arguing how Old Testament stories and images prefigured those in the New Testament. After the Reformation, however, interpreters felt comfortable seeing biblical situations as prefiguring conditions of contemporary life. The English Puritans who settled New England, for example, were wont to see themselves as the antitype of the children of Israel, founding a new Jerusalem (319).

This Protestant version of typological interpretation was particularly useful for the establishment of the African American Church. As Snow explains: "When the slaves embraced Christianity, they found in biblical narratives a way to express their own experience profoundly and metaphorically. Biblical stories of suffering prefigured their suffering; biblical stories of victory over impossible odds prefigured their hopes. In the story of the Children of Israel in Egypt, they discovered

---

Paul" (Crossan, "The Search for the Historical Paul," n.p.). Crossan maintains that Paul's later statements about slavery, in which some might see the apostle's taking either a neutral or an affirmative stance toward the institution, come from letters that Paul might not have written (for example, Ephesians 6:5–9) or certainly did not write (Titus 2:9–10).

the central type of their experience, which prefigured their own deliverance from slavery" (319).

According to Snow, King regularly invoked Protestant typology in his sermons and essays. One sermon cast Mahatma Gandhi as an antitype of Moses and the British colonizers as antitypes of the Pharaohs. Another sermon portrayed the apostle Paul, in his letter to the Romans, whom he was ultimately unable to visit, as a type for believers who have not reached all their goals (319–20). A notable sermon, "Paul's Letter to the American Church," offers King the opportunity to assume the persona of Paul and preach against racial segregation in the American church (320). Ultimately, Snow argues that King's "Letter from Birmingham Jail" was an antitype, adapting and expanding the genre of the Pauline epistle, the type.

In short, in the African American Church, the apostle Paul has always been more than simply an arbiter of what to wear to services. Devout churchgoers would know implicitly that a Pauline injunction for women to cover their heads was a metonym that resonated with the apostle's historical and continuing relevance for their faith, their church. As the contemporary African American scholar Kendra King puts it:

> It seems that the Apostle's reminder to Timothy experienced a new birth in the twentieth century through the political activism, ingenuity, and truth-to-power messages of the Black church, which used the pulpit to call America back to herself in terms of African-American social, economic, and political equality. Moreover, it has been the continued activism of the Black church and its leaders that has helped to ensure the equitable treatment of African Americans in the twentieth century through Paul's three-pronged strategy of power, love, and stableness of thought. (172)

Hearing from Estee: Well-Planned Questions, Rich Responses

Unlike Wilson's conversation with the Kidds, Goss's interview with Mrs. Thomason was carefully scripted. Goss's research had provided ample background material on the significance of Sunday hats, the women's reasons for wearing hats, and the influence of the civil rights movement on the tradition. Goss, a Delta native herself, was thoroughly primed to investigate a topic that she had come to know and see in action in her home region.

1. First of all, why do you feel that hats are worn to church?
2. First Corinthians 11:5 says that a woman should cover her head when at worship to symbolize her obedience to God. If that was the only reason to wear hats, then all Christian women would wear hats to church. Why do you feel that black women in particular have embraced this command so wholeheartedly?
3. You mentioned that the pastor would say you don't come into God's house inappropriately dressed. How would you dress to go to a friend's?
4. I would like to share a quote with you from the book *Crowns*: "Countless Black women would rather attend church naked than hatless. For these women, a church hat, flamboyant as it may be, is no mere fashion accessory; it's a cherished African American custom, one observed with boundless passion by Black women of various religious denominations. A woman's hat speaks long before its wearer utters a word. It's what Deirdre Guion calls 'hattitude' . . . there's a little more strut in your carriage when you wear a nice hat. There's something special about you." If a hat says a lot about a person, it says even more about a people—the customs they observe, the symbols they prize, and the fashions they fancy. And that's from *Crowns* by Michael Cunningham and Craig Marberry. What does the term "hattitude" mean to you?
5. Are you familiar with the Red Hat Society social group?
6. The Red Hat Society is a predominantly white social group that insists on fun, frivolity, and sisterhood at all ages. It is based on a line from the poem "Warning" by Jenny Joseph that reads, "When I am old, when I am an old woman I shall wear purple with a red hat which doesn't go, and doesn't suit me." They are distinguished by their bright red and purple outfits,

which they wear to functions and meetings. One of the only stipulations that they have is that if you are under fifty you wear light purple and pink instead of the red and purple. You reserve that until you're over fifty, which they call "The Birthday." How does the "hat culture" in black churches compare with this?

7. On February 11, 2007, twenty-six black churches in the Baltimore area held "Red Dress Sunday," where parishioners were encouraged to wear red outfits in order to raise awareness of the increased risk for African Americans to develop heart disease. The day was filled with medical lectures and community events that spread knowledge of heart-disease prevention and treatment. In the church you attend, are there any such events held?
8. Can you describe the most outlandish hat you ever saw?
9. What is the social etiquette on giving and receiving hat compliments?
10. Is there a distinction between hats that you wear in the spring and hats you wear in the winter?
11. How, if at all, do you feel the use of hats in the black Delta churches is any different from the rest of the South?
12. Do you yourself wear hats to church?
13. What does your favorite hat look like?
14. Do you know how many you have?
15. This past Sunday was Easter. How, if at all, are Easter Sunday hats different from regular Sunday hats?
16. It has been said that women from the Church of God in Christ denomination have the most beautiful hats. What do you think about that statement?
17. What would you do if one of your friends came up to you and said, "Now, Thelma, I just got this hat. What do you think?" And this is not a nice hat, to put it nicely. What would you do—how would you react?
18. How do you feel that the use of hats, gloves, and other accessories like pearls and handkerchiefs was influenced by the civil rights movement?

19. When the "liberated black woman" of the 1970s started wearing Afros and dashikis to church, how do you feel that that was received by the "pearls and handkerchiefs" set?
20. I've learned that hats, especially favorite, nostalgic, or costly hats, were handed down to posterity. Culturally, what do you feel is the significance of this?
21. Do you think that you would give your hats to your daughters if they didn't want them?
22. Contemporary services, where worshipers attend in jeans, are increasing in popularity. How do you feel about this, and what does it say for the future of hat usage?
23. African tribes are some of the most beautifully adorned people in the whole world. Comparing the two cultures, how do you feel that this African tradition of decoration compares with the modern black American practice of "stylin'" at church?
24. Is there anything we didn't cover, or that you would like to add?

As the excerpts from the interview show, Mrs. Thomason was an extremely generous informant, providing Goss with perspectives on religion, race, and Arkansas culture that would eventually make their way into Goss's final project of three poems. Notice, however, that the interview excerpts Goss provided to us show her veering away from the careful script of planned questions and tapping into a rich conversation with Mrs. Thomason.

ESTEE GOSS: First of all, why do you feel that hats are worn to church?

THELMA THOMASON: Okay, well that's a two-way question because hats now are not in demand and that's reflected in the church. Up here for our congregations in Fayetteville, maybe three people wear hats to church. If I go home to Arkansas City, everybody in church has on a hat. So, they haven't changed. They still think that the head should be covered. . . . Here now, hats are not the "in thing" anymore. But I feel like, since I was reared like that, and was trained and told why and how I should wear a hat, I still wear my hats when I can, because I still think that women should be fully dressed. See, I'm one of them fully dressed women. You should be fully dressed with your hat. . . . But you should always have your head covered in church. That's out of total respect for who you're serving, and respect for yourself, too. . . .

EG: First Corinthians 11:5 says that a woman should cover her head when at worship to symbolize her obedience to God. If that was the only reason to wear hats, then all Christian women would wear hats to church. Why do you feel that black women in particular have embraced this command so wholeheartedly?

TT: Because they're still sticking to the old whole Bible, you know. Back then the black women believed anything the minister said. There wasn't a whole lot of reading, but there was a whole lot of listening to what the ministers said. They talked about being submissive to your husband; they talked about being appropriately dressed when you come into God's house, and they [the black women] listened, and they listened well. And they just did it. There were not a lot of questions. . . .

EG: I would like to share a quote with you from the book *Crowns*:

> Countless Black women would rather attend church naked than hatless. For these women, a church hat, flamboyant as it may be, is no mere fashion accessory; it's a cherished African American custom, one observed with boundless passion by Black women of various religious denominations. A woman's hat speaks long before its wearer utters a word. It's what Dierdre Guion calls "hattitude . . . there's a little more strut in your carriage when you wear a nice hat. There's something special about you."

If a hat says a lot about a person, it says even more about a people-the customs they observe, the symbols they prize, and the fashions they fancy. And that's from *Crowns* by Michael Cunningham and Craig Marberry. What does the term "hattitude" mean to you?

TT: Hattitude means to me that I stuck to whatever my belief was. I still believe that we should wear our heads covered up in church. I grew up like that. From the time I was seven, I can remember, until where I am now, that you should always go appropriately dressed to church. And then, you don't show up in God's house looking like you just left the honky tonks, as they would call it. So that's the reason. And when we wear hats that shows that you still believe—you still have that belief that there's going to be a better thing happen to you. . . . We still believe deeply that you should have that within you to be responsible now to dress the right way to go to church to worship. Don't go worship the same way you go buy groceries. Don't go worship the same way you go visit a friend . . . this is the Sabbath day, I was told. And it still is—respect the Sabbath day. Now I know that the Sabbath day is made for man, but back then, it was known as God's day. You didn't cook, you didn't wash, you didn't iron, you didn't do anything. You went to church. And believe me, we were there all day. So, see that came up in me, and that will never be gone. I cook on Sundays, because I have no choice, but, the other stuff still sticks with me—before I leave the house, I'm dressed. I'm ready. And you know, you feel naked [without a hat], if that's the way you came up. . . . And you're used to that. Well, I was used to doing these hats all my life, and still wear [them] and that's the way I taught my daughter. . . . My mom, she's ninety-one. She's still decked up in her hat on Sunday, and she'll tell you, "That's not the right color," because she knows what she likes, and she likes her hats. I asked her, "Mom, would you go to church without a hat on?" She said, "I'd go, but I'd feel real strange." So it's a belief, it's a deep belief. . . . The identity that they were taught—that their grandmother passed to their mother, and their mother passed to them, and just keeps going on and on—it's a cycle.

EG: Do you yourself wear hats to church?

TT: Every time I get a chance.

EG: Is there a distinction between hats that you wear in the spring and hats you wear in the winter?

TT: Yeah! You got summer hats, winter hats, fall hats, all kinds of hats. You don't wear a straw hat in the winter. . . . Now, fall hats would be more like the felt hats . . . the stronger type hats. The crushable hats, you would wear in the wintertime. And in spring, you wear bright hats, bright colors, maybe some flowers, maybe the veil—just something very light looking. Not dark. Darkness is for the winter, springtime is light, and summer gets even lighter. You can wear ones with just the brim, and this part would be up. You know, your crown is out. You can wear summer hats strictly for the sun if it's out. I don't like the sun to get on me, so I wear wide-brim hats. There are all kinds of hats. And they cost all kinds of money.

EG: I know. I was trying to shop for one, Good Lord! Three hundred bucks, easy.

TT: That's right!

EG: And that's for a little pillbox with a little piece of net on it.

TT: Where you buy hats, though—I'll give you this tip. The winter has just ended, you go to Dillard's, and you look at all the hats that they didn't sell for the winter, and you buy a couple of winter hats. At the end of summer, when they didn't sell all those and it's getting ready for fall, go buy you some summer hats. See, how you can keep up like that?

EG: How do you feel that the use of hats, gloves, and other accessories like pearls and handkerchiefs was influenced by the civil rights movement?

TT: Well, that civil rights movement was something great. But at first it showed unity. They were all together. It was just a beautiful sight to see people that, for once in your lifetime, just got together. You knew where you came from. . . . But you take those people out there that stuck together and said okay, this is just me, and I'm showin' it the way I am. They showed it the way they were. They were dressed with their hats and whatever, I don't know 'bout them pearls, but the hats, and the gloves, was okay. And for me, I didn't see the purpose of marching with gloves. I would have had my hands just loose. I'd have had a hat on, but I wouldn't have—it probably would have been a work hat, um, you know, I wouldn't have been decked up. But, they were just showing true—true to the cause. That's what that was. And I think some of them went out and bought a new hat and stuff like that but you know, um, they were trying to—there's time to show unity, for once.

EG: And this is something that marks your culture as a people—something that unifies the women.

TT: Exactly! That's what that was, and it was a beautiful thing.

EG: African tribes are some of the most beautifully adorned people in the whole world. Comparing the two cultures, how do you feel that this African tradition of decoration compares with the modern black American practice of "stylin'" at church?

TT: Well, see, that's still—there's no belief. If you stylin', you just goin' for the style. You goin' to church to be seen. I think that—I don't know too much about African cultures. From what I see on TV, I really like everything I see that they wear.

EG: There should be a company or system of some sort that has this big hat swap. You know? If it ran from across the country, once they wear the hat three times, boom, get a new one.

TT: That's right. That's right. Now, having said that, in Eureka Springs, they have the vintage hats. . . . She has beautiful hats. Sometimes she'll call and say, "I have two or three of these." I'll drive up there, and she has them and the price is sometimes wrong, but if you drive that far, you just going to get it anyway. But that kind of place is there. . . . I'd probably have every hat in the world if they did that, because I'd want all the fancy hats! But that would be a good thing to have, though, if we would do that. But now, in this area, I don't think there'd be enough hats coming in. I think if you were in the area of Chicago, or New Jersey. . . .

EG: Or Atlanta!

TT: Atlanta! Yes! And Memphis. Pine Bluff [Arkansas] is not bad, though. They show up every service with their hats on. . . . They have a lot of pretty things down there, and they wear a lot of pretty hats. And where they get the shoes, I'd like to know, too, because there's some fancy shoes. But when you get old you can't wear heels, so that's that.

Final Project: Three Poems

Respect

Don't be fooled by this dress I have on,
For I have scrubbed floors and burped my babies,
Don't be fooled by this pearls I have on,

For I have mowed the yard and changed the oil,
Don't be fooled by this shoes I have on,
For I have chased after dreams and runaway hats,
Don't be fooled by this polish I have on,
For I have whupped my claws out more times than I care to
tell,
Don't be fooled by this sweater I have on,
For my heart has been chilled by a friend's betrayal,
Don't be fooled by this face I have on,
For I have wept over my share of grievances,
But my children, this hat is what it seems,
For I am a Queen and this is my crown.

Hat Hunt

I went to by a hat to wear for you today,
I wanted something that I could use racing day,
But as I shopped online, a problem I did see,
A plain hat would be fine, to watch an Oaklawn spree,
But if to church I went, amid the black queens best,
Straight back home I'd be sent,
Their hats outshine the rest,
Ebay ended my search, it serves both black and white,
I now could go to church, and dress myself just right,
So here I stand for you, all decked out in my hat,
To honor these black queens, and show I'm down with that.

On the Black Woman in Her Hat

A soul so rich and deep that vast skies cannot contain it,
A being so savory and spiced a whole sea cannot sterilize it,
She walks with the rhythm of Africa—to the beat of her very
own drum,
This ornament she wears so proudly sets her apart—a canvas
to project herself onto.
This crucial accessory that represents so much,
Unites her with her mother, friends, and sisters.

Through injustice and hardship, these hats are symbols of her
creed.
The truths these women cherish are unalienable,
Even if their hats are.

Religion, Church, Customs: Reasons to Call the Delta Home

All three student projects in this chapter focus ultimately on some aspect of the African American Church's role in the political and cultural fabric of the Arkansas Delta. Goss's project illuminates this dimension of Delta life in a slightly different way than does the Brinkley writers' or Wilson's. While she was a participant in the ADOHP, Goss was a long-standing resident of Searcy, the county seat of White County in east-central Arkansas, the home of Harding University, a traditionally conservative fundamental Baptist institution, and one of the few cities in the region to grow in population from roughly nineteen thousand to almost twenty-three thousand between 2000 and 2010. Searcy is also one of the most predominantly Caucasian towns in the region; nearly 87 percent of its residents are white. Goss, intensely proud of her Latina family background, grew up as an ethnic minority in Searcy, where only 4.6 percent of the citizens are of Hispanic or Latino heritage. As a person who viewed the African American Church as an outsider, and whose own heritage was a bit outside the mainstream culture of her hometown, Goss used her final project to celebrate African American women's wearing of hats to church as a symbol of stability in a region undergoing substantial change. Goss's project celebrates the wearing of hats as emblems of intergenerational pride. Goss's poems are literate emblems of her understanding of part of the social composition, the social text, of the Delta. They embody what Gruenewald means when he talks about reinhabitation: an initiative to "identify, recover, and create material spaces and places that teach us how to live well in our total environments" (2003, 9). And certainly the poems represent authentic intellectual work on Goss's part: They evaluate rather than simply report. They emerge in a real genre. Their speakers, their characters, are alive, and are not simply academic abstractions.

4

Food and Foodways

Traditions Worth Saving and Reliving

AS WE EXPLAINED IN CHAPTER 2, many student projects in the ADOHP capitalized on the epideictic. These projects, with their central goal of vivifying and illuminating the values and mores that have created a quality of life distinctive to the Delta, show the argumentative burden of the epideictic. Epideictic texts do not simply celebrate, they must also argue: These values, these ways of life, are *worth* maintaining.

Such arguments were clearly visible in a range of ADOHP students' projects about food. As several students discovered, food in the Delta plays a fascinating cultural role, perhaps more strikingly than in other predominantly rural, agricultural states. The projects featured in this chapter—Laine Gates's examination of body type and ethnicity, Marcie Manley's study of Shadden's Barbecue, and the Marvell High School Family and Consumer Science project on family dinners in the 1940s—bring values associated with food as a cultural force in Arkansas into fascinating focus. The food projects, by and large, were students' incursions into a social text that is packed with meaning, redolent with connections to family, ethnicity, class, health, history, and community. In authentically intellectual projects, students chose to take up such topics as "healthy" foods in Lee County, pork barbecue in rural Phillips County, and family meals in Marvell not only to celebrate their values and entertain readers, but also to interrogate and try to make sense of the role that food and foodways play in their homes, their towns, and their region. Moreover, as with all projects contributing to a critical pedagogy of place, these students' projects aimed to ferret out what was and is worth saving about food and food culture in any reinhabitation of the Delta. In what follows, a brief prelude establishing rural Arkansas as a locus for southern food culture sets the table (as it were) for the students' projects.

"Nothing Fancy, but It Sure Is Good, Especially for Working Folks"

The old saw "I don't know much about X, but I know what I like" no doubt has been applied to more topics than one could catalogue: "I don't know much about art, but . . . ," "I don't know much about music, but . . . ," "I don't know much about travel, but. . . ." The aphorism might appropriately be applied to food in Arkansas. If one were pressed to identify a cuisine with a geographic location, Texas or Oklahoma could claim beef brisket, Tennessee or Alabama could say pork barbecue, Chicago could go with deep-dish pizza, Omaha or Kansas City could hold on to steak. But what about Arkansas? There seems to be no dish that qualifies as distinctively Arkansas food. A real Arkie might say, "I don't know much about food, but I dearly do love it," in all its many manifestations.

In a charming article in *Oxford American*, the journalist Sam Eifling (2010) poses the simple question, "What Do Arkansans Eat?" Characterizing Arkansas as a "smallish, landlocked state with Missouri's backwoods at its roof, Mississippi's catfish pipeline to its east, culinary powerhouse Louisiana to the south, and Texas' beef-pork-pepper riot at its southeast corner" (2), Eifling suggests that the essence of Arkansas cuisine escapes definition. "When I put the question of the state's culinary identity to my uncle, a lifelong Arkansan whose jobs have pulled him all over the state," Eifling writes, "he was stumped: 'I have eaten food in every county in the state. If there's something distinctly Arkansan, I haven't found it.'" The uncle did mention one possible exception, however, "the annual Coon Supper in the Delta town of Gillett, where the state's pols made a show of enjoying barbecued raccoon" (3). This event, held during the second week of January every year since 1947, is, as the former US Senator Dale Bumpers noted in a speech on the Senate floor, "one that an Arkansas politician misses at his or her own peril" (Tolbert 2001).

At the risk of falling into an abyss of figuration, let us propose that the Gillett coon supper represents a synecdoche embedded in a symbol. As synecdoche, the barbecued raccoon is a part representing the whole. The part: it's a particular food item, a wild animal, known not as a culinary delicacy but as a pest, a scavenger, an invasive rodent, so ridiculously abundant that poor folks can always find one to kill and eat. The whole: it's rural southern food in general, a range of animal and vegetable entities that one wouldn't normally think about eating—pig intestines, pokeweed, fried cornmeal, and so on—but that sustain a poor, hungry population when other more refined and delicate foods aren't available. As with all symbols, the very concept of "rural southern food" has embedded in it, and evokes, a broad array of semantic and psychological associations: poverty and hardship, dependence on the land, perseverance, pride. One might suppose that politicians show up at the Gillett coon supper because barbecued raccoon tastes good. A more plausible reason, however, is that attending the event shows constituents that the politician is one of them, that he or she understands what is involved with feeding a hungry population with meager resources.

The southern foodways scholar Beth Latshaw (2009) attempts to demonstrate this proposition empirically. Citing data from the Southern Focus Polls conducted by the Odum Institute and the Center for the Study of the American South at the University of North Carolina in 1992 and 1995, Latshaw offers reports on how frequently residents from different regions of the United States consume southern food, whether and how long those consumers have lived in the South, whether those consumers identify themselves as southerners, how those consumers self-identify by religious affiliation, and how those consumers differ according to race, income, and level of education. Latshaw notes that both "black and white southerners often interpret southern food in a metaphorical sense, as symbolizing the perseverance of 'the southerner' and his/her homeland or the ability to make an artful cuisine out of mere scraps" (116). Latshaw quotes John T. Edge, the former director of the Southern Foodways Alliance, who notes that southern food is "totemic to white and black Southerners" because "both see it as reaching back to the tough times they survived" (116). Even traditional Arkansas folk music resonates with the themes of scarcity and hardship about food in the state. Consider these verses from a song initially called simply "The State of Arkansas" but later referred to as "The Arkansaw Traveller":

> My name is Bill Stafford, I come from Buffalo Town;
> I've travelled this whole wide world over, I've travelled this wide world round;
> I've had my ups and downs in life, but better days I've saw;
> I never knew what misery was till I came to Arkansaw.
>
> It was in eighteen hundred and two, in the early month of June;
> I landed in Hot Springs one sultry afternoon;
> Up steps a walking skeleton and hands to me his paw,
> Inviting me to his hotel, the best in Arkansaw.
>
> I followed my conductor into his dwelling place,
> And poverty was pictured in his melancholy face;
> His bread it was corn-dodger, and his meat I could not chaw;
> And that's the kind of hash I got in the state of Arkansaw.
>
> He fed me on corn-dodgers as hard as any rock;
> My teeth became all loosened, and my knees began to knock;
> I got so lean on sage and sassafras tea that I could hide behind a straw;
> Indeed I was a different man when I left Arkansaw. (Schrock 1992, 174).

(For the uninitiated: a corn dodger is a small cornmeal cake, usually fried hard in a skillet, ideal for dunking in bean juice or "potlikker," the liquid left over from boiling vegetables.)

But, of course, the scarcity of food in Arkansas and throughout the rural South has never been equally distributed throughout the population. As the Southern Studies scholar Marcie Cohen Ferris (2009) succinctly puts it, "food reflects power structures and social change" (10). In other words, the profit motive for the agricultural-business-industrial ownership sector has generally been more important than providing working-class consumers with nutritious, healthful food: Rich folks generally don't go hungry. Poor folks do. Ferris offers two historical touchstones to exemplify her point. First, in the long run-up to the Civil War, "The plantation elite's commitment to cotton and tobacco—rather than food production—ignored the hunger and malnutrition that generations of poor white and black southerners endured. . . . The majority of poor and working-class white and African-American southerners remained hungry and ravaged by diseases associated with contaminated feed and water well into the twentieth century" (11). Second, in the 1930s, the pictures taken by photographers working for the Farm Security Administration show that "the South was in crisis. People were making do, but just barely. Barely enough food, barely enough room to eat, barely enough dishes to eat from, and barely a stove for preparing food" (13).

Laine Gates and Act 1220: Food Becomes a Political, Personal, and Family Issue

These complicated, conflicting feelings about food—the reveling in its variety, the totemic identification with it, the concern about its availability—took a decidedly political and personal turn in 2003 in Arkansas, a turn that in the following several years motivated the work of Laine Gates, a University of Arkansas student who took the class as an undergraduate and then became part of the teaching team. In 2003, the Arkansas Legislature passed Act 1220, the childhood obesity law, and the act was signed into law by then-Governor Mike Huckabee. The provisions of Act 1220 were renewed in the Arkansas Department of Education's "Rules Governing Nutrition and Physical Activity Standards and Body Mass Index for Age Assessment Protocols in Arkansas Public Schools" on February 13, 2012. One part of this law, generally overlooked in public discussions, removed vending machines from elementary schools, required professional education for cafeteria workers, put greater scrutiny on contracts between schools and soft-drink companies, and created parent advisory councils to consider health and nutrition issues. The most visible and contentious feature of the law, however, was the requirement that the state Board of Education "promulgate rules and regulations" for schools to include, as part of a health report to parents, the body mass index (BMI) percentile by age for each student. In Arkansas, every student in kindergarten and grades 2, 4, 6, 8, and 10 must have his or her BMI assessed by school personnel unless the student's parent or guardian provides a written letter of refusal. School districts are required to communicate the BMI information to parents and guardians in a "private and confidential manner."

BMI is a calculation based on a person's weight and height; some healthcare professionals use BMI to estimate the effect of weight on health. For example, the higher the BMI, the greater the risk of some diseases, including high blood pressure, coronary artery disease, stroke, osteoarthritis, some cancers, and type 2 diabetes. To calculate BMI, one squares the number representing a person's height in inches, uses that number to divide the person's weight in pounds, and then multiplies that number by 703. So for a person weighing 155 pounds and standing 5 feet, 8 inches (or 68 inches),

155 divided by 4,624 (that number being 68 x 68) = .03352076
x 703 = 23.56 BMI

Whereas some controversy initially developed in Arkansas over the schools' taking on the responsibility of calculating each child's BMI, considerably more hullaballoo was stirred up by the assignment of children to BMI percentiles, categorizing youngsters as "underweight," "healthy weight," "overweight," or "obese." According to a formula used by the Center for Disease Control (CDC), a child age nine is classified as "underweight" with a BMI under 14, "healthy weight" with a BMI between 14 and 18.8, "overweight" with a BMI between 18.8 and 21.2, and "obese" with a BMI over 21.2. A sixteen-year-old is classified as "underweight" with a BMI lower than 17.2, "healthy weight" with a BMI from 17.2 to 24.2, "overweight" with a BMI from 24.2 to 27.5, and "obese" with a BMI over 27.5.

In 2010, the latest year for which Center for Disease Control data were available, 16.2 percent of Arkansas children aged two to five were classified as "overweight" and 14.1 percent of this same age group were classified as "obese." In the 2010 study, 15.7 percent of students in grades nine through twelve in Arkansas were classified as "overweight" and 14.4 percent as "obese." These figures complement those released by the Trust for America's Health and the Robert Wood Johnson Foundation (2011) showing that Arkansas is the ninth "most obese state in the nation," after Mississippi, Alabama, West Virginia, Tennessee, Louisiana, Kentucky, Oklahoma, and South Carolina.

Arkansas parents whose children's BMI puts them in the overweight or obese categories receive a letter informing them of the child's percentile status. In the years immediately following the passage of Act 1220, according to the Center for Health and Health Care in Schools, some parents were taken aback by these letters, "viewing them as a criticism of their parenting." In the years since 2003, however, "increasing number of parents (are) now appearing in the offices of pediatricians, armed with the letters and asking what they need to do to help their children" (Center for Health and Health Care in Schools 2013).

Gates on the Delta Food Culture: BMI, Body Type, Ethnicity, and Nutrition

Laine Gates, now director of outreach for the Arkansas Support Network, an organization that advocates for adults with disabilities in Springdale, Arkansas, played a rich role in the ADOHP by studying the "human" side of the BMI controversy. She parlayed her project for the ADOHP class into her undergraduate honors thesis, which she presented at a national anthropology conference and which was published in the conference proceedings, and later into her master's thesis. Once she entered the MA program in cultural anthropology at the University of Arkansas, she served as a member of the ADOHP teaching team for three years. Here is Gates's summary of her undergraduate thesis:

> As rates of childhood obesity have skyrocketed in recent years, state and federal policymakers have developed public school-based programs to fight "America's pandemic obesity problem" (Tillotson 2004, 617). These programs have focused on simply promoting "healthy" lifestyles within the school setting without attempting to explore the cultural or political factors that underlie childhood obesity. One such program was the cornerstone of former Arkansas Governor Mike Huckabee's Healthy Arkansas Initiative, Arkansas's Act 1220 of 2003, more commonly known as the "BMI Initiative." African American females in the Arkansas Delta have one of the nation's highest rates of obesity, as defined by BMI Initiative data (Arkansas Center for Health Improvement 2006). Working as part of the Arkansas Delta Oral History Project in the spring of 2007, Gates interviewed African American teenagers in the Arkansas Delta in order to better understand the cognitive schema employed in organizing perceptions of food and health.

As Gates argued, these "political and cultural factors" are deeply embedded in the socioeconomics of food and foodways in the rural South in general and the Arkansas Delta in particular.

The oral history portion of Gates's project involved interviewing two teenagers from the Delta, Montre Thompson from Pine Bluff and Katiedra Body from Marianna, querying them about their attitudes about what constitutes "healthy food." But as a prelude to reporting these interviews, Gates developed several points about the history and politics of food in the Delta that are germane to the attitudes stirred up by Act 1220.

First of all, Gates dug deeply into data available from healthcare organizations in the state, finding that overweight and obesity rates in the Delta are generally eight to ten points higher than elsewhere in the nation (Arkansas Center for Health Improvement 2006). The Delta, not surprisingly, also has higher rates of high blood pressure, diabetes, stroke, cancer, and heart disease. Low birth weights, high infant mortality rates, and infrequent medical care add to the region's poor health profile.

Second, Gates, a good cultural anthropologist, investigated issues related to food availability, both currently and historically. In most Delta towns, she reported, convenience stores outnumber supermarkets, and fruits and vegetables are relatively expensive. Delta diets are long on carbohydrates and sugars, short on vegetable, fruit, and dairy products, and fried potatoes make up one-third of all vegetables eaten (Champagne 2004). Historically, the cheapest and most easily preserved foods for poor people in the American South have been pork and cornmeal; thus, these became the core staples of the Delta diet. Pork, considered by nineteenth-century doctors to be "high energy" and thus suited to slaves and laborers, was ubiquitous, and every part of the animal was used—down to the intestines and feet. Certain types of poultry, mostly chickens, were also present, but were usually reserved for Sundays and special occasions if they weren't sold. This limited availability (combined also, perhaps, with the preeminent symbolism of the chicken in West African culture) contributed to the view of chicken as a prestige food (Carney 1998; Semmes 1996). In their own small garden plots, Gates learned, slaves grew turnips, sweet potatoes, cowpeas (black-eyed peas), cabbage, collards, pumpkins, okra, onions, and squash. Slaves also fished and hunted; the game most often caught included rabbit, opossum, and raccoon. Most of these products, however, did not contribute significantly to diet, as they were usually sold or used by the plantation owners.

Third, Gates looked at government initiatives related to food and food security in the Delta. She argued that New Deal relief programs led to a breakdown of the home production of food and to a greater dependence on store-bought foods. Younger generations who were lucky enough to be employed in federal programs like the Works Progress Administration (WPA) had far less time for and interest in gardening, she maintained, whereas older generations still placed prestige on self-sufficient food production (Bennett, Smith, and Passin 1942). The change from a subsistence to cash economy meant that canned meats were substituted for wild game and fish and candy bars replaced home canned fruits. Homegrown vegetables, wild greens, fish, and game such as squirrel, opossum, raccoon, and frogs became stigmatized. This shift in foodways was further affected by the mechanization of agriculture and a changing definition of success—from the possession of land to the possession of cash. Welfare payments and the movement from commodities (which were, ironically, surpluses given away to benefit the agriculture industry by driving up prices—still effectively the leftovers of plantation owners—to food stamps in the late 1960s sealed the dependence on purchased (and less nutritious) foods (Levenstein 2003). In fact, this transition from agricultural surplus to food stamps is credited with conducing conditions of starvation in the Delta by the 1960s. Participants in the federal food stamp program were required to purchase a month's supply of food stamps all at once, and most people who needed the stamps were not able to come up with the sufficient funds to buy them.

Fourth, she interrogated how people's attitudes bumped up against the anti-obesity strictures of Act 1220. Gates maintained that African American cultural attitudes concerning body image are frequently suggested as a possible contributing factor to obesity, and studies indicate that there is less social pressure for African American women to be thin (Hawkins 1997). Particularly in rural areas, she found, there is greater pressure to remain slightly overweight and to display self-acceptance, even in cases where women express personal dissatisfaction with body image. African American women and girls are subjected to conflicting ideals of the body every day. Some black women express "preferring" a small-to-medium-size body, but identify a larger body as signifying better health (Liburd et al. 1999). Gates related the story of an African American father in the Arkansas Delta who refused to have his daughter take part in the BMI measurement and who said: "Sissy's no different from anyone else in the family." According to Gates, African American respondents in a recent study published in *The Journal of General Internal Medicine* mentioned the importance of maintaining a perceived "healthy" weight in case of illness as a reason not to lose weight.

Of course, Gates's conclusions in her project came to life most vividly in the perceptions of her two interviewees, both high school juniors from Delta towns.

Hearing from Montre and Katiedra: What Does "Healthy Food" Mean?

Gates's interviews with Montre and Katiedra about concepts of food and health provided a lively contemporary perspective, a snapshot of how these historical and sociopolitical conditions in the Delta are manifest in two teenagers in the first decade of the twenty-first century. Like a good anthropologist, Gates aimed to study Montre and Katiedra not only as individuals but also as participants embedded in various cultural groups. Here are some salient points Gates made about her two subjects.

First, Montre and Katiedra inhabited relatively different types of food networks, associations of people from whom they got and with whom they shared food; however, Montre's network was clearly more embedded in a food-sharing community. Both students lived in economically similar situations, and each resided at home with both parents. Montre's father was a pastor and his mother was a stay-at-home mom. Both of Katiedra's parents were employed by the Lee County school district. Montre was active within his church community, and had an extended network of relatives and other adults with whom he interacted often. Katiedra's family, on the other hand, attended church regularly, but was not particularly active within the church community. In addition, Katiedra's social interactions were focused primarily on immediate family, though many members of her extended family lived close to Marianna.

Montre's situation in a more tight-knit food network was reflected in his responses to Gates's queries. When asked what kinds of foods he considered unhealthy, Montre responded, "fast foods restaurants is what I would say isn't good for you, but as far as home . . . I don't really know a food that wouldn't be good for me. It's how I make it or how whoever makes it." When asked to list healthy foods, Montre listed chicken (including fried, depending on how it is prepared), yams, corn, green beans, macaroni and cheese, mashed potatoes, and numerous desserts, saying, "because it soothes the soul. They don't call it soul food for nothing."

In addition to belonging to a closer food network than Katrieda, Montre had another food-culture advantage. His mother was an avid gardener, tending to a garden that provided the Thompson family with access to numerous fresh vegetables. When asked where his family got its food, Montre's first response was his mother's garden, his second response was the gardens of others in their church community, and his third response was the local grocery store. He also was able to name numerous specific species of native fish and game to which his family often had access through other community members, even though neither Montre nor any of his immediate family was a hunter.

Montre further differentiated "healthy" foods from "nonhealthy" foods by pointing to their methods of procurement and preparation: "'cause a lot of like greens and stuff that we eat—it's grown from the ground. It's not like you go to the store and it's been pasteurized and all of that nutritionalized and it's like the potatoes, like the stuff that is grown and you cook it yourself, which means you can add things and take away things . . . and you can make it healthier than what it actually is from the basic . . . you can make it healthier than what it is." Through hours spent in the kitchen with his parents, Montre was also able to give detailed instructions on cooking different types of foods, including a made-from-scratch blackberry pie, beginning with picking the blackberries.

Katiedra, although similarly close to her parents, reported that she was able to cook only simple things, such as rice or pasta. When asked about foods considered "healthy," Katiedra listed spinach, tomatoes, celery, salad, and soup. When asked about "unhealthy" foods, Katiedra responded, "Greasy foods like a lot of fried chicken and fried okra. If it's greasy, it'll just ruin your body in so many ways."

Although the two are in similar economic situations, Montre's degree of immersion in his community allowed him greater access to fresh, "healthy" foods, whereas Katiedra and her family relied almost entirely on store-bought commodities. But paradoxically, the social system that afforded Montre greater access to healthy foods corresponded to a positive valuation of foods considered unhealthy. Katiedra's ideals of health, based on not wanting to "ruin the body," correspond to her family's relative isolation within their community, thus diminishing access to "healthy" foods.

Though her primary purpose was to study the history and culture of foodways in the Delta, Gates ended up portraying the political shortsightedness of the BMI Initiative promoted by Arkansas Act 1220. Though not wanting to diminish its potentially admirable goals—to improve the health of overweight Arkansas citizens and thus to reduce healthcare costs—Gates ultimately argued that such simple nostrums as "be thin, reduce your BMI, and get healthy" were culturally naïve and easier said than done.

Gates's intelligent and consummately academic project achieved great acclaim, both at the University of Arkansas and at the national anthropology conference where she presented her work. Her methods stand in contrast to the delightfully personal approaches taken by the projects highlighted in the remainder of this chapter.

Barbecue and Family Meals: Valued Foods in Sociopolitical Contexts

Despite the psychologically charged valences connected to food and foodways in the Delta, relatively few of the student projects focusing on food brought the social, economic, political, and personal tensions involved with food to the table. Instead, they epideictically reveled in the role that food has played in the Delta to bring disparate ethnic groups together, to gather folks from the working classes for social solidarity, to strengthen family bonds, and to connect families to their churches. Yet even the seemingly warm fuzziness of the food projects belies the social tensions existing below the surface. Marcie Manley's project on Shadden's Barbecue took shape in large part because of the rough-and-tumble low-class-perhaps-no-class reputation of the revered food shack and its status as the paragon of pork barbecue, the ultimate working-class food in the Delta. The Marvell High School family-dinner-for-the-preacher project could happen now, one might argue, only because family meals and "special" meals are qualitatively different—to the chagrin of some older folks—than they were a half century ago.

Marcie Manley, Shadden's, and the Temple of Barbecue

When Marcie Manley, then a junior at the University of Arkansas and now a respected television journalist in Little Rock, decided during year one of the ADOHP to study the history and sociology of Shadden's Barbecue, she knew she was uncovering a Delta legend. Housed in a hundred-year-old ramshackle store several miles east of Marvell on US Route 49, Shadden's was the demesne of one Wayne Shadden, who for forty years cooked up legendary barbecue–pulled pork and pork ribs—and served it with "the coldest beer in the state." Shadden's was known for many things: it was rumored to be a gambling joint, sometimes drawing a couple hundred gamesters into its parking lot on Saturday nights. It was famous—in legends clearly apocryphal—as the location where Levon Helm, who eventually went on to start The Band of "Up on Cripple Creek" fame, got his start, picking a guitar and singing the blues on the front porch. It was renowned as the place with one waitress who would take your order and bring it to you, two coolers where you could help yourself to a soft drink or a beer, and a small but important grocery counter where you could buy three things: white bread, pickles, and Shadden's special sauce. But most of all, it was known for Wayne's cooking. When Wayne died on May 21, 2010, the Helena *Daily World* mastered the art of understatement in his obituary, which simply said, "Wayne was a good cook and well-known for his barbecue. He was a Navy veteran, a member of the Veterans of Foreign Wars and the American Legion."

Fortunately, Marcie, who grew up in Marvell herself, had the opportunity to interview Wayne three years before his passing. Here is Marcie in her own words, in excerpts of a retrospective interview conducted in 2012, on why she chose to study Shadden's, what she learned from the project, and why she thinks investigations like hers are important.

- Being from the Delta, a lot of my experiences growing up revolved around food—with family dinners, potlucks, backyard picnics, and the like. It was how people got together.
- And then there was the legend of that little shack outside Marvell that has great barbecue. And it was said to be where Levon Helm got his start—even though Levon is from Turkey Scratch, which is about 8 miles in the opposite direction from Marvell than Shadden's.
- I thought, what better way to match up the two things that are important in that part of the Delta—food and music.
- Shadden's had popped up in columns by foodies and travel gurus many times before my interview.
- Wayne Shadden died in 2010, and the store closed. In my interview, I had asked him if he had any plans for the future of the place. He didn't. His children lived out of state, and they had no interest in returning to run a hundred-year-old barbecue shop. But people are still talking about missing it.
- Mr. Shadden's wife had gone to school with Levon, and Levon even stayed with them for a time. But to Mr. Shadden, Levon was just another guy from the area. His attitude toward Levon mirrored his own attitude about himself: He wasn't important. He was just a good guy who was a pretty good barbecue cook. Levon picked up music just like Mr. Shadden picked up barbecue.
- Mr. Shadden kept pictures of *Coal Miner's Daughter* up at the store. When they were filming that movie, he would load up the truck full of barbecue and drive it 50 miles up to near Memphis, where they were filming.
- I think that the longer time progresses, the more negative the image of the Delta becomes. The perception of the Delta is "low this and low that"—low performing schools, low employment. People tend to leave the Delta behind them—it's a place you come from but never go back to.
- But if you're from the Delta there are things about you that you can't shake. There are things worth remembering there, things that are important. Highlighting places like Shadden's makes you

realize that people get their starts in small places. There's value in recognizing what your region has contributed. The Delta is a place that is as rich in history as it is in farmland.
- There is a nostalgia—we shouldn't overlook the seriousness of the actual, contemporary reality, but there are things coming out of the Delta that are worth remembering.

Though she doesn't mention the term, clearly Manley understood the epideictic argument in her project, suggesting that a celebration of Delta barbecue in general and Wayne Shadden and his restaurant in particularly should play a role in any reinhabitation of the Delta. She was clearly determined to solicit an interview with Shadden that would yield this type of celebratory piece.

Hearing from Marcie: The Interview

Though she was working with a notably terse interviewee, Marcie's interview with Wayne Shadden was a huge undertaking, about seventy-five questions that ranged over Wayne's personal history (for example, US Navy veteran and former cook at the Veterans of Foreign Wars [VFW] before opening his own place), the history of the building as a place to dance and gamble outside in the parking lot, his regular customers (and his dislike of the "too many dopeheads" that show up now), his role as the prize-winning cook in barbecue contests at the legendary King Biscuit Blues Festival, his celebrated sauce (at the height of his business he would make about 300 gallons a month), and the apparent lack of interest his children showed in returning to the Delta to run his business after he was gone. The following excerpt, touching on the Levon Helm legend at Shadden's, gives a wonderfully representative taste of the whole interview:

MM: So do you have a lot of people who stop by on the road? Out of town people, tourists?

WS: Oh yeah, yeah. Lots of folks from out of town. The casinos—when they opened up—I really had some business then. Just, people just talking got it going.

MM: Where have the furthest of your customers been from?

WS: New York, everywhere. Been people from everywhere.

MM: Any famous folks?

WS: Yeah, Levon Helm, Hillary Clinton. All those folks have been through here.

MM: Now, Levon grew up just down the road—

WS: Yeah he grew up over here, Turkey Scratch. He went, well he finished school here. They, he and my wife, graduated together.

MM: Oh, okay.

WS: Yeah, so that's how I got to knowing him. (*coughs*)

MM: How closely did you know him?

WS: Oh real close, real close.

MM: You mentioned earlier that he lived in your house for a while.

WS: Yeah, I had this vacant house down here, and he moved in it and stayed there. Stayed there a couple of years. Just came in and out. You know, when he came home, he'd be there and stay there.

MM: What was he like?

WS: A likeable guy. (*laughs*) I mean, he liked to party and all that stuff. Play music. Well I had as high as three hundred people outside there. He'd set up right out there on the porch there. And people from everywhere'd come to hear him. (*laughs*)

MM: You showed me that photo album, that's from Loretta Lynn's film. Y'all catered that event.

WS: We catered that up there when we were up there on her ridge while she was making that movie. *Coal Miner's Daughter.*

MM: What all did y'all do up there with that?

WS: Just watched them film. There was a lot of filming. And eat and drink. Bout all it was. (*laughs*)

MM: Y'all did cater it though, didn't you? I mean, I saw those pictures.

WS: Well, I cooked the meat here and hauled it up there in the truck.

MM: All the way to Nashville?

WS: Yep, well I'd say it was about 50 miles this side of Nashville. Right there where her ranch is between Memphis and Nashville.

In the following, notice how Manley, much to her credit, captures the rich but elusive and iconic character of Shadden in her narrative work.

The Final Project—"Is It All in the Sauce?"

By far, the best flavor (pun intended, of course) of the Shadden experience came in Manley's final project, a wonderful feature story about the interview, the restaurant, the ambience. Notice that Manley chooses not to use the first person but still includes herself as an engaging character in the piece. Notice, as well, how she exploits omniscience, getting into the psyche of both Wayne Shadden and the young interviewer. But consider especially how Marcie shapes her own burgeoning identity as a journalist by writing an essayistic narrative, very much cut from the same cloth as the "literary journalism" of the late twentieth century (Sims 1984) and very much a nontraditional choice of genre for a mainstream college English course. Notice how Marcie moves well beyond simple reportage into the realm of the construction of knowledge that is emblematic of authentic intellectual work, to create the iconic character of Wayne Shadden and his famous establishment.

Is It All in the Sauce? The World Famous Shadden's Barbeque

He watched the blue smoke curl up from the end of his cigarette. Wayne Shadden liked watching it snake toward the ceiling as he waited for her to arrive. He looked at the Marlboro in his hand, seeing the orange, burning rim give way to another millimeter of ash. A lot like life, he thought, the image of a burning cigarette. Life had moments of burning clarity that progressed for only a certain amount of time before all that was left of a person was his ashes. The smoke of his legacy would disappear forever, with perhaps only the smell of its contents left behind.

He shook his head and laughed at himself. He was too damn old if he could bring himself to think such things. Having met the girl who would interview him the day before, he had been feeling his age ever since. She had dropped by to meet him before they got down to business, he figured. She walked in, somewhat shy that day before. She told him she wanted to hear his story, the story behind this place of his.

He didn't know what the hell he would tell her. There wasn't much he knew about this place. He had only run it for the past thirty years, and he didn't see how that made him an expert on anything.

Still, he had given in to her request. He thought the idea of leaving something of himself behind was nice, and if he had thought of it, he probably would have considered it poetic in a way. God knows, nobody else would be coming along to ask him about his life. Sooner, much sooner than he would like, his stint here at Shadden's Barbeque would come to an end. That much, he knew.

So he waited, unconsciously taking his thumbnail to task on the peeling plastic covering the counter. He was nervous. He shouldn't be, he chided himself. She was only twenty years old. If anyone should be intimidated, it should be her. She was practically an infant. But he knew, as he shifted himself in his chair, that he would be the one with sweaty palms. He would just have to compensate by remaining (how would they say it?) cool and collected. The day was hot enough that he could blame the perspiration of nervousness on the sweltering heat that permeated the little shack. He had installed a new window unit last week, but the small appliance barely seemed to make a difference, and he doubted it would even be able to cool his bathroom in the Delta heat.

His thoughts drew to an abrupt end as he heard the screen door screeching open. The interviewer had arrived. She had said her name was Molly, and she seemed to be a sweet girl. She was related to the Mandrakes up in Aubrey. Shadden knew her grandpa, so he knew she came from good people. He also knew for himself that the family didn't have much to do with the quality of the offspring these days. He furrowed his forehead and wondered what the heck was making it so tough for her to make it up the shanty steps. Then he saw the bulging brown leather bag hanging to one side and the bag of goodies she had clasped in her left fist. He couldn't make out what was in the plastic sack, but whatever she was lugging was hefty. He couldn't bring himself up out of his chair. Instead, he preferred to let her labor with her cumbersome task of making it through the small wooden door. He laughed a little to himself as she struggled to shove it open. One of the floorboards had warped over time, and it tended to catch the old door, making it difficult to get it shoved open. She did it though, with a look of determination, and without saying a single cuss word. Shadden could tell she wanted to, but what kind of impression would that make?

She did finally make it through the door, and with a heavy sigh, freed herself from her load. Both the leather satchel and the plastic sack settled to the floor with an unceremonious crash. She winced a little, apparently having forgotten the fragile contents she had carried. Through her perils, he had progressed to light another cigarette and he grinned at her through the haze. She cocked her head sideways and in a direct, but southern manner, asked him if he wasn't aware of the law prohibiting smoking in businesses in Arkansas. He laughed heartily, and she was definitely aware that it was at her, not with her by any means.

"I've owned this place for thirty years. I've smoked for longer 'an that. If Huckabee wants to tell me where I can smoke a cigarette, I can tell him where he can shove it," Shadden grumbled.

Surprisingly, she laughed. Not a fake laugh either, he thought, but a full-hearted, gut laugh. She looked at him slyly, and asked, "Well do you mind if I join you?" And she pulled out a pack of her own. She lit the end and blew the smoke from pursed lips. She tilted her head back and asked him if he was nervous. Her drawl was pretty thick, and he was sure that she didn't talk like that at school. Something about her told him she was pretty good at sliding in and out of her Delta belle personality. He answered her, telling her about the numerous times he had been interviewed like this before. He could tell by her eyes that she noted that he neither confirmed nor denied the fact that he was nervous. Giving in to opportunity, she shrugged her shoulder and flicked the end of the cigarette.

"I've done news interviews before," she said out of the side of her mouth as she settled back on the stool, "but this is different. This makes me nervous, so you'll have to forgive me if I blunder around a bit. It might take me a while to get my feet under me on this whole thing."

He assured her it would be all right, realizing that she had given him a free pass, and they finished their cigarettes by making a few comments about the weather or how the crops seemed to be doing. They were both stalling, and finally she drew the foreplay to a close. She went about setting up her equipment like a professional. She carried one cassette recorder, one digital recorder, and a video camera. All of this she pulled out of her leather satchel, along with three microphones and a note pad. Suddenly, Shadden began to feel beads of sweat rising up on his neck. It had begun.

From the plastic sack she pulled two different floodlights, a string of extension cords, and a sheet. She explained that if the interview went on long enough it could get dark outside, and then they'd need the extra lighting. Shadden nodded as if he understood. Made sense to him, he reckoned. Jim at the back table snorted and coughed, which was his way of grabbing someone's attention. Molly acted surprised, but Shadden knew she had already taken inventory of his entire store and everyone in it in the five minutes she had sat there sharing a smoke and shooting the bull.

Shadden was right. As Molly peered up at the frumpy man in the back of the store, she was taking in details she had missed during her initial perusal. She noted the well-worn but clean wooden floors that led to an uneven table surrounded by mismatched chairs. The man Shadden called Ole Jim wore Coke bottle glasses and a plaid work shirt. He had suspenders that gave a notion of holding his pants up, though Molly doubted they would fall, given the man's bulging belly below his waistband. He cocked his hat back, and took a napkin to his sopping forehead. Molly had forgotten to leave the door open, thus cutting off any ventilation in the store. Jim was telling her in a subtle way, she realized, that she should remedy the mistake and soon. She checked her equipment and went to the door, cracking it open.

The fresh air gushed in, splashing over her face with the coolness of running water. She hadn't realized that sweat was running down her back, or that the Delta mugginess had begun to stifle her. She had been intent on looking like she knew what she was doing. She was trying to appear professional. She was trying to keep from throwing up. Her nerves were wound tight, and though the man behind the counter seemed as pleasant and docile as her own grandfather, there was something about interviewing someone that made her anxious beyond explanation.

She was about to ask the man to give her his memories. She was requesting that he provide her with his life story, something so extremely personal that she wasn't sure she could ever hand hers over with as much grace and ease as he apparently was capable of doing. A pickup truck zoomed by on the highway, and she realized she had been gazing out the door in a trance. She was caught in her own thoughts, but she was brought back to the old shack and the sounds of the highway outside.

Resettling herself on the stool at the counter, she pushed "record" deliberately, knowing Shadden was preparing himself for the onslaught of questions. She started easily; they began with superficial questions like where he was from and when he was born. These questions didn't bother Shadden. Everyone has a beginning—everyone has a place they come from. This was nothing new for anyone to know, and so he didn't feel like he needed to worry about her perception of him. It was easy enough to say he was born in Texas in 1933, and when she asked him how he got to Arkansas, it was easier still to say that his parents had moved here to get a job farming. He was too young to remember the Depression as the nightmare people say it was. He didn't remember the empty refrigerators or the grumbling stomachs. He didn't remember his daddy working nineteen-hour days to produce a crop that would get only a few cents to the bushel. No, he had been only a little tyke then. He didn't have any recollection of what life must have been like for them. She didn't ask that question, though, maybe because she figured he wouldn't know. She was at the university, so she could obviously add and subtract. He reckoned she knew what she knew, and was only going to ask him about what she needed to learn. That was fine by him, he consoled himself—fine by him to a T.

When they got to the meat of his life, that's when the pressure began to build. His hands got clammy and his tongue got a little thicker. He tried to pay attention to the words she was saying, but people had begun to stream in and out of the store. Most of the shops in town closed at five, and a lot of folks came out at around five-thirty to pick up some grub. Each time the door opened and screeched closed he was aware that there was another member of the audience. They were all perplexed over what this young girl was doing with all this fancy equipment in Shadden's store. They were hungry and they wanted to order, but they weren't sure that they should interrupt either.

Buzz came in from the kitchen at the back, pad in hand. He was poised to take an order from whoever wanted to get their chow to go. Even he paused in his regular duties, focusing in on the old man and the young girl, sitting on opposite sides of the counter, looking at Shadden's life from opposite ends of a telescope. To her, his life seemed to be bigger than any story she could make up. To him, his life had become a small speck in the scheme of things. Life moves on, and new lives begin. It was the way of it. He had had a good life. He had lots of people he'd met, famous people even. He knew she wanted to hear about Levon Helm. He could tell in her face that she'd gotten a whiff of the news that Shadden had known him. Levon had even lived in a house of his. Everybody knew that Shadden's wife and Levon had graduated high school together, and after that the two men were close, like brothers, many said.

They'd been in the interview about twenty minutes. He reached up behind his chair to a shelf, pulling down a battered yellow photo album. He tossed it to the counter with a thud, followed by a cloud of dust.

"Take a look at these here pictures. We got about twenty people in this place. Between you wanting the door closed and the crowd that's gathered in here, I'm beginning to roast. I'm an old man, I can't get too hot. So you sit here and take a gander at them, maybe they'll give ya some questions. I'm gonna get these people their barbeque so they can head on out of here," Shadden told her.

The people standing around gave a sigh, mixed feelings evident. They were glad to be getting on, glad Shadden would take a minute or two from something that seemed so important to make sure they got dinner to their families. Miss Delia was waiting at the back of the room. She hadn't said a word. Shadden knew she worked down at the cotton gin keeping the books, and he knew she had two little toddlers at home. People like her frequented his store, and he knew all of them and their circumstances. She came in every Wednesday. It was a treat for the kids. She sometimes brought them in to see him. Cute little buggers—and they liked their barbecue and grape soda, both of which he kept stocked on a regular basis.

He'd always had a soft spot for his clientele. Ever since he started barbecuing at the old VFW, he'd been sure to remember all of his customers' faces and try to remember every story they told him. It made a quilt in his mind. Every person got a block or two, and their stories are what built the colors and patterns in his mind. He loved hearing those stories, and he loved making people happy. His barbecue seemed to have done the trick down at the VFW. So he kept cooking up his pork and slathering on his sauce. Funny to think now he owned his own store and his sauce was in grocery stores for sale. He even had people call and request orders of it. He'd oblige them, packing up however many bottles they wanted and shipping 'em out. People said he didn't charge enough. Two dollars and fifty cents wasn't near enough for what they got, people argued. Yet he couldn't bring himself to mark it up any higher. Wasn't no need to rob a man blind for barbecue sauce. The fact that anyone wanted to order it bewildered him a bit, anyways.

The last one of his customers was waiting in front of him at the register. He rang up the four sandwiches and a six-pack of beer. The woman was two dollars short, and he let her get by with it. She'd pay him back the next time she came in. They always did. He looked over at the girl on the stool, and he noticed she was taking notes. She had talked to a few of the customers, and now he wondered what all she had gotten out of it. He kept up appearances of being disinterested. He sat back down, lit a cigarette and waited for her hand to stop its fanatic squiggling over the paper.

He asked, "So, you get what you wanted?"

"Well, I guess so," she said. "To be honest, those pictures were really fascinating. I had no idea you and your family knew Levon so well, or knew any of these people at all."

He laughed a bit and pointed to the icebox that was about three feet behind her.

"If you're thirsty, which I know ya are, you can grab a beer out of there, and I'll tell you all about it."

She reached into the icebox that looked as old as the man in front of her. Yet when she stuck her hand in to pull out one of the amber bottles, she felt cold air against her skin and the sting of ice-chilled glass against her fingertips. Amazing, she thought, how some things can withstand the test of time. With that thought running over in her head, she looked at Wayne Shadden. The crags in his face made him look like a map that had been opened and refolded too many times. It gave him an air of knowledge, like every wrinkle in his face and on his hands held a secret. She almost felt bad for wanting to delve into those memories, those life secrets. She felt, as she popped the cap from the bottle and saw the misty vapor rise from the brew, that she was exploiting him.

She forced her eyes to return to his face, ending her contemplation on the bottle and returning her mind to the discussion at hand. The old photo album he had given her to review contained dozens of pictures of Levon, Shadden and his family, along with the cast and crew of the film depicting Loretta Lynn's life. She recalled watching it once or twice before. Sissy Spacek was Loretta Lynn, and Tommy Lee Jones had portrayed her husband. As far as she could remember, Levon had played the part of Loretta's father, the coal miner. If her memory served her, the title of the film had been *Coal Miner's Daughter* and that might even have been a title of one of Loretta's songs.

Shadden confirmed all this, noting that the film had been called by such a title, and it did depict Loretta Lynn's life. Filming, he said, had been on her ranch about 50 miles outside of Nashville, in his words, "50 miles this side of Nashville toward Memphis."

Shadden recalled Levon inviting him up to the movie set. They'd need food up there, and Shadden figured he could provide some barbecue for the likes of famous folks. He cooked it all right there at his pit, packaged it up and hauled it to the set. He remembers driving up in his truck, the smell of hickory-smoked meat wafting up to his nostrils every now and again. It was 1979, and only two years earlier he had opened his barbeque shack. Now he was catering to major movie stars. Life's funny that way, he supposed. For several days they stayed there. Just about all the memories of that stint near fame involved eating, drinking, and watching the famous folks at work. His kids had enjoyed running around the cameras and microphones. His daughter had loved rifling through the costumes and playing hide and seek in the trailers and dressing rooms. He remembered sitting around the picnic tables, teasing Levon and taking in Loretta's pretty laugh. They had seemed like a family, and that was the best part about it.

Levon had brought Shadden a lot of memories. He could still recall the lanky teenager Levon had been. Taking his guitar out on the porch, he would play for upwards of three hours out there. People would just start showing up to hear him play. Shadden never could figure out how word traveled so fast. But it did, and he would have people out there in front of his barbecue shack, demanding that Levon keep on playing and calling for barbeque and beer. The crowd would be so thick full of people from all over that you couldn't stir 'em with a stick. And they would all stay until Levon's fingers gave out and his voice had gone hoarse. Nowadays, Levon rarely came down. He still played concerts up in New York, but his fame with The Band had brought a lot of followers, and the time he spent at home brought him little peace. Back in the days before he was famous, Levon would come and spend a few days with Shadden and his family. Now, too many hangers on wanted a piece of him. Too many people wanted a brush with fame. Levon had had his brushes with fame, now he just wanted a life to himself.

Molly's eyes seemed a little wet, and he wondered if he'd said something wrong. She assured him that she was just moved by his memories, and how he could take something so simple and make it profound. He laughed, and for the first time it wasn't at her. He had really enjoyed that comment, and they both realized at that moment that she wasn't there to exploit him. She was there to share his memories with him and anyone else who would listen. He didn't have to give them away; they would still be his memories. It was kind of like his barbecue. He put it on the grill, and he was responsible for letting it simmer and slowly ripen into a bold-tasting barbecue. Each time he did it, he put his heart into his food. Then he let other people walk out of his place with a piece of it. That's what this was like. He was allowing her a glimpse. He was giving her a sample. He was providing her a taste of the flavors and textures that made his life what it was and what it is. No harm in that. He'd been doing that all his life.

He noticed she'd emptied her beer, and he motioned for her to grab another. She grasped two cold bottles by the neck, conveniently popping the caps off in one swift motion. She sat a bottle before him. He hesitated, and she smiled. He took the bottle, knowing he would have indigestion later, and clinked his to hers.

"So, is that all ya got Missy? Or are you going to start asking some real questions?"

She shook her head and laughed. The old man had a sense of humor, and she was beginning to get the feeling that he liked her.

"We've only been at this for about an hour now. I figure I can go as long as you can. But since we're relying on your memory, I don't know how much longer we'll be able to get anything out of you," she sassed back at him.

He laughed and coughed a bit. Those damn cigarettes were catching up with him. Still, he took a swig of his beer, grabbed a cigarette, and lit a match.

"Darlin' we've got cases of beer and cigarettes for days . . . if my memory doesn't last, those will. Fire away."

Marcie Manley was a young woman when she conducted her ADOHP inquiry on Wayne Shadden and his restaurant. But the genre she chose for the final project, we think, creates an older, wiser, more contemplative and retrospective narrative persona than her youth might be expected to convey. As she clarified in the retrospective interview cited above, she clearly sees small, family-owned Delta food shacks in general, and Shadden's in particular, as part of the fabric that needs saving. "It's All in the Sauce" isn't troubling in its nostalgia, we would argue. Its achievement, allowing Marcie to engage in a cultural study, producing authentic intellectual work, makes a strong case for reinhabitation.

If there is a touch of a more mature sophistication than expected in Manley's project, just the converse—a sprightly, youthful optimism—is evident in the work done with family meals by the students from Marvell High School.

What's Cooking in the Delta? Soul-Food Cooking in the 1940s

The students from tiny Marvell High School, located in a town of about eleven hundred people in rural Phillips County, clearly had a great sense of humor. Here's the first page of their final product, created during year one of the ADOHP:

Ingredients:

1	Tape recorder	1	Dedicated teacher
1	Eighty-year-old woman with a story to tell	12	Eager students
		42	Questions

Mix together. Add a pinch of creativity. Serve immediately and enjoy.

And the students followed this recipe precisely, allowing visitors to the year-ending celebration of the ADOHP to dine on a classic meal of southern cooking served on an outdoor stage overlooking the Mississippi River in Helena on a sultry afternoon.

Most of the high school classes that participated in the ADOHP were history, government, or English classes. At Marvell High, Delores Smith bravely volunteered her Family, Food, and Consumer Science course for the project. To their credit, Smith and her students were able to use oral history methods as teaching and learning tools while still covering the state-mandated curriculum for this content area.

To achieve this merging of oral history and consumer science, Smith and her charges—particularly the principal authors Phylicia Martin, Avery Hall, Robin Robinson, Marquitta Truitt, and Kasheda Daniels—decided to focus on a history of cooking in the 1940s. With this topic, the Marvell students were able to record the story of Sarah Bobo, an eighty-year-old cook from Hoop Spur, Arkansas, and learn the recipes, techniques, and basics of cooking that she employed. Once they had done their background research and conducted the interview, they concluded that a play would be the best way to convey this fascinating material to an audience.

Wanting their play to be the best possible, Smith and her class recruited help from Cheryl Scott, a teacher from the drama department. The cross-disciplinary collaboration resulted in "Southern Cooking from the Good Ole Days." In the production, they cooked two dinners: a common, everyday supper that African American families in the Delta would have eaten during the 1940s, and a more elaborate and formal meal that the family would have prepared and served when the preacher came to visit. At the end of the performance, the students served up the menu for the "fancy" dinner to the audience: fried chicken, chitterlings ("chittlins"), corn on the cob, strawberry cake, fresh lemonade, and sweet potato pie.

Soul-Food Cooking in the 1940s and Sarah Bobo

Though it remains popular today, soul food derives from a distinctive culinary heritage. African American slaves struggled to maintain some of their original culture through food, so southern slaves established their own cooking culture using foods that were similar to foods that were part of their African and West Indies heritages. Slaves were generally allotted the parts of livestock that the plantation owners did not want to cook and were given the most undesirable parts of the meal, the leftovers from the plantation house. The slaves learned to develop recipes using the discarded scraps and their own homegrown vegetables. Even after emancipation, many freed slaves were poor and could only afford the least expensive cuts of meat. Subsistence farming yielded fresh vegetables, while fishing and hunting provided fresh fish and wild game.

One might say that Sarah Bobo, whom the Marvell students interviewed, had lived with soul food her entire life. Bobo was born in

Hoop Spur on April 28, 1924, the daughter of Robert Henry Jackson and Grover Kelly Jackson. The oldest of five children, Sarah had one sister, Odessa, and three brothers, Moses, Thomas, and Robert. The family earned a living by farming, and it became Sarah's responsibility to clean and cook for the family when she was nine years old. Sarah eventually married Leroy Bobo and began a family and continued the tradition of cooking soul food.

The Students' Perspective: Wide-Ranging Interview Questions

The Marvell students clearly discovered early on what a gold mine they had in Bobo, and the interview questions show evidence of a large, curious group who wanted to plumb the depths of her experiences and knowledge. The interview contains the following forty-two questions, covering family relationships, farming, cooking methods, and meal preparation. Notice how all the questions in some way touch on issues one would expect to find in a Family, Food, and Consumer Science course, but notice as well how the interview format allows the material to come alive in ways that "textbook learning" simply can't.

1. Where were you born?
2. Could you tell us your parents' names?
3. Could you tell us your profession—your job?
4. As you were growing up, who had the biggest responsibility for managing your food in your household?
5. Where and how did you buy things like meal, flour, and sugar—the things you couldn't grow at home?
6. Where did you get it from?
7. How was the merchant different in those days compared with a store today?
8. Was the merchant operating in a building like a store in those days?
9. What were the foods that y'all ate the most?
10. Can you tell me what your traditional breakfast meal was back in the '40s?

11. What foods today bring back childhood memories?
12. What do you eat now that you used to eat when you were a child?
13. How old were you when you first started cooking?
14. Who taught you how to cook?
15. Why did you start cooking at an early age, or was it mandatory, or did you want to learn to cook, or did you have no other choice but to cook at nine years of age?
16. What can you tell me about the food harmony? Lye harmony, I believe they used to call it.
17. Back in the day people cooked with different things to put flavor in food. Could you name some of the things that were used?
18. What kinds of stoves did they use for cooking?
19. Did you have baking sheets when you got to bake a sweet potato in those types of stoves back in those days?
20. What is your definition of soul food?
21. Was tomato dumpling a favorite back in those days? Do you know anything about tomato dumplings?
22. Do you suppose you could teach some of these young ladies how you all did it back then?
23. How did you measure your ingredients in the 1940s?
24. Where did you get your recipes from?
25. How were the holiday meals different from your everyday meals?
26. What times of the day was the meal prepared for the family?
27. What was considered a traditional Sunday meal that makes it different from Monday through Saturday meals?
28. What foods treated colds?
29. Were there any other home remedies that food may have been used for, such as spider bites or cuts?
30. Once you grew up and started your own family, how was it different from when you cooked at home?
31. What do you know about rationing?

32. Did you grow gardens after you got married? What was it like to have children with a family and work outside of the home and prepare meals for the family?
33. Were you afraid of worms, or were the greens full of worms and stuff during those days?
34. I heard you mention earlier that your father, when you were at home, would buy and raise corn. Was corn being raised for you to cook and eat or was it raised for livestock?
35. What kind of meat did you all eat and how was it prepared?
36. How were most of the meals prepared? Like did you fry it, boil it, smoke it, or what?
37. How did you fry the food? Like what kind of oil did you use to fry foods?
38. How long did it take you to cook your first meal?
39. What was some of your favorite things you cooked the most?
40. Can you tell me what a hoecake of bread is?

Sarah Bobo's Voice: Excerpts from the Transcript

Bobo, of course, provided a human perspective on the material, offering in her responses the outlines of a social text about families and food in the Delta that these students were not only studying but also were living out their own contemporary versions of.

PM: (Question #1) Where were you born?

SB: I was born in this little place called Hoop Spur, Arkansas, but they call it Elaine, Arkansas. I was born in 1924, April 28, and I am eighty-two. Next month, I'll be eighty-three.

MT: (Question #7) How was the merchant different from those days compared with a store today?

SB: Um, they seem like they were more aggressive with the food then. They, um, try to make you get this and get that and table spreads and they didn't seem to be friendly.

KD: (Question # 9) What were the foods that y'all ate the most?

SB: The most food we ate was beans, rice, potatoes, salt pork, and, um, sweet potatoes, greens we can raise out in the greens, we put them up in a jar. We didn't have frigerators and, um, we had an icebox, and we can our hog meat. My father would kill hogs, five to six hogs; we canned that meat. My mother would, and mostly had was what we raise—chicken and hogs. We raised greens and we put them up in a jar so we had that to eat in the winter.

MT: (Question #10) Can you tell me what your traditional breakfast meal was back in the '40s?

SB: Um, we would have salt pork and potatoes and biscuits, sometimes rice and salt pork and syrup and we had milk to drink and, um, we had milk with the sweet milk. We churned it and made buttermilk, so we had buttermilk to drink. We didn't like the cow's sweet milk so we drank buttermilk and also our mother would give out the syrup; she would make water syrup. She put sugar and, um, a cup of sugar and a cup and a half of water and, um, she'll put a little flavor in it to make it have taste.

KD: (Question #27) What was considered a traditional Sunday meal that makes it different from Monday through Saturday meals?

SB: Because, um, Sunday they try to have something good to eat like chicken, um, steak, um, pork chops, and we didn't have that during the week. We had it on Sundays.

Final Project: *Southern Cooking from the Good Ole Days*

Hamlet tells the Players in the Shakespeare play that "the play's the thing," but that isn't quite true with *Southern Cooking from the Good Ole Days*. While the script creates rich, rounded characters and incorporates a substantial amount of the actual interview with Bobo—using dialect features that the students themselves tried to capture in the transcript—the most spectacular thing the play accomplished was introducing the "special" meal that the Marvell students cooked and served to the audience assembled on the banks of the Mississippi in Helena.

Southern Cooking from the Good Ole Days

Introduction

Scene 1: Mrs. Sarah Jackson Bobo as a Little Girl
Scene 2: The Resulting of the Trip to the Market
Scene 3: Mrs. Sarah Bobo Cooking Her Family's Sunday Meal
Scene 4: The Sunday Meal with the Preacher

Southern Cooking from the Good Days

Performed by Marvell High School Students
April 20, 2007

The Cast

Mrs. Kelly Jackson	Klensha Boyd
Mr. Robert Jackson	Jarvis Wilson
Sarah	Robin Robinson
Odessa	Marquitta Truitt
Robert	Avery Hall
Mrs. Sarah Bobo	Diedre Speight
Mr. Bobo	Jarvis Wilson
Sarah Ann	Phylicia Martin
Bertha	Nakisha Booth
Dorothy	Diesha Gamble
Michael	Avery Hall
Sylvester	Cedric Gum
Preacher	Rickey McCraney
All Children	Phylicia Martin, Nakisha Booth, Diesha Gamble, Avery Hall, Cedric Gum

Narrator - Quinisha Robinson
Play Coordinators - Mrs. Cheryl Scott and Ms. Delores Smith
Stage Coordinators - Edra Marshall and Kelvin Sims

Scene 1

NARRATOR: Mrs. Sarah Bobo was born April 28, 1924, to Mr. and Mrs. Robert Jackson in a little place called Hoop Spur, Arkansas. It is now known as Elaine, Arkansas, located west of the Mississippi River, where soul-food cooking is a way of life. Mrs. Bobo had one sister, Odessa, and three brothers, Moses, Thomas, and Robert. Mrs. Sarah Bobo will celebrate her eighty-third birthday this month. However, being the oldest girl of the family she had the biggest of the responsibility of cleaning and cooking, which started when she was only nine years old.

MRS. KELLY JACKSON: Sarah, we're fixin to leave for the market. I gotta go with daddy. You know he hates dealing with those 'gressive merchants.

SARAH: Yes, mam.

MRS. KELLY JACKSON: Now make sure you clean up after breakfast, you hear.

SARAH: Yes, mam.

MR. ROBERT JACKSON: (*sticking his head in the door*) Come on Kelly!

MRS. KELLY JACKSON: Y'all be good!

(*Sarah fixing breakfast, then begins to put food on the table*)

SARAH: Robert, Odessa, y'all can come eat!

(Robert and Odessa enter and sit at the table)

ROBERT: Not again! Why we always got to have salt pork, potatoes, and biscuits?

SARAH: We don't always have potatoes, sometimes we have rice.

ODESSA: Robert, be quiet for Sarah don't give us none of that syrup mama made.

SARAH: You got that right! (*places the syrup on the table then gets the milk*)

ROBERT: Why you get buttermilk and we gotta drink cow milk?

ODESSA: Sweet milk, Robert.

ROBERT: Same thing!

SARAH: Robert, you better try being grateful fo you don't get no supper tomorrow.

ODESSA: Yeah and you know tomorrow's Sunday, so we gone have (*rubbing her stomach*) greens, black-eyed peas, cornbread, okra, and fried chicken.

SARAH: Now say yo grace and eat.

ROBERT: Lord, I know I haven't been real sweet but bless the food we bout to eat tomorrow I'm gone be very good for real so don't let me miss my Sunday meal. Amen.

(Lights Out)

Scene 2

NARRATOR: Back in the day many people bought grocery that would last them, what we now call bulk items. While growing up at home, Sarah noticed how her parents raised gardens and bought food from the market. Later, she and her husband, Leroy Bobo, used many of the same methods.

(Mr. and Mrs. Jackson entering the house)

MRS. JACKSON: Sarah, Robert, Odessa, we're home. Robert help your father get the flour and sugar.

ROBERT: Awe man! Those bags weigh a hundred pounds.

MRS. JACKSON: *(unbagging the other grocery)* Ya'll all eat breakfast?

BOTH GIRLS (SARAH & ODESSA): Yes mam.

MRS. JACKSON: And Sarah you did an excellent job cleaning up, so tomorrow we gone have tomato dumplings.

ODESSA: Alright!

SARAH: Thank you, Mama.

(Mr. Jackson and Robert Jr. coming back in)

MR. JACKSON: Kelly, did we get everything on the list?

MRS. JACKSON: I believe we did. We got 2 pounds of brown beans, northern beans, and black-eye peas. We got sugar and flour and salt pork and meal.

MR. JACKSON: Well, fine! Me and the older boys will gather some more greens and corn first of the week.

Scene 3

NARRATOR: During the 1940s Mrs. Sarah is married and has a family of her own. Although she sometimes give the responsibility of cooking to her oldest daughter, Dorothy, she is a wonderful cook and takes great pride in her Sunday meals.

MRS. SARAH BOBO: Children sit down at the table. I don't want yo Sunday best all dirty fo we go to church.

MR. BOBO: Kids, the pastor's comin fo dinner and I want ya'll on yo best behavior. Don't you go embarrassing me and Sarah.

CHILDREN: Yes, Sir!

SARAH ANN (*one of the children*): Mother, what we gone be having?

MRS. SARAH BOBO: Ya Daddy killed two chickens, so we gonna have a basket full of chicken, fried potatoes, corn, greens, cornbread, and a sweet potato pie.

MICHAEL (*one of the children*): Almost like Christmas!

MRS. SARAH BOBO: No we not having dressing and lots of cakes and pies; just one sweet potato pie.

SARAH ANN (*one of the children*): No tomato dumplings?

MRS. SARAH BOBO: (*laughing*) Not this time. Maybe next Sunday. Yeah! Next Sunday I believe we'll have pork chops, rice and gravy, biscuits, and tomato dumplings.

BERTHA (*one of the children*): What ya cooking now, Mother?

MRS. SARAH BOBO: I'm putting my greens on befo we leave, but I can't seem to find my pickling spice anywhere. (*Sarah pauses still searching for the pickling spice*) Leroy, you seen my pickling spice? How in the world am I gone season my greens. (*pauses still looking*) Dorothy, I need you to finish my pie while I go down and see if Ms. L. E. Peoples has some pickling spice.

SYLVESTER (*one of the children*): Don't worry, Mother, Aunt Jessie Mae got some fo sho.

DOROTHY (*one of the children*): Mother, how do I make this pie?

MRS. SARAH BOBO: First ya pour in a fist full of sugar, add a chunk of butter, a pinch of nutmeg, and a dab of this vanilla flava.

DOROTHY (*one of the children*): (*repeating the directions nervously*) You say pour in a fist full of sugar, a chunk of butter, a pinch of nutmeg, and a dab of vanilla flava.

MRS. SARAH BOBO: (*getting her purse and scarf*) Be sure and taste it to make sure it's sweet enough. Tell yo daddy when he come out the washroom I'll be right back.

MR. BOBO: (*entering dressed for church*) Where's Sarah?

SYLVESTER (*one of the children*): She went down Aunt Jessie Mae's to get some seasoning fo the greens.

MR. BOBO: I done invited the preacher man and Sarah ain't even got no pickling spice. Now how she gone season tha greens. Come on kids, load up, it's time to go to church.

(Lights Out)

Scene 4

NARRATOR: Sunday dinners are one of the most prevalent times when soul food is seen on tables. They are a time for families to get together and often invite guests. These massive Sunday dinners were a welcoming part of family and social life. Collard and mustard greens, cornbread, kale, ribs, fired chicken, chitlins, yams, and okra are all excellent examples of what may be found at a Sunday soul-food meal.

(After church at the table eating Sunday dinner)

MR. BOBO: Children, dinner time!! (*children come running*)

(Pastor and Mr. and Mrs. Bobo already seated)

MRS. SARAH BOBO: Bow your heads while the Reverend blesses the food.

PREACHER: (*very seriously*) Lord, we thank you today (*pause*) for good bread, good meat, good lawd, lets eat!

PREACHER: Well, Mrs. Bobo I must say you done yoself a fine job. These is the best greens I don ever ate.

MRS. SARAH BOBO: My thank you!!!

MR. BOBO: Well, Reverend, God gotta a way of working things out.

CHILDREN: (*laughing*) Sure does!!

MRS. SARAH BOBO: (*bringing the pie to the table*) Reverend, make sure you save room for sweet potato pie.

PREACHER: (*looking at the pie*) My God! God is good. (*everyone laughs*)

We have included the script for *Southern Cooking from the Good Ole Days* exactly as the students from Marvell High School performed it and submitted it to us, and we must admit that we blush a bit at the students' naïve and honest use of dialect. That feature notwithstanding, we see in the play and performance a richly collaborative project in which the students created a genre—probably an unfamiliar one to them—that allowed them to embed themselves in experiences involving food, foodways, and faith that folks in the southern end of the Arkansas Delta had lived out for decades and that the students seemed to believe were worth preserving.

Southern Food: Identity for Delta Folks, Identity for ADOHP Students

Students who chose to write about food for their ADOHP projects certainly learned about its identifying power. Foods and foodways that lead to overweight and obesity produce an identity that the state promulgates. Foods and foodways that center on small-town life and local music conduce a "one of the locals" identity for people in the know. Foods and foodways that focus on family and faith shape an identity for the family members and the faithful.

Students who chose to write about food also learned, we believe, something about how their choice of genre not only shapes an identity for them but also how different genres bring exigent topics to life in effective ways. Laine Gates's study of Montre's and Katiedra's views on healthy food was part of her undergraduate thesis project, so the academic paper did the job, and Gates's work established a solid, respectable persona in the piece. In contrast, Marcie Manley wanted to create an "insider" identity for herself—a persona of a budding journalist who had grown up "in these parts" and knew all the legends. Her feature story does the job. Finally, we suppose contemporary high school students could read about how family meals used to be a tradition in rural America. We suppose that these students could learn in their history courses that preachers at small rural churches used to get part of their compensation in the form of meals served at parishioners' homes. We suppose that students could talk with their parents, or among themselves, about how family meals or "preacher" meals are different now than they used to be. We suppose that students and their families might conjecture whether a return to such meals might be a signal of strength and sustainability in their communities. We think all these ideas came to life effectively for the students as players in the Marvell High School script.

5

Race, Resistance, and Schooling in the Heart of the Delta

WE SUPPOSE it's not surprising that, during the entire span of the ADOHP, one issue—actually, one set of issues—was never completely absent from the students' projects: race, racial tension, and racial violence in the Arkansas Delta. Three factors combined to keep these issues on a front burner for ADOHP students. First, whereas natives of Northwest Arkansas tend to identify themselves as Ozark mountaineers—a sturdy, mostly Scots Irish stock whose loyalties were divided in the American Civil War—the rest of the state, particularly the half sitting east of Little Rock, has always been thoroughly southern. Indeed, the Arkansas historian Willard Gatewood (1993) refers to the Arkansas Delta as "the deepest of the deep South." As we noted in chapter 2, even though Arkansas did not have the substantial plantation culture that one associates with the antebellum South, Arkansas was a slave state, and a substantial portion of the state's African American population has family connections to slavery. In a typical year of the ADOHP, about 60 percent of the participating high school students were African American. Second, one of the most iconic events in the American civil rights movement happened in Arkansas, the federally mandated desegregation of Little Rock Central High School in 1957. In 2007, year one for the ADOHP, the high school and the city of Little Rock sponsored a huge fiftieth-anniversary commemoration, a multiday event that drew substantial national and international press coverage. The story of the Little

Rock Central desegregation resonated throughout the project. Third, for ADOHP students whose folks had lived in Arkansas for a couple of generations, the famous *Brown v. Board of Education* decision of 1954 had played a significant role in their families' lives. A substantial number of the students had parents, grandparents, great aunts or uncles, or even just older acquaintances who had attended schools that had been forced to desegregate by the *Brown* ruling. Moreover, a considerable number of the students had knowledge—some of it first-hand—about the private school movement that emerged in the Delta in the wake of the *Brown* decision.

Given these circumstances, the ADOHP students, particularly the high schoolers, seemed especially prone to write about race. Since high schools participated in the project for two years, it was not unusual for the student projects in the first year to be dominated by issues related to race. We must note from the outset that all of the members of the ADOHP teaching team at the University were white, but several of the participating high school teachers were African American. The members of the teaching team were curious, perhaps naively, about why race was still such a salient issue, some fifty years after the Little Rock Central desegregation, and we brought up our curiosity regularly with our high school colleagues. A conversation with a University of Arkansas history professor, an African American who had grown up in the Delta town of Dumas, Arkansas, and attended a high school in the 1980s that was overwhelmingly African American, provided an illuminating anecdote related to this question. Members of the teaching team asked the professor to estimate what percentage of the curriculum he had experienced had any connection to African American history or culture. "How about zero percent," the professor responded. This anecdote coheres with our judgment—held by the University of Arkansas teaching team and the high school teachers—about the students' proclivities: they wanted to think, learn, talk, and write about race, but their schooling up to this point had offered them relatively little opportunity to do so.

The three student projects featured in this chapter provide this opportunity. The inquiry by Lee County High School students into a community boycott that emerged in the wake of school desegregation there in 1972, Dave Prater's "public-radio" essay about the rise of the all-white private academies in the Delta, and the two-year study of race-related issues by Pine Bluff High School students—examining not only school desegregation but also the decay of a downtown business area—all provided ADOHP students the chance to write themselves into the social text composed by racial turmoil in Arkansas during the last quarter of the twentieth century, to ferret out elements of this aspect of their region's history that might be worthy of keeping alive for the sake of reinhabitation, and to engage in truly authentic intellectual work, constructing knowledge that they had had little encouragement to synthesize and contemplate. The projects featured in this chapter differ a bit from those highlighted in the chapters about religion and food. In this chapter, readers will find relatively little of the nostalgia-tinged epideictic discourse common in the previous chapters. The consensus among student writers in this chapter seems to be the history of racial issues and tensions in the Arkansas Delta needs to be kept alive, but certainly not revered in any way as "the good old days."

Before Little Rock: Jim Crow in the "Deepest of the Deep South"

Even though the geography of the Arkansas Delta places it firmly in discussions of the Deep South, the Delta has received relatively little attention to its racial history—certainly less than the attention paid, for example, to Little Rock's or Mississippi's. But make no mistake: the Delta is the Deep South. Notice how Gatewood explains the moniker he uses: "To an extraordinary degree, the Arkansas Delta represents in microcosm the distinctive environment, behavior, and historical experience of the South. In few other areas have the tensions characteristic of southern society been more obvious than in the Arkansas Delta. These tensions have manifested themselves in various ways—between man and the physical environment, between whites and blacks, between rich and poor" (5). Gatewood's explanation embodies the facets that made race such a problematic and intriguing topic for ADOHP students: economic issues, social customs, and simple human necessity.

To be sure, a great deal of strife in the Delta has been manifest in black and white relations, and this chapter necessarily focuses on these racial relationships. Mostly, we look at race relations through the perspective of black inhabitants and citizens, and we do so with the recognition that this is an important but partial perspective. We do not mean to extend any particular stereotypes of Delta residents—regardless of race—or the South itself. Reviewing black resistance and the white response during the Elaine, Arkansas, race riot of 1919, Kieran Taylor (1999) reminds us how misguided it would be to portray Delta blacks as "passive victims" and to portray whites as "a monolithic mob of reactionary hatemongers" (267). In what follows, we acknowledge the distinctiveness of Delta residents and communities while also recognizing the complexity of human behavior when it applies to custom, livelihood, and fear—even if we cannot attempt to fully unpack such complexity.

The racial history of the Delta must begin, of course, with slavery. Although the French and Spanish brought black slaves to the Delta, it was the Louisiana Purchase of 1803 that brought slavery in Arkansas to a level comparable to other areas of the early United States. The historian Fon Louise Gordon (1993) clearly details the "powerful and flourishing institution" of slavery in antebellum Arkansas: "From 1820 to 1850 the percentage of increase of the slave population was greater than that of any other slave state: 1820–30, 182 percent; 1830–40, 335 percent; 1840–50, 136 percent. . . . In total slave population among slave-holding states, Arkansas rose from fifteenth in 1820 to twelfth on the eve of war" (101). The Delta was undoubtedly the center of slavery in the state and would create racial demographics that made it unique in the state. Gordon again: "While only 35 percent of the white population and 46 percent of slaveholders lived in the Delta, 67,286 or 61 percent, of the slave population lived there" (101). After emancipation, these demographics gave African Americans a brief period of relative power: "During Reconstruction from 1868 to 1874, blacks in Arkansas participated in government, assumed the responsibilities of citizenship, and affiliated with the Republican Party. The Party drew its greatest numerical strength and loyalty from the black electorate" (103). Yet the resurgence of the Democratic Party and the beginnings of Jim Crow laws in the 1890s and the turn of the twentieth century would further degrade blacks' role in politics and their civil rights. Disenfranchisement and corporeal violence were in full sway. Ninety-three blacks were lynched in the Arkansas Delta from 1889 to 1918 (112).

This is not to say that blacks did not organize in resistance. Jim Crow and the economic disparities of sharecropping forced many poor, rural blacks to form unions such as the Progressive Farmers and Household Union of America (PFHUA). This agricultural union sought to advance some social and economic gains of the post–World War I era in the Delta. Growing black farmer and sharecropper participation in PFHUA would be a catalyst for the Elaine Race Riot, also called the Elaine Race Massacre, in Phillips County during late September and early October 1919. The historian Kieran Taylor (1999) offers this description of the PFHUA: "Emerging most strongly from the rich cotton land south of Helena, several hundred African Americans joined the union, organizing lodges in the towns of Mellwood, Ration, Hoop Spur, Elaine, Old Town, Countiss, and Ferguson. Black workers rallied to the union cause hoping to combat their landlords by striking for higher wages, withholding cotton in hopes of a more equitable settlement, and suing corrupt plantation owners. The secret phrase to gain entrance to the meeting at Hoop Spur was reportedly "we have just begun" (274–75).

It was at a PFHUA meeting on September 30, 1919, at the Hoop Spur Lodge, just 3 miles north of Elaine, where approximately one hundred blacks, mostly sharecroppers, met to discuss their plans to secure higher wages from white landowners. This meeting took place amidst an especially racially tense period in the Delta, "as earlier nationwide strikes led planters in the area to believe that the organization represented a significant, and possibly violent, challenge to their economic and social hegemony" (McCollum 2011, n.p.). Three white men approached the meeting, where armed guards stood outside the building, and shots rang out. It is unclear through historical accounts where the first gunshot came from, but one white man was killed and another injured. White citizens responded quickly. By the next day, several posses formed to put down the "conspiracy" and "insurrection." On October 2, US troops were sent to Phillips County to bring order to the riots. Grif Stockley, a lawyer who grew up in Lee County adjacent to Phillips County, has thoroughly researched the Elaine Riot and believes that as many as 1,000 whites from other counties, Mississippi, and Tennessee rushed to Phillips County and participated in the fray. Stockley questions the initial report from the US commander that only two black residents were killed: "Estimates of African American deaths, made by individuals writing about the Elaine affair between 1919 and 1925, range from 20 to 856." Stockley continues, "If accurate, these numbers would make it by far the most deadly racial conflict in the history of the States" (Stockley 2001, xiv). In the legal wrangling that followed, 122 blacks were charged with crimes. Twelve men were convicted of murder and sentenced to death. However, after a six-year court battle spurred by the National Association for the Advancement of Colored People (NAACP), the men were released between 1923 and 1925.

The Elaine Race Riot/Massacre crystallizes for us the Jim Crow era of the Delta, which casts more than a shadow over the present. Stockley frames Elaine and Jim Crow in this context: "One thing is certain. The entire truth of the Jim Crow era and segregation will never be known until both blacks and whites summon the courage to battle the emotional anxiety that will accompany the discussion of these times" (xxi). As the student projects in this chapter make clear, even after integration, there exist a history and legacy of organization and resistance in the Delta places that harken back to some of the darkest times in the Delta. The story of the Marianna boycott, as uncovered by ADOHP students from Lee County High School, provides a stark example.

After Little Rock: The Specter of Segregation in Lee County, "Crossing the Color Line"

Imagine this scene: It is the morning of January 13, 1972. Chaos has descended on your high school. All you can hear is your fellow classmates screaming and running from the sharp teeth and snarling muzzles of police dogs. As you dodge the explosive force of the fireman's water hoses all you can think about is—when will this nightmare end?

This was a scene that eleven students at Lee County High School encountered vicariously thirty-five years later in their ADOHP project. The students were revisiting the racial tensions that resided in their small East Arkansas town in the late 1960s and early 1970s, turmoil that would end finally in May 1972, but only after a substantial boycott of Marianna, Arkansas, businesses by the local African American community and a sit-out by students at the high school.

For many of the ADOHP students at Lee County High School, participation in the project represented their first substantial introduction to this watershed moment in their community's past. For their final project, the students created a portfolio, an accumulation and examination of data from their oral history project. The components of this portfolio were the students' brief explanations of what oral history is, what the 1972 boycott in Lee County was, and what they perceived the historical value of their project to be. After these explanations came sections entitled "What Does Your Interview Say" and "What We Learned," in which the students tried to make sense of their interview by asking themselves these questions:

- Is the interviewee's account more a representation of his or her present thinking than of his or her past?
- Has there been a great loss of memory of the particular events?
- What influences—personal, cultural, social—might shape the way the interviewees expresses themselves?
- What background and interests do the students bring to the topic of the interview?
- How might the purpose have shaped the content, perspective, and tone of the interview?

To accompany their interview portfolio, the Lee County students also performed a short skit that artistically expressed the information that they received from their interviewees: B. R. Simmins and Julia "Ju Ju" Hughey.

The Little-Known Story of the Marianna Boycott

For most casual students of school desegregation, the Lee County incident represents a footnote. The Little Rock High School crisis of the 1950s has garnered most of the attention given to school desegregation in the state of Arkansas, and deservedly so. Its relative obscurity, however, doesn't diminish the importance of the Lee County High School story for residents of this East Arkansas county, particularly for African Americans. The story gathers additional importance when one considers the school sit-out in the context of the events that had preceded it for nearly a decade.

The racial history of the region is important. Lee County was created in April 1873 from the adjoining counties of Phillips, Monroe, St. Francis, and Crittenden and was named in honor of Confederate General Robert E. Lee. Although a significant majority of the population has always been African American, from its inception Lee County's white minority population exerted dominance over the political, social, and economic affairs of the county. The inherent tensions accompanying this power structure created in Lee County a hotbed of political, social, and economic resistance.

Beginning with Reconstruction, African American militiamen under the command of the State Militia Commander General D. P. Upham, along with white militiamen, suppressed Ku Klux Klan activity in the Militia War (1868–69) in eastern Arkansas (Jones 2012). After Reconstruction, African American populism emerged as a force in Lee County, exacerbating tensions between political factions, economic classes, and most important between the races. In the 1880s and 1890s, and especially with the Cotton Picker's Strike of 1891, violence often accompanied expressions of resistance (Holmes 1973). In the twentieth century, African Americans began taking larger steps to challenge the system of white supremacy in Lee County. Much of the challenge coincided with the midcentury rise of the civil rights movement that was emerging in the Arkansas Delta and straining race relations. In Lee County, the strained relations were intensified by a series of events: the establishment of Volunteers in Service to America (VISTA) programs in the county, a boycott of white businesses, and the sit-out at the high school.

VISTA, an antipoverty program, emerged from President Lyndon B. Johnson's "War on Poverty" and Economic Opportunity Act of 1964, and in the following year, Arkansas began running its own VISTA programs. The mission of VISTA emphasized the idea that trained volunteers would help people help themselves. This meant that many of the VISTA programs that were established in the Arkansas Delta would ultimately challenge racism and its compatriot, classism.

Perhaps the most controversial Arkansas VISTA project was the Lee County Cooperative Medical Clinic. As we noted in earlier chapters, the Arkansas Delta was (and still is in some ways) a land where cotton is king, and the cotton industry, from its earliest years until the early twentieth century, was shaped by plantation agriculture. But as mechanization and the rise of agribusiness turned the "simple agrarian iniquities of sharecropping into the starvation and degradation of labor displacement" (Schwartz 1988, 188) poverty conditions in the Delta worsened, especially in Lee County. According to a 1968 study, Lee County was one of the six poorest counties in the nation (73 percent of the county's population was living in poverty), had an infant mortality rate of more than twice the national average, a school dropout rate of 72 percent, and nearly half of the adult population was defined as illiterate (Schwartz 1988).

In August 1969, a VISTA program headed by Dr. Dan Blumenthal began working to establish the Lee County Cooperative Medical Clinic at Marianna to provide health services to the county's poor. The response from Lee County's white population was immediate. Many viewed Dr. Blumenthal's and VISTA's involvement at the local level as an attempt by outsiders to insert themselves into the county's socioeconomic status quo. To make matters worse, several of the doctors on the local medical board opposed this effort. Refused admission to Lee County's Medical Society, Blumenthal was automatically barred from membership in the Arkansas Medical Association and not allowed to treat patients or use equipment at the Lee County Memorial Hospital (Jordan 1969). In response, Blumenthal and the thirty-three other VISTA volunteers worked tirelessly to establish the clinic, which opened its doors in March 1970. Olly Neal, an administrator at the clinic and an African American born in Marianna, reported to the *Arkansas Gazette* that the clinic and the work of VISTA had a tremendous effect on the local African American community, asserting that "Blacks are made aware on a daily and hourly basis that they are second class citizens and that whites are first class citizens" and that the clinic and VISTA had provided the local community with some level of community control and self-respect (Jordan 1969, 8A).

Despite this increasing awareness of racial inequities, the black population of Lee County seemed slow to respond to VISTA initiatives like the clinic. Jerry Hornsby, a General Electric project coordinator in East Arkansas, believes that local African American leaders were reluctant to shake up the established white order. According to Hornsby, "A level of militancy had not been reached. You had only white VISTAs agitating for improvement. The anger in East Arkansas had not yet become focused, the organization had not yet developed, the leadership not yet emerged. The Delta of 1969–70 was a kettle that had just begun warming. It still had a way to go before boiling over" (qtd. in Schwartz 1988, 196). But the simmering tensions in Lee County started to boil in May 1970 and continued to do so throughout 1972. Dr. Blumenthal and his VISTA successor, Dr. Ralph Wolf of New Orleans, and four local African Americans filed a federal suit against the Lee County Memorial Hospital in May 1970 claiming that refusal of service to Blumenthal's patients was unconstitutional. This move prompted Lee County citizens on both sides of the color line to jockey for positions within the county political establishment. Although the county's African Americans had limited political success, the VISTA program received a boost when a lawsuit against Lee County Memorial Hospital was decided in April 1971 in favor of VISTA, securing the use of the hospital to treat patents beyond the scope of the Lee County Cooperative Clinic (Schwartz 1988).

Finding a Voice: Boycotts in Marianna

With this small success gained by VISTA against an antagonistic white establishment, Lee County's African American citizens resurrected their legacy of resistance. The community felt empowered by VISTA, and they found their voice. This empowerment was soon tested, as an incident at a local pizza restaurant resulted in an economic boycott that paralyzed white downtown Marianna businesses, convincing the white minority that outsiders were once again stirring the racial pot.

In early June 1971, Quency Tillman, an African American, was arrested for refusing to purchase a $2.06 pizza she did not order. The County's African American community objected to this humiliation and began a boycott of at least forty white-owned businesses in Marianna's downtown. After eight days of the boycott, a group of African Americans working under the name of Lee County Concerned Citizens worked with the NAACP to draft a letter to be presented to Marianna's Chamber of Commerce. The letter urged the Chamber to arrange a meeting to address multiple grievances identified by Lee County's African American community as critical to "avoid[ing] the inevitable conflict between the races which will follow if it continues" (Stockley 2009, 381–84). The grievances reflected a growing consensus among local African Americans regarding discrimination in employment as viewed through the national civil rights lens—namely, the failure to hire African Americans in county and city offices, banks, and drugstores. This consensus extended into education as well: the complainants maintained that the hiring of teachers, principals, and school secretaries should be based on merit and performance, not on race, and that African American students should be treated on an equal basis with their white counterparts (Stockley 2009).

During June 1971 the boycott remained peaceful, but in July the nonviolent tactics of the protesters suffered a setback. On July 14, 1971, two of the boycott leaders, Rabon Cheeks and Prentis Neal, brother to Olly Neal, were passing out leaflets when they claimed the county judge Haskell A. Adams purposely ran a red light and tried to run them down. After failing to convince either the police chief or the county sheriff to file charges against Judge Adams, the two boycott leaders proceeded to the county courthouse. Adams followed Cheeks and Neal to the courthouse, and once there pulled a gun that he had in his pocket and threatened the pair in front of other witnesses. Adams was then charged by the prosecuting attorney, but only on charges of carrying a concealed weapon and assault. Adams later claimed that the brakes on his truck locked, causing the truck to slide (Stockley 2009). Not long after Adams had threatened Cheeks and Neal, three white-owned businesses were damaged by arson. Unknown assailants fueled increasing tensions by firing shots at local police patrol units, including the deputy sheriff's car. Many locals believed this to be the culmination of the county's increased racial tensions.

Unfortunately, these events proved only to be the calm before the storm. After the trial of Judge Adams, to which he pleaded no contest and received only a fine, violence broke out in the vicinity of the Lee County Courthouse Square. It was reported that a group of whites affiliated with the county's White Citizens Council were carrying baseball bats, kicking and hitting several individuals, including Al J. Daniel, a white Little Rock lawyer who had served as counsel for a number of Lee County's African Americans involved in the economic boycott ("Violence Follows Trial at Marianna" 1971).

Throughout the month of July racial tension was at its peak. Whites patrolled streets under the name of the "Good White Citizens of Lee County" to make sure that African American citizens who wanted to patronize downtown businesses could do so without being harassed by boycotting African Americans, contending that the African American protesters had used violence and intimidation to intensify the boycott. Additionally, both print and television news reporters had been harassed and driven out of town by Lee County's white citizens. In response to the escalation of violence by both African Americans and whites, Governor Dale Bumpers sent state police units to deal with racial problems and imposed a curfew. The boycott, which did not officially end until July 1972, resulted in the closure of eleven businesses, and at least five buildings were damaged by fire (Schwartz 1988, 245).

During the whirlwind of violence that engulfed Lee County, both African American and white citizens suggested that the racial problems that existed in the county were extensions of issues arising from the newly desegregated Lee County school system and the presence of VISTA. Although there is no evidence to suggest that VISTA volunteers had a role in the boycott, eleven VISTA volunteers were in Lee County at the time, and all were assigned to the clinic. At this time, the Lee County Cooperative Clinic was receiving more aid, and notoriety, than at any time in its previous history, due in no small part to the Association of Citizens Council of Arkansas and the Arkansas Farm Bureau, both of whom claimed that VISTA workers were associated with militant groups engaged in agitating the local communities (Schwartz 1988). An editorial appearing in the November 27, 1971 *Arkansas Gazette* titled "VISTA Is Welcome in Arkansas" captures this dynamic perfectly: "VISTA has made many of the poor in Arkansas—and especially the Negro poor—aware of their own just due that had been theoretically there for a century but in practice has not been enjoyed. For the first time in the lives of many poor, they are exercising their right in a free society to petition pubic officials for redress of grievances and to register and vote on political judgment day. If all this rubs some local power structure a little raw, then perhaps that's the way it ought to be" (4A). Undoubtedly, tension still existed because of VISTA's presence in the county, but it seemed for the moment that VISTA and the Lee County Cooperative Clinic were becoming permanent fixtures. Therefore, the new battleground to test Lee County's citizens' dedication to resistance shifted to the newly desegregated school system.

"Be It Resolved": The Lee County High School Black Student Boycott

In Marianna, around 8:30 a.m. on Thursday, January 13, 1972, 200 to 250 African American students sat down in the halls and the principal's office at Lee County High School to protest unfair conditions for African American students at the school and submitted fourteen demands for changes in the school's operations. Local law enforcement, the state police, and the fire department were called to the school to disperse the demonstration. The actions of the authorities in this instance mirrored broader social events, coming on the heels of violent overreaction to protests at Kent State and other campuses nationwide in the preceding two years. Juanita Write, an African American student, recalled that the "fire-department turned the water on us and we all started running and I lost my shoe . . . I was running back to get it and the police slapped me across the face and I fell and then he hit me in the back of the head and I fainted ("Marianna Blacks Protest at School" 1972, 1B). This was only one example of alleged brutality used against the African American students and two reporters, one white and one African American, both of whom were employed by the West Memphis newspaper *Many Voices* during this incident. At the end of the day on Thursday, twenty-two African American students and the two reporters of *Many Voices* were arrested for misdemeanors and charged with creating a disturbance in a school area ("School, City Reported Quiet at Marianna" 1972).

In the days after the incident, more details about what transpired came out in the newspapers. The confrontation began when fifteen African American students, as a group, wanted to discuss several demands contained in a petition to be presented to Principal Bob Blankenship. It is alleged that Blankenship agreed to talk to five representatives of the group, but not the whole assembly. The following excerpt is taken from the petition addressed to Principal Blankenship and others, including Governor Bumpers:

> Be it resolved that on this day January 13, 1972, we the black students of Lee Senior High School agree that these demands be met in good faith of sound judgment and of sound mind. Be it resolved that if our demands are not met properly there will be a continuous boycott of classes, lunchroom programs, assemblies and all activities at Lee Senior High School. Why should we blacks celebrate and commemorate the births and deaths of other known leaders and not

> that of our great leader the Rev. Martin Luther King, Jr., or other outstanding black figures contributing to all mankind regardless of race, creed, or color? ("Marianna Blacks Protest at School" 1972, 1B)

The students refused Blankenship's offer. A few went back to class, but the majority refused to move from school grounds. As a result, local law enforcement, the fire department, and the state police were called to neutralize the situation. Many students were reported to have received injuries in the melee that followed. The total number of confirmed student injuries is unknown because of conflicting medical reports. White officials at the time reported that no students were injured. However, Olly Neal, the administrator of Lee County Cooperative Clinic, confirms that multiple students were treated at the clinic following the incident. H. C. Dial, Lee County's superintendent, later agreed that at least twelve students were treated for injuries ("250 Blacks Confront School Officials at Marianna" 1972).

After the altercation, tensions in Marianna escalated again. Firebombs were thrown at the deputy sheriff's and the sheriff's house. One went off, with no injuries; the other was found in the yard and did not go off. In response, Mayor John Oxner ordered a temporary curfew on the town. The day after the firebombing incidents, a caravan of African Americans including civil rights activists and parents went to Little Rock to discuss with Governor Bumpers's staff their grievances regarding the response to the demonstration. One member of the caravan, Gertha Trice, worked as a laboratory technician at the Lee County Cooperative Clinic. According to Trice, "many black students were beaten and chased into and through the woods by club-swinging city, county, and state police and non-police alike" ("Curfew Ends in Marianna" 1972, 11A). Attesting to the vicious brutality, Trice said that in one instance a field tractor was borrowed and students were chased with it across fields. Additionally, it was reported to the governor's staff that at a mass meeting at a Baptist church in Marianna parents had decided to withhold their children from classes until action was taken to address their grievances. The African American school faculty that accompanied the caravan asked the governor's staff that charges against the students be dropped, claiming that white school officials had "sacrificed progress that had been made at the school to a moment of angry impulsiveness" ("250 Blacks Confront School Officials at Marianna").

Pressure from the Delta Coalition, an African American activist group, and this meeting forced the Department of Education to create a six-person team to investigate the racial situation at the school, and led the director of the state police to investigate the department's involvement in the alleged brutality toward students at the demonstration. The biracial committee from the state education department recommended that charges be dropped against the African American students arrested at the demonstration January 13, and that the parents of the students abandon their demands that the superintendent and principal be dismissed. It also recommended that a task force representing Governor Bumpers should be formed to mediate the controversy by bringing together the school board and the African American student leaders ("250 Blacks Confront School Officials at Marianna").

Throughout the month of February, school officials and the faculty who continued to teach their classes reached out to the boycotting students and their parents to urge them to return to school. Unfortunately for Marianna, the school boycott seemed to members of both races to be another staging ground to test their commitment to resistance and civil rights. Lee County, at this point, already had a private white academy. The public school population was 80 percent African American even though African Americans comprised only a little over half of the county's total population. Racial tensions were peaking owing to the ongoing boycott of white-owned businesses in downtown Marianna; the county had all the components in place for a violent racial confrontation. Hopes to avert this confrontation were raised when Governor Bumpers offered to appoint a task force of three whites and three African Americans to work with Marianna residents to end the deteriorating situation. Governor Bumpers insisted that both sides request assistance before such a committee would be appointed because he believed that such a request would indicate that both sides desired a solution. The following day, Lou Mann, president of the Marianna School Board, and Olly Neal, a leader of the African

American community and business administrator at the Lee County Cooperative Clinic, indicated they supported the governor's idea for a mediation task force (Stockley 2009, 383).

From March through August both sides sought to blame the other for the county's racial tension. Organizations such as VISTA, Lee County Concerned Citizens, the Citizens Council, and newspapers such as the West Memphis paper *Many Voices* were continual targets of both sides in the escalating confrontation. But at the end of the school year the sit-out ended, removing from Lee County one of the most painful symbols of social change in Delta society. Trials were held for students arrested during the demonstration. Fifty students were found guilty, thirty-four were found innocent, and thirty-three cases were dismissed for lack of evidence.

"Crossing the Color Line"—The Student Project at Lee High School

We find it remarkable that the students at Lee County High School had apparently never been afforded the opportunity to investigate this rich vein of their region's history, so we were delighted that it was the topic taken up by Ruth Marshall's high school English class for the ADOHP. In fact, Marshall's students had a direct link to the 1972 student boycott—their teacher. Marshall was a student at Lee High School on the day that the boycott began. Although Marshall was not one of the students that sought a conference with the principal and did not sit out of school for an extended period of time in protest, she had vivid memories of how the boycott began—"kids were running down the halls," she recounted—and how the fire department hosed students (one of whom was her sister, who was a protestor) in a scene reminiscent of the civil rights annals.

In a retrospective interview, Marshall spoke about how the topic of the 1972 boycott came to drive her students' work. After brainstorming ideas for the ADOHP project, Marshall opened up to her students about her personal experience on that tumultuous day in 1972, which inspired them to learn more. "I knew there were people still around that had experienced it," she explained to us. And so, sparked by their teacher who had *lived* a part of this history, a small group of students set out to learn more about experiences and attitudes on segregation and race in their small Delta town.

The students—Katiedra Body, Xavier Davis, Jasmine Dukes, Bennieka Farris, Ryan Galvan, Adrianna Green, Giorgio McCall, Tyisha Nelson, Carnora Smith, Shankekwa Taylor, and Abraya Walker—and their teacher located two persons to interview from the community. One was B. R. Simmins, a former student at Lee High School and a participant in the school sit-out in 1972. The other was Julia "Ju Ju" Hughey, the white owner of Marianna Parts Company during the boycotts of 1971–72, who was better known to the community as "the NAPA dealer." The interviewees were asked the same thirty-seven questions, which covered a range of relevant topics: integration, racism, violence, personal views of race relations, community support, and personal reflections. The transcript of the interview with B. R. Simmins corroborated some of the newspaper accounts we cited earlier in this chapter. Additionally, students were privy to the ironic and poignant sense that Simmins gave concerning being on school grounds some thirty-five years after the boycott:

QUESTION 1: What was your role in the boycotts?

SIMMINS: I was a student at the time at Lee High School and there were fifteen demands that we had at the time. We didn't feel we were getting equal treatment at Lee High School. We decided we would talk to our principal about our questions and demands, and we had asked for permission to talk to him, but on that day he refused to talk to us. So we decided to sit in front of his office until he did talk to us, and he never did.

QUESTION 3: How did it affect students, parents, and anyone else in the community?

SIMMINS: Well because Mr. Blankenship, our principal, refused to talk to us (*clearing her throat*) and Mr. Franklin Montgomery somehow was called out with this big fire truck and his men. We were sitting inside the building here at Lee High School; it's ironic that I'm here today, and he had Mr. Franklin Montgomery, who's still alive, ordered his men to poor [*sic*] gushing water on students who were outside the building and also, as I remember, it was January 13 and he also ordered them to poor [*sic*] water on the children down in the hall. Also, it was just all uncalled for, negative, evil, and racist.

QUESTION 5: What happened to the students who missed the entire semester?

SIMMINS: Well, all the students missed the semester out of school including myself. I'm trying to remember some of the students who went to choose to go to West Memphis, some of the students chose to move out to St. Louis, some of the students went to Little Rock, some of us missed the whole semester, and our parents, some of our parents were teachers and some of the teachers volunteered to teach us in a church.

Additionally, the students learned through this microlevel interaction the extent to which black community members had to go to provide education to the boycotting black students. In this sense, oral history became for these students a living history, both rich and more critically complicated than perhaps they could have imagined.

One particular aspect of the topic's complexity emerged during the interview with Julia "Ju Ju" Hughey, who provided a merchant's view of the color lines drawn in the community during 1971–73. Here are some excerpts from the interview with Hughey:

QUESTION 7: What circumstances led to the boycott?

HUGHEY: Well, it was dissatisfaction over merchants not hiring enough blacks. They [blacks] used to come into our stores and apply for jobs and brought forms to fill out. Some of the whites had black personnel, but they would say, "Well, we are not hiring right now." That's what really kind of started it, was unrest about not hiring enough blacks.

QUESTION 9: How did the boycott affect the community?

HUGHEY: It was kind of heartbreaking to see the community fall apart, in particular when they has [*sic*] to call the National Guard in. All the merchants in the community were upset about it, and they did their best to stop it. And the children were not out of school the whole semester. School was open to those who wanted to come. So there is a question there about that. Nobody missed school because unless they wanted to.

QUESTION 11: Was there any violence that you know of?

HUGHEY: The only violence that I knew of was some of them [blacks] made Molotov cocktails; I think that's what they called them. And Lou Mann, who is dead, owned the house where my granddaughter Heather lives now, and they shot into his house (he was on the school board at the time), which I thought was terrible. No one was hurt, and to my knowledge, no one was killed during the whole thing.

In some ways complementary and in some ways contrasting, these two oral history accounts offered a ground-level view of the racial tensions of integration in Lee County schools that helped the students situate (and challenge) their understanding of this not-long-lost piece of Delta history.

From the transcripts, the students were able to compose and format a brief, yet formal, reflection of their experience in the writing project and performed a skit at the local gathering of ADOHP in Helena at the end of the project. The students' writing brings out some of the nuance and frustration of race relations in Lee County—then and now. Here is the concluding section of their skit:

> If there is to be harmony in the world, then there must be a willingness to communicate intelligently with each other. By no means should there be a separation among the races because of a superiority complex. When people are not willing to accept change, then negative results occur. The 1972 boycott in Lee County is a prime example of the destruction that can be caused by unwanted change. Desegregation in Lee County brought major changes within the community due to the attitudes of all parties involved.

Learning about unwanted change and lack of communication may be of some value to Lee County adolescents and teens as they still face a cultural climate brisling with racial tension. As recently as 2012, the 8th US Circuit Court of Appeals acted on a previous district verdict stemming from a charge levied at the Lee County School District from a former employee. The plaintiff was one of the minority of white administrators on the school board and the charges appear to be firmly related to race. According to one news report, the racial tensions within the board led to two white members "reassigned to lesser jobs after blacks claimed a majority of the School Board seats in 2007" (Brantley 2012, n.p.).

Given the ongoing racial climate in Lee County, we wanted to know from Marshall what she thought of race relations in the county and what the students learned from this literacy project. Marshall noted that "younger people really don't pay it any attention" and they are "more apt to mingle." However, she also acknowledged that with older residents, remnants of past racial tensions are more clearly demonstrated. This raised another question: "How do you feel about discussing, reading out, and doing projects on race in your classroom?" Marshall replied that her high school students seem "comfortable" discussing race, although she sees this type of pedagogy of place as being "momentary," as students "don't dwell on" these racial issues in any sustained cultural or curricular forums.

Marshall's response points to what we see as a salient feature of the traditional school curriculums and subsequently one of the possibilities of a critical pedagogy of place: "My thing is a lot of kids don't know their history," she said. "And when they don't know it, they are more passive. They don't try to make things better." Marshall linked this "passivity" in student learning to lack of intellectual "activity": "They hate to read, and they don't seem to interact with the world very much, including their parents, beyond the Internet." We hope that sustainable projects like ADOHP can actively engage students' literacy interests and help engender critical consciousness of the places in which they live and learn.

Finally, Marshall's candid comments gave us a glimpse into another pressing concern about racial binaries in Lee County and the Delta at large—continued racial segregation. One drawback Marshall sees in projects like ADOHP in her school is the lack of white students that are able to collaborate with black students owing to racial demographics. She recognizes that her school is "heavily segregated," in the respect that Marshall only has around two or three white students in seven class periods in most school years. Marshall attributed this de facto segregation to the success of Lee Academy, a predominately white private school, and the KIPP (Knowledge Is Power Program) public charter school in Helena, both of which attract students away from Lee County High. Marshall worries that there will always be a sense of racial separation in Lee County, as "one generation seems to pass beliefs on to the children and so on." This singular example of perpetual segregation connects directly to another ADOHP project, David Prater's radio essay on the private school movement.

"The Nine-Hundred-Pound Gorilla": Marvell Academy and the Rise of the Private School Movement

In the 1960s and 1970s in many areas of the South, efforts to eliminate segregation in public education had been stymied by the massive withdrawal of white students from the public schools and the concomitant establishment of a private school system. This was especially true in Arkansas, which still reeled from the federal government's forced desegregation of Little Rock Central High School in 1957. This retreat of white students into private schools or academies was most obvious in the Delta, whose counties had the highest percentage of school-age African Americans. As one ADOHP high school student put it in a post to her writing group, "The schools are still segregated. All the white kids go to Lee Academy."

One particularly prominent example of this movement in Phillips County occurred in the small town of Marvell. Like its neighbor to the north, Lee County, Phillips has earned a reputation for racial confrontation and resistance. Although the Elaine Race Riots, described above, are perhaps the most well-known expression of racial resistance and confrontation in the county's history, the response of the county's white and African American citizens to *Brown v. Board of Education* is also worthy of note. After the *Brown* decision in 1954 and the desegregation of Central High School in Little Rock in 1957, Phillips County public schools remained segregated. During the early part of the 1960s, the Student Nonviolent Coordinating Committee (SNCC) targeted Phillips County, along with other counties, to protest the county's efforts to thwart desegregation. Activists sought to gain full integration of public facilities and to increase African American political participation. SNCC encouraged African American parents to enroll their children in schools that had been open to only white students before federal and state law had been changed from "separate but equal" to "freedom of choice."

This resistance to de facto segregation in the education system troubled many whites. Marvell, a small community in Phillips County with a population of 1,916, responded with the establishment of Marvell Academy, which opened in two frame houses in 1966. Some of the school's founders were members of an ambiguously named "Citizens' Council," a group that maintained that "integration is the corruption of the true American heritage by alien concept and ideology" ("Private Schools: The Last Refuge" 1969). Other whites in Marvell supported the academy by claiming that the new school would preserve the quality of education, which appealed to a genuine fear that African American students would inhibit the educational progress of white students.

It was this cultural phenomenon that prompted David Prater, an undergraduate at the University of Arkansas, to focus on Marvell Academy for his ADOHP project. After conducting extensive background research on the private school movement, Prater made contact with one of the founders of Marvell Academy, Charles Loeschner, a farmer from Marvell. Loeschner and nineteen other farmers had dug into their personal finances to open Marvell Academy in 1966. Loeschner himself had to borrow money to contribute his $2,500. For "fifteen or sixteen" years, Loeschner sat on the school board, and at the time of the interview his daughter Laurie was in her fourteenth year on the school board. The interview, containing seventy-two questions and covering such topics as education, private schools, farming, auctioneering, and Marvell Academy, showed Loeschner to be a hardworking

Delta farmer, dedicated to his children and their education and to his community.

Prater, who during his time at the University of Arkansas worked at the student-run radio station KXUA, created an audio segment modeled on the Chicago Public Radio show *This American Life*. His radio essay is a deftly crafted piece incorporating sociohistorical commentary, narration, and blues music with audio excerpts of the interview. The following bit from the opening reveals the tone:

> PRATER'S NARRATION: (*blues music playing*) It was almost conspiratorial the way he talked about the education he gave his children. He never mentioned race. He never mentioned the *Brown* decision. He never mentioned the public school or the subsidized housing project next to it. . . . Charles Loeschner was a founding member of [Marvell Academy] and sat on the board from 1966 until 1981 when his last daughters graduated.

Yet the transcript later shows that Loeschner *does* briefly mention the public school. In fact, Prater's narration that follows sets up an interesting excerpt from one of Loeschner's responses:

> PRATER'S NARRATION: Loeschner will indirectly tell you why Marvell Academy was founded, but it is evident from what was going on in Arkansas and the South that there's something that he doesn't want to talk about.
>
> LOESCHNER: Well, it was important . . . very important to me because I wanted my kids to have a quality education. I didn't feel like the public schools could do that . . . could give the quality education that I want my children to have.
>
> PRATER: Okay, is there any particular reason why?
>
> LOESCHNER: Not particularly.

It seems that Prater crafts the beginning of the essay to feed the audience's expectation that Loeschner will reference race as the primary reason for the private school. However, this bombshell moment does not materialize.

Instead, Prater's essay takes on the sophistication of a public radio piece in which the subject of the essay and his or her experience are too complex to be neatly wrapped up in stereotypical terms. As an interviewer who is on Loeschner's home turf (Loeschner buys Prater a hamburger at the local café during the visit), Prater's *own* relationship to this controversial issue becomes more complex. Here the narration continues: "The most remarkable thing about these private schools in the Delta is how the community supports them." Loeschner goes on to explain how the funds for Marvell Academy are raised:

> LOESCHNER: People donate certain items, farm items and different things, and, uh, you would sell those items at a school sale that night. They would have a catfish supper or steak supper, something like that. Then after, they would have a little auction. Well, that money—started out I think the first auction we done raised $20,000—we been doing this now, I would guess, probably twenty years . . . maybe twenty-five. Ah . . . I just got through doing an auction. I think it raised $110,000 the other night. That all goes to the school.

While Prater's narrated commentary acknowledges the financial and community commitment needed to keep Marvell Academy's doors open, it also recognizes the irony and complexity of the racial implications: "The easy and typical answer would be white racism, to stereotype the farmers [whites who send their children to the academy] in the Delta as nothing more than atavistic, to blame them for problems that are nationwide." But the essay explains that both Marvell Academy and the Marvell public schools have been successful in preparing their students for national tests—something corroborated by Ruth Marshall's interview. Prater's essay also implies, though, that the town of Marvell itself is as split along race lines as the schools: "Policies and decisions within local government bodies often come to a 5 to 4 vote along racial lines. There's not an easy answer to this problem. Blaming either side has failed to produce harmony within racially mixed communities." Ultimately, Prater's essay reaches a more balanced (if not somewhat conciliatory) tone: "It is much easier to ignore the nine-hundred-pound gorilla then try and carry it."

To us, Prater's essay is a solid example of youth cultural studies. It embodies a nontraditional genre, the radio essay, that truly *assays* its topic in an associative and open-minded fashion. In terms of authentic intellectual engagement, the essay constructs knowledge by probing into the foundational nature of Delta segregation academies, not relying solely on staid stereotypical representations. Writing himself as an embedded observer into the social text of racial relations in the Delta, Prater frames an issue involving real people with real lives on *both* sides. Most important, Prater's essay contributes to a critical pedagogy of place in bringing out a human connection to the taint of segregation that still pervades much of the Delta. Student work like this demonstrates the difficult nuances involved in asking local residents and students to consider *decolonizing* and *reinhabiting* places that have such familiar sociocultural structures in place.

"Maybe This Release Was Necessary": Pine Bluff and Retelling the Race Narrative

If the trials of desegregation and boycotts are laid out in the work of the Lee County High students and if Prater's piece has the advantage of physical and theoretical distance, then perhaps we can look at the student work from Pine Bluff High School as an explicit attempt to wrangle with competing narratives of racial tension. Although there are stories of racial tension in Arkansas that contain more bloodshed and news-report imagery, race and resistance in Pine Bluff comprises a narrative rarely told. Pine Bluff is both an epicenter for African American leadership in the Delta and an integral thread in the tapestry of storytelling that came from ADOHP student work.

Pine Bluff, a municipality of about forty-seven thousand (down from about sixty thousand in the early 1990s), sits on a bend of the Arkansas River about 60 miles southeast of Little Rock. Founded by French explorers in the early nineteenth century and incorporated in 1839, Pine Bluff has always been a nexus where farming, lumbering, and river transportation have converged. The city earned a dubious distinction in 2013: the web-based newspaper *Inquisitr*, describing the effects of "the economic downturn and rising gang activity" that "led to 18 murders . . . through all of 2012," named Pine Bluff "America's Most Dangerous Little Town" (Johnson 2013).

In this rough-and-tumble environment, Brenda Doucey, a veteran teacher of English, journalism, and creative writing at Pine Bluff High School—the largest of four public schools in the region—led a cadre of juniors and seniors through two years of ADOHP work, the first culminating with a portfolio of student work about the desegregation of Pine Bluff High School in 1963 and the second producing a video about the decay of businesses in downtown Pine Bluff. Both projects invited students to write themselves into the social text of racial history in their town, to interrogate what aspects of life and commerce might be worth reinhabiting in Pine Bluff, and to engage in rigorously authentic intellectual work.

Like many small cities in the South, Pine Bluff experienced a rough birthing of the civil rights movement. Throughout the 1950s, African American efforts concerning civil rights, both within the South and beyond, were largely focused on implementing *Brown*. These efforts thrust *Brown* into the consciousness of the small-town South. Soon, boycotts and protests were no longer confined to the larger southern cities; rural African Americans found their voice and proved willing to physically and vocally express their frustrations with the slow pace of change in even the most remote corners of the South. This certainly was the case for Pine Bluff, where desegregation was met with entrenched white resistance.

With the second largest African American population in Arkansas, Pine Bluff had cautiously delayed the desegregation of its public schools until administrators knew how desegregation was going to play out in Little Rock. Political and social resistance to these changes was intense, due in part to the establishment in Pine Bluff in March 1955 of a segregationist organization called White America Inc. At the time, Jefferson County, of which Pine Bluff is the seat, was one of only seven Arkansas counties where the African American population either equaled or exceeded its white population. Understanding the precariousness of their political and social situation, the local white citizenry resisted the threats they believed were inherent in the rising civil rights movement. Segregationist organizations such as White America served as a potent means for transforming social unease into political action.

By 1956, Pine Bluff had announced plans to begin integration, but school and civic officials thought it best to delay implementation for two years. Beginning in the fall of 1958, Pine Bluff would implement a grade-by-year plan starting with the first grade (Lewis 2008). In the aftermath of the turmoil surrounding the integration of Little Rock's Central High, this announcement prompted segregationists from roughly twenty-one counties to convene in Pine Bluff and form the Association of Citizens' Councils of Arkansas (ACCA). This move led the school board to postpone the implementation of its plan for another five years (McMillen 2007).

During the five-year delay, parents of African American students, the attorney Wiley Branton, and the Pine Bluff branch of the NAACP challenged the Pine Bluff school board. In late 1960, the NAACP filed a petition signed by sixty-six parents requesting a special meeting with the school board to discuss desegregation. At the meeting, the African American parents and Branton pressured the school board to announce their desegregation plans. The school board refused, standing by its statement that it was not yet ready to disclose that information. In 1963, the school board voted to implement a voluntary desegregation plan and to begin the integration of grades one and two (Lewis 2008).

Brenda Doucey: Another Witness to History

Brenda Doucey lived through these troubled times. Similar to Ruth Marshall's students at Lee High, Doucey's students at Pine Bluff High School had an advantage in brainstorming ideas for an ADOHP project—Doucey had experienced integration as a white high school senior at nearby White Hall High School. Investigating the Pine Bluff desegregation scene "was really just my suggestion," Doucey reported, in a retrospective interview. "I let everybody discuss the topics, and the kids voted." As with Marshall's class in Lee County, the students ran with the idea. Like Lee County High, Pine Bluff High School, although from a larger school district, remains to this day clearly segregated in terms of the race of its students. Nearby private schools and the suburban White Hall School District pull white students away from Pine Bluff High.

The similarities between Lee County High and Pine Bluff High don't extend far, however. The integration of Pine Bluff, White Hall, and the other small surrounding districts did not generate the vivid examples of tension that occurred in places like Little Rock and Marianna. This less-highly-fraught atmosphere might be attributable to some of the aforementioned persistence of African American leaders in Pine Bluff and efforts to avoid one-sided handling of inevitable integration issues. Whatever its source, we see in the Pine Bluff students' projects a sense of freedom and cooperation that is not overtly apparent in other projects about race.

The first project from Pine Bluff High shows interesting evidence of these features. The final product was a portfolio representing the work of several students—Camille Brunson, Jennifer Caldwell, Daniel "Big Gould" Harris, Daniel Johnson, Cierra Lee, Alexis Millenbaugh, Kye Meadows, Andrea Walker, and Cedrick J. Williams—in Doucey's AP English and journalism or newspaper classes. (Many students had her in multiple courses.) The general approach of the portfolio may best be summarized by the students' "Special Thanks" that accompanies the Table of Contents: "We would first like to give thanks to God for providing us the opportunity to live in such a great country where we can live and learn freely. To our teacher Mrs. Doucey, you are the best and thanks for pushing us to achieve greatness. . . . Last but not least to the University of Arkansas for providing us and starting this wonderful project as a look back on our BLACK HISTORY, AMERICAN HISTORY, and MAKE HISTORY [*sic*]." In addition to acknowledging their spiritual, pedagogical, and institutional literacy sponsorship, these students believed they could make history in their project—a testimony, we believe, to being allowed to engage in nontraditional, nonhierarchical inquiry, to construct new knowledge, and to think deeply about the cycle of decolonization and reinhabitation that Pine Bluff has experienced.

In the portfolio, the students balanced their historical accounts collected through interviews with community members with imaginative renderings of what the integration of White Hall School (their teacher's alma mater) might have felt like to those who lived it. The students drew attention to an interview they conducted with Doucey about her senior year. The interview corroborates historical accounts that the integration of White Hall was fairly peaceful, except for one situation. Doucey admitted that black students were "intimidated" from attending graduation in 1963 in a symbolic and literal negation by a large proportion of the white student community. This move on the part of the white students seemed to symbolize the harmful, if ultimately nonviolent, discrimination black students faced. There is a poignant moment in the students' account of their interview with Doucey where she admitted that "she would have tried to welcome the blacks to the school if she could do anything different [*sic*]."

In his contribution to the portfolio, Daniel Harris offers a poem, "A New Change," that creates a narrative point of view placing the reader in the mind's eye of a black student entering White Hall School for the first time:

> A change now is very hard, especially on my senior year
> I don't want to go but our school end is near. . . .
> White Hall is the school that I'm going to next week
> How will I get through integration, how will the other
>   students treat me?
> Will I get hit from behind, will they lock me up somewhere?
> Will they put anything in my food or treat me unfair?
> Will they let me live to graduate or trip me down the stairs?
> Will I get in fights every day or will they let me play sports
>   with them?
> Now it's my first day and everything looks fine, but as I walk
>   down the hall
> I'm still thinking will I get hit from behind.

Drawing on interviews with community members, Harris channels the fear of the faceless assault from behind or the darkly legitimate fear of not being allowed to graduate.

Similarly, other Pine Bluff students, through interviews, research garnered from the city and school libraries, and Internet inquiries, created meaning with texts that hint at their budding historical and political consciousness. For instance, they produced a fictionalized version of the *The Pine Cone*, the name of their current student newspaper, set in 1971. Among the topics for news stories were a racial debate over the prom theme that erupts in riot and the black community's protest of the elimination of a black history program. Moreover, an editorial written by Daniel Johnson considered the sociocultural implications of the "sudden and recent integration of the district." Johnson's editorial embodied the point of view of a Pine Bluff High student in 1971, although the race of that fictional persona is not clear. However, the voice was simultaneously powerful, bitter, and hopeful: "This is what happens when years of racist thoughts come to a head in an integrated community. Maybe this release was necessary. Maybe this is an event that will go toward the eventual . . . acceptance of one another in the future or maybe thirty years [from] now we will still be caught with stupid looks on our faces." Other editorials took on such personas as the religious white student who felt she could spend time with a black friend in certain company and an unidentified-race student (whose voice was created by Kye Meadows) who hoped the recent trials would not lead to future tribulations: "The overall goal of integration was to bring everyone together and work toward a common goal. I feel this goal was accomplished, and a lot of barriers have been knocked down."

Although most accounts in our research show that the racial barriers at Pine Bluff were not as daunting as some smaller places in the Delta, time will tell if the goals of the area will indeed be a model of common trust. In the retrospective interview, Doucey opined that the area is "very accepting" of all races and ethnicities (not just black and white); yet, the "nine-hundred-pound gorilla" of neosegregation still exists in Pine Bluff and surrounding communities. What is certain is that the work from Doucey's students was risky, rhetorically complex, and justifiably hopeful. Though far from perfect, we believe wholeheartedly that the ADOHP work on race reveals an authentic and engaged learning experience for the Delta and University of Arkansas students. In terms of the epideictic, the students are able to learn not only about a past that they do not wish to preserve—a rhetoric and reality of segregation—but also about the courage and spirit of hard-fought integration and the resistance that was needed to generate these inconceivably tumultuous events. Perhaps what the students learned about a critical pedagogy of place is that full *reinhabitation* and *decolonization* does not take place in one, two, or perhaps three (their own?) generations. However, we can see some seeds for these goals planted in these intergenerational narratives of inquiry, exploration, and critique.

Telling the Stories of Race in the Delta: Critical Race Theory—Controversy and Potential

We have tried to create as balanced a picture as possible of race and resistance to racial discrimination in this chapter. Yet many readers will acknowledge that a great deal of the student perspectives in this chapter were those of African American students. This fact results from a demographical and sociocultural reality in Delta public schools, one we believed needed to be highlighted in this chapter. With that said, we offer a brief coda on how race might be treated in projects such as ADOHP. If we stand by our commitment to engaged and authentic student work and a critical pedagogy of place, we cannot avoid finding stories that are both fruitful and fraught with local and institutional concerns. Therefore, we have considered how other theories of race, schooling, and politics might inform future readings of this chapter's texts and other initiatives like ADOHP. Critical race theory offers a lens that could plausibly enrich future historical and literacy projects.

Critical race theory (CRT) began in law schools in America as an attempt to foreground race in legal and political matters, led by such scholars as Derrick Bell, the first African American tenured faculty member at Harvard Law. Though we cannot do justice to the theory in this limited space, we can briefly delineate some of the major tenets of the theory as it has been applied to legal studies, public policy, and education. Edward Taylor, a sociologist of education, describes the theory this way: "CRT is grounded in the realities of the lived experience of racism which has singled out, with wide consensus among whites, African Americans and others as worthy of suppression. CRT thus embraces the subjectivity of perspective and openly acknowledges that perceptions of truth, fairness, and justice reflect the mindset, status, and experience of the knower" (Taylor 1998, 122).

CRT is not without critics. Many may recall the political backlash President Obama received for embracing Bell in a video that surfaced of a 1991 Harvard Law function where Obama introduced Bell. Bell's writing and viewpoints and CRT itself have been vehemently criticized for being "too cynical, nihilistic, and hopeless" (Taylor 1998, 124). However, we see potential in CRT, not merely for its subversive confrontationalism, but also because it champions an experientially based approach. Taylor explains how the sharing of personal narrative contributes to CRT: "One powerful way to challenge the dominant mindset of society—the shared stereotypes, beliefs, and understandings—is the telling of stories. Stories cannot only change the status quo, but they can help build consensus and create a shared, communal understanding. They can, at once, describe what is and what ought to be" (122). At the heart of ADOHP is the discovery and telling of such stories. We cannot pretend that all of these stories of race and resistance helped students, schools, and communities reach any sort of consensus. However, we do feel invigorated by the glimpses of storytelling and student learning that sought to examine what was and what might be.

6

Toward Rural Sustainability

Outgrowth and Extensions

AS WE REFLECT on the experience of the ADOHP, we reach two important and related conclusions about it. First, although we congratulated ourselves (and received congratulations) for undertaking a literacy outreach project in an economically challenged region of the state, we would be overstating our accomplishments to claim the ADOHP as an economic revitalization project. As Kim Donehower (2014) notes, rural literacy initiatives are generally (and too frequently) characterized "in terms of economic development and the ways that mastering new technologies of literacy can 'bring rural communities into the 21st century' and allow them to 'compete on the global stage'" (98). In contrast, Donehower, referencing a concept from Deborah Brandt's *Literacy in American Lives*, describes her advocacy of rural literacy initiatives as embodying a means "to sustain the processes of intersubjective life" (103). In other words, Donehower sees rural literacy work as connecting people to people as much as (or more than) connecting people to texts and technologies. We see the ADOHP fostering this same intersubjective liaison.

Our second conclusion amplifies the first. As testimonials from participating University of Arkansas students, high school students, and high school teachers throughout this book suggest, one of the most valuable (and occasionally thorny) aspects of the ADOHP was the contacts that it fostered among students and citizens of the Delta, students and mentors at the University of Arkansas, and interview subjects from throughout the state. This connectedness, Donehower argues, is a vital key for sustaining rural communities: "Rural communities who wish to sustain themselves in the current economic, political, and cultural climates must enact a delicate balance, stemming outmigration by solidifying local identity and pride-of-place while not isolating themselves from the rural, urban, and suburban communities with which they must be interdependent" (108). Borrowing verbs from the social scientists Robert Putnam and Michael Woolcock, Donehower maintains that rural residents, to promote sustainability, must "bond (connect with people in immediate and similar situations), bridge (create more distant ties to like persons), and link (reach out to unlike people in dissimilar situations)" (108). She concludes: "If literacy is inherently about 'sustaining the processes of intersubjective life' (103), distinctive, home-grown literacy groups and activities . . . have great promise for rural sustainability" (108).

Our goals in this final chapter are simple: to describe projects that have grown out of the initial impetus provided by the ADOHP, projects that embody the intersubjectivity and connectedness that Donehower lauds, and to urge educators in all regions to consider the possibility of replicating and extending the work of the ADOHP, particularly in communities that would both receive and give benefits by virtue of engaging in the projects.

The ADOHP Lights a Fire: The Augusta and McGehee Stories

Something about the theory and method of the ADOHP must have captured the fancy of educators and citizens at large in two small communities in eastern Arkansas. These two communities, Augusta and McGehee, have continued to generate initiatives that guide citizens to tap into the region's collective memory, to construct knowledge based on it, and to create engaging texts celebrating values the community apparently thinks are worth saving. Both communities were early participants in the ADOHP, and both capitalized on developing close, personal contacts with the ADOHP teaching staff.

ARCare and "The Augusta Miracle"

In this section and the next, all first-person pronouns refer to David Jolliffe, not to the coauthors. I have been lucky since 2007 to participate in what I call the Augusta Miracle: the story of a small town whose citizens agreed to work together to improve education, literacy, and its quality of life. (See Jolliffe, "The Community Literacy Advocacy Project" 2010b).

During that year, Dr. Steven Collier, executive director of what was then called the White River Rural Health Center, came to me with a proposition. Augusta, population around 2,200 and the home base of White River Rural Health's network of small-town clinics, had just suffered substantial job losses with the closing of a manufacturing facility on Route 64, the main drag through town. The region was losing its population, the performance of students on standardized examinations was plummeting, and a malaise, a general feeling of decline, hung in the air. Collier knew something had to be done to get Augusta and Woodruff County back on a path toward success.

A year earlier, he and others had convened the Augusta Recovery Initiative Committee, a group of citizens from all walks of life who were determined to revitalize the town, the county, the region. The committee met for about a year, thinking its focus should be economical—how to bring the economy back to life. After about a year of meetings, however, the committee decided that the economy was just a symptom. The group decided that the Augusta Recovery Initiative should focus on education and quality of life in the region, doing all it could to ensure that students in the public schools received a challenging, leading-edge education, availed themselves of all the resources necessary to be admitted to and succeed in college, and considered strongly the possibility of giving back to Augusta and Woodruff County after they had graduated. The committee reasoned that a revitalized economy would follow from an improved educational system and the better quality of life that such an improvement conduces.

At a purely coincidental meeting about health care and literacy in the Arkansas Delta, Collier asked me if I could help. I jumped at the chance. I immediately resonated with Augusta, a small town and county seat on the White River in east-central Arkansas, quite similar to my hometown, New Martinsville, West Virginia, a small town and county seat on the Ohio River at the base of the northern panhandle of my native state. I liked Collier; I liked everyone from Augusta and Woodruff County whom he introduced me to.

I told Collier and the others: If we want to improve education and the quality of life in Augusta and Woodruff County, we cannot simply look to the schools. They can't do it on their own. We have to look to the whole community; not only the schools but also the churches, the library, the civic organizations, the government agencies, the businesses and industry. Everybody in the town and the county has to pledge: "Whatever I can do to improve teaching, learning, reading, writing, thinking, performing, whatever I can do to enrich the life of the mind and the quality of life in the town and the county, I will do it."

Collier and the committee took the bait. Together, we established the Augusta Community Literacy Advocacy Project, dedicated to listening to folks from all corners of Augusta and Woodruff County and finding out what they wanted to do to bring reading and writing into their lives in a more meaningful fashion. In a stroke of genius, Collier appointed Joy Lynn Bowen, a retired teacher whom everyone in the region knew and trusted, as the education director and community literacy advocate. Since that time, Joy Lynn and I have worked nonstop to bring citizens young and old to the world of the word in Augusta and Woodruff County.

What we have accomplished is substantial. We have run events, both single-day workshops and multisession classes, for parents and childcare providers on how to make homes more literacy-conducive for preschool children. For the elementary school, we have sponsored family readings of the principal's book of the month. For the high school, we involved the students and their teacher Cindy Gutridge in the ADOHP in two early years of its tenure. In addition, at the high school, we have run regular sessions to help students score better on the ACT examination, a necessary hurdle for people who want to go to college in Arkansas, which now ranks forty-ninth among the fifty states in the percentage of adults who have a postsecondary degree. At Augusta High School, we recruited at the high school a young playwright, Lori Browning, whose work was performed as part of the Arkansas New Play Festival sponsored by TheatreSquared, a professional company based in Fayetteville. We sponsored a Teen Shakespeare and Team Shakespeare project in which students from Augusta High School, along with counterparts from high schools in two neighboring towns, McCrory and Newport, spent five entire Saturdays studying *The Tempest* and, via improvisation and creative writing, produced their own 40-minute version of the play that we then performed outdoors on the banks of the White River. (See Jolliffe 2012 for more on this project.)

Each time we've had a major accomplishment with the Augusta Community Literacy Advocacy Project, the folks at ARCare have sponsored some kind of public celebration—a lunch, a reception, a dinner—to honor the participants. I have appropriated a term from the communication theorist David Procter and described these celebrations as "civic communions" (Jolliffe, 2010b). Indeed, just as the communion service in Christian churches celebrates the life of the church with bread and wine, so do ARCare's civic communions commemorate the spirit of the town's and the region's citizens, their accomplishments, their initiative.

One palpable and well-received outgrowth of the Augusta story was *The Veterans of Woodruff County: Stories and Memories of Service to One's Country*, a seventy-page book published in 2012. The book, filled with narratives about military veterans provided by the vets themselves or their families, plus a rich array of photographs, represents a robust vein of citizen involvement in the Community Literacy Advocacy Project. About a year after we launched the initiative, Jeannie Waller, a doctoral student in English specializing in rhetoric, composition, and literacy at the University of Arkansas at Fayetteville, came to me with a desire to do something with citizen writing groups in Augusta. I liked the idea immediately, but we needed a context, a reason to get citizens writing *about* something. Fortunately, a retired judge in Woodruff County, Burl Simmons, provided the impetus. Judge Simmons had long wanted to build a monument to the citizens of the county who had served in the military, and he proposed to raise funds to construct such a monument on the front lawn of the courthouse. Why not, I posed to Waller, Bowen, and the Recovery Initiative Committee, put out a call for folks throughout the county to contribute stories and essays about veterans—about their family members, their friends, in many cases about themselves? Surely, a stone monument on the front lawn of the courthouse would honor veterans. How richly would they be honored as well by the resonating memories and memorabilia the veterans had left to their loved ones, their families and friends?

Waller picked up the idea and ran with it. *The Veterans of Woodruff County* manifests a proposition that scholars and teachers of writing know to be true but that struck the citizens of Augusta and the surrounding county as surprising: namely, that writers are not only those esoteric souls who publish fiction, poetry, drama, and journalism. Writing doesn't happen only in lonely garrets or artists' enclaves. Writing lives, writing thrives, when ordinary folk have a need to express themselves, a context that will welcome that expression, and an audience who longs to learn what the writers feel, think, believe, and know.

Since the completion of *The Veterans of Woodruff County*, ARCare and the Augusta Community Literacy Advocacy Project have continued to expand by sponsoring literacy-focused challenge projects for high school students in selected communities served by the healthcare organization. In 2013, for example, ARCare challenged juniors and seniors at Augusta High School to do three things: to write a substantial essay about what might happen if small towns in the Arkansas Delta could see themselves as regional collaborators rather than as rivals (the reason for that topic will be made clear below); to take the ACT examination, ideally more than once, and do as well as they could on it; and to engage in a community service project. After examining ACT scores and grade-point averages and having the students' essays evaluated anonymously by experienced teachers outside of Augusta,

ARCare selected five students to participate in a trip to the Stratford Festival in Stratford, Ontario, where they saw fine productions of *Romeo and Juliet* (there's the connection to the essay prompt), *The Who's Tommy*, and *Fiddler on the Roof.* On the way home, the students, who were accompanied by Bowen and me, stopped off at Niagara Falls simply as tourists. The trip to Canada was the first time out of the country for all five, the first time on an airplane for four, and the first time out of Arkansas for three.

In 2014, ARCare posed a similar challenge to high school students from Cherry Valley and Southside, Arkansas, two communities with ARCare clinics. These students did the same tasks the Augusta students had done the year before, but their essay prompt required them to interview adults in their communities and ask them to describe, without naming names, what they thought were the characteristics of an ideal political leader. The seven students selected went on a trip to Washington, DC, where they met one of their US senators, toured historical sites and museums, and saw an excellent production of *Richard III* at the Folger Shakespeare Theatre—thus enabling them to see a less-than-ideal political leader in operation. Again in 2015, ARCare challenged students from Cherry Valley and Southside to read and write about issues related to community health care (a theme that ARCare wants students in their communities to understand), and the eleven students who rose to the challenge enjoyed a long weekend in Dallas, visiting museums, seeing a production of Moliere's *The School for Wives*, and spending a fascinating afternoon with the poet Greg Brownderville, who hails from tiny Pumpkin Bend, Arkansas, but who is now on the creative writing faculty at Southern Methodist University. As I write this, Bowen and I are soliciting applications from students who will participate in this year's challenge and visit Chicago in February 2016.

The Augusta-ARCare connection to Cherry Valley, moreover, has spawned another literacy-outreach project. With assistance secured at a statewide conference sponsored by the Brown Chair, one of the teachers at Cross County High School in Cherry Valley, Matthew

Swensen, founded the first-ever peer-tutoring writing center in an Arkansas high school. The veterans' book, the reading and writing workshops, the challenge trips, and the peer-tutoring writing center, I maintain, have altered the literacy landscape of Augusta, Woodruff County, and surrounding burghs, giving residents a range of contexts that invite them to see themselves as investigators, to produce genres that do important public work, and to foster—and ultimately sustain—a richer quality of life.

McGehee, the Artistry of Billie Seamans, and Community Literacy

The small town of McGehee, Arkansas, population around 4,200, located in the southeast corner of the state, has also continued to capitalize on the ADOHP connection. Like Augusta, McGehee had been an early participant in the ADOHP, and like Augusta, McGehee benefits from the unflagging efforts of a dynamic educator in Yogi Denton, the eleventh- and twelfth-grade social studies and English teacher at the high school. McGehee also has the good fortune to be the hometown of Anne Raines, director of tutorial services in the Enhanced Learning Center at the University of Arkansas, who was a central member of the ADOHP teaching team during the project's five-year run.

In the spring of 2013, Denton approached me with an idea for a new school and community literacy outreach project. Through her church, Denton had gotten to know the amazing story of Billie J. Seamans, who was about to turn ninety-two and who every Sunday morning at church sat two pews in front of the Denton family. Seamans has been a photographer for his entire life. Prior to World War II, he apprenticed to a local photographer in McGehee who took mostly family and school portraits. At the outbreak of the war, Seamans enlisted at his earliest opportunity—his father was the head of the local draft board, and all four Seamans boys went to the war. Seamans, a diminutive man, was assigned to the Army Air Corps and flew over a dozen missions as the ball turret gunner in B-17 raids over North Africa and Italy. Each of these missions had on board a photographer, whose pictures of the bombing raid would be shown to central command at the end of each mission to determine whether the appropriate targets had been hit and whether a new run should be ordered. Relatively early in Seamans's time as the ball turret gunner, the photographer on his plane was killed when the plane was hit. Given his experience as a photographer and his stature—he was small enough to fit into the photographer's small space on the bottom of the plane—Seamans was "promoted" to photographer, a position he occupied for several dozen missions in the North African and Italian campaigns. And what glorious pictures he took, capturing not only the results of the bombing runs but also panoramic shots of aircraft in flight and life-on-the-streets shots of neighborhoods and people (especially endearing were the children) in Italy.

Returning to McGehee after the war, Seamans used the GI Bill to study what he calls "the physics of photography" at Southern Arkansas University in Magnolia and at an arts school in Dallas, and he soon developed a career as a freelance photographer that lasted for the next four decades. His primary employer was International Harvester, the manufacturer of tractors and other heavy equipment used in the cotton, rice, and soybean fields of the southern Delta. International Harvester simply wanted photographs of its equipment being used in the fields. Seamans gave them more than that: he gave them art, taking pictures of tractors, bailers, and combines set in the rich, fecund milieu of the region. Photography aficionados at the University of Arkansas, viewing Seamans's agriculture shots for the first time, likened them to the Depression-era pictures of Dorothea Lange and the US Southwest photos taken by Ansel Adams. In addition to providing photographic vistas of the region's agriculture, Seamans also took thousands of pictures of family and community life in McGehee and DeShea County—shots of hunting expeditions, ball games, church picnics, civic club meetings, holiday parades, you name it. And in every one of the thousands of photos he took from the 1940s through the early 2000s, one sees the eye of an artist behind the lens.

Denton saw the rich possibilities for a literacy project in the Seamans story. In preparation for the McGehee High School's homecoming celebration (called Owlfest because the school mascot is an owl) in 2012, she worked with Brandi Anthony, who teaches in the Environmental and Spatial Technologies program at the school, to create large poster-sized reprints of several of Seamans' best life-in-McGehee pictures from various stages of his career. Denton placed these photographs throughout the American Legion hall and stationed a pair of her students beside each photo. When visitors to Owlfest (and, yes, people really *do* come back to McGehee for homecoming) stopped to look at the pictures, the students would take oral histories from them, asking the visitors to tell them what stories, memories, and legends the photograph evoked for them. The students, of course, recorded these conversations and later transcribed them. In addition, Denton arranged for her students to interview Seamans on multiple occasions, asking him to tell them what it was like growing up in McGehee, going off to war, coming back to raise a family, and taking thousands of beautiful photographs.

The culmination of this substantial effort was the publication, jointly by the Brown Chair in English Literacy and McGehee High School, of *Keeping a Moment: Through the Lens of Billie J. Seamans* (Varnell 2013), a sixty-page book containing over a hundred of his photographs, three complete essays by teams of McGehee High students, and three transcripts of interviews with Seamans. The book was unveiled at Owlfest 2013 in October. Seamans was the grand marshal of the homecoming parade, at which McGehee High students wore T-shirts with the book cover reproduced on them. One week later, Seamans learned that he had been designated to receive the Governor's Lifetime Achievement Award from the Arkansas Arts Council in recognition of his six decades of artistry.

We are not sure whether the last seed planted by the ADOHP has blossomed. But we can assure all comers that literacy, social text, place, and authentic work all certainly converged in Augusta and McGehee, emerging from the seeds planted by the ADOHP. We are always willing to entertain an idea from one of our participating communities for a similar project.

Branches from the Same Tree: Potential "Cousins" of ADOHP

The previous sections suggested that ADOHP has played the role of parent to children. We'd also like to suggest that the project could spawn cousins, projects similar to ADOHP but with slightly different foci and emphases. We think the greatest measure of any educational project might be meeting the standard of replication and transfer.

Should other parties borrow from ADOHP and attempt to replicate it much in the same way teachers are encouraged—by the Professional Learning Communities movement, for example (see DuFour and Eaker 1998)—to listen to their colleagues and approach similar teaching problems together? In short, yes. We believe the ADOHP is consummately clonable and transferable. Some advice from the educational theorists Yvonna Lincoln and Egon Guba (1985) guides our thinking. As they write, "If there is to be transferability, the burden of proof lies less with the original investigator than with the person seeking to make an application elsewhere. The original inquirer cannot know the sites to which transferability might be sought, but the appliers can and do. The best advice to give to anyone seeking to make a transfer is to accumulate empirical evidence about contextual similarity; the responsibility of the original investigator ends in providing sufficient descriptive data to make such similarity judgments possible (298)." Clearly, the feasibility of transferability hinges on the explanation of the project, something previous chapters take up extensively, so we think the argument for morphing the ADOHP becomes an easy one to make.

Obviously, if one were to try to create a project similar to the ADOHP, the question of funding becomes salient. As chapter 1 noted, the ADOHP was funded with income from the endowment for the Brown Chair in English Literacy. Although the project itself was designed to create lasting, repeatable effects regardless of the funding, it certainly started with financial capital, a generous gift to the University of Arkansas. As we grappled with the idea of spreading this work to other situations that may not have the financial starting blocks this project enjoyed, we considered, through a lens of sustainability, how others might still be able to create ADOHP-like relationships between students and their communities. Projects like the ADOHP are not fly-by-night efforts; they hold the potential to create change in a generation of young people, their teachers, and the involved communities.

With a hopeful attitude, therefore, we'd like to highlight what other educators are doing in a similar spirit, urging that these types of projects emerge whenever and wherever possible. What do projects look like in secondary schools and colleges, and how can they, at each level, incorporate the fundamentals of ADOHP while taking on different formats? We offer two examples of this type of work in different settings. In each of these contexts, we see versions of the three primary hallmarks of ADOHP: youths inscribing themselves in the social texts of a salient topic in their culture, deploying the resources of place in their learning, and accomplishing authentic intellectual work.

Telling Their Stories

In secondary schools, a range of projects currently operate in ways that suggest an alignment with ADOHP. For an exemplar, we wanted to find something that was particularly congruent with our goals and readily applicable for a wide range of practicing teachers. Surely the example of completing interviews and documenting oral histories of the elderly is done in a number of schools across the country. What Suzanne Myers, an English teacher from Atchison County High School outside of rural Effingham, Kansas, offers in her example is the logistical thinking to make this kind of project work in other scenarios, for other purposes, and with different audiences.

As many good projects do, Myers's began as she observed in her students a disconnection with their community. "I wanted to find a way to get them out into the community that was both academically meaningful and helpful to the folks in the community as well," she said (Myers, interview, December 13, 2009). Her students attended a single high school in a small rural school district, one that encompasses an economically diverse population. The school community resulting from these influences was isolating, but it didn't have to be.

In her goal to help the students identify with their surrounding community, Myers considered several options (making menus for locally owned restaurants, creating pamphlets or brochures for area businesses) before deciding on working with a local nursing home. She had volunteered at a nursing home when she was in college and remembered what that experience had meant to her; she also remembered there being a shortage of contact with the outside world for the nursing home residents. "I wanted my students to interview the residents and get ideas about their lives since many had lived in the region and had been connected to it for a long time." Myers's idea was to have students collect stories from nursing home residents and then present them like a journalistic article, modeled on National Public Radio's popular *This American Life* radio show. On *This American Life*, the host Ira Glass interviews people and collects stories that focus on a central point or idea. Myers wanted the experience to be more than just an interview, more than outreach into the community; she wanted her students to be challenged to think for themselves and to construct meaning out of many smaller pieces of data.

Myers began the project by having her students listen to segments of *This American Life* and then instructed them on the intricacies of performing interviews. As we did in ADOHP, Myers found that her students generally lacked questioning ability and needed practice with question types and the process of an interview in general. Her role in the classroom, as she saw it, was to help her students prepare for the interview by practicing questions in interview scenarios with their peers. The next step in the process was to secure transportation and recording equipment. Myers was able to get support from her school district to bus the students to the nursing home for two hours (estimated cost, $150). She relied on students for recording equipment, mainly their cellular phones; in some cases, students chose not to record their interviews because they anticipated it would create a different feel for the interview itself.

In scheduling the participants, Myers worked with a nursing home activity coordinator as the central point of contact. She had the students complete the one-hour interviews in pairs, the interviews taking place in the residents' rooms or in common areas around the facility. The activity coordinator attempted to schedule interviews with residents who did not have family members in the area and received few visitors.

After the interviews, each pair of partners spent about another five days working on analyzing transcripts, discerning the thesis of the interviews themselves, and then creating cohesive presentations of their material to the class. Though the students' final products needed to fit the criterion of being organized around central ideas like the *This American Life* interviews, Myers gave students options—videos, audio, scrapbook—on how to present their interviewee to the class, similar to the "literacy license" that we incorporated in the ADOHP.

The project represented a challenging assignment for these students, a "good thing," according to Myers, who said that school was often too easy. Students had a difficult time taking raw data and synthesizing it for an audience that wasn't there. The whole idea of looking at little sound bites or words on a page was often frustrating for these students. The interview process was also difficult for the students because they had not planned the questions very well. The interview itself, which sometimes included awkward periods of time after the questions ran out, reinforced their need to develop critical questions and a general spirit of inquiry.

Of course, in work like this, the interviewees benefited in myriad ways. Certainly nearly forgotten members of the community were given an opportunity to tell stories and to interact with members of the younger generation, who ideally were conveying stories and ideas that would outlast their fragile bodies.

According to Myers, several students came out of the interviews impressed and in awe of what their subjects had accomplished. As she noted, adolescents are sometimes too self-absorbed and materialistic and to be able to recognize the contributions of community members like the nursing home residents. The project allowed students to connect with the community by connecting with the interview subject. Myers also believes that her students benefited from being able to collaborate with a peer on this project, especially since most of the pairs struggled to come up with questions and then turn their interview into a new product. Without the support of a peer, Myers contends that the process of the interview itself and the product each pair created might have been too difficult, even for her honors sophomores.

In reflecting about the project and considering whether others might replicate it, Myers remained enthusiastic about the process and the social and educational learning that occurred through the project. Besides having a dedicated teacher, it didn't cost much to make either happen. "I achieved instructional goals related to language arts content while the students seemed to really understand the contributions of a dying generation of people. I could have never taught them that if they hadn't experienced it."

As a teacher, Myers felt her students were a bit unprepared to effectively execute the interviews, and in future years she intends to spend more time on the interview process. In addition, a few groups of her YouTube-generation students reportedly might have taken things a little far with their projects in trying to make them entertaining. But these interviewing deficits and adolescent social development miscues were small drawbacks to a project ripe with positive vibes.

In thinking about repeating the project, Myers also mentioned a district-level concern that other schools might also face. Specifically, her district's common pacing goals—every teacher teaching the same page of the novel, same concept, on the same day—might have hampered this organic, community-minded project before it could begin. While making this work, Myers had to think only of her own students and limitations. But she feels that if she were to attempt this with her students in the future, the educational climate might mandate that all students in a grade get to do it or none of them do. Myers maintains, and we concur, that students should do projects like this at the discretion of each teacher who gives full consideration to the ability and orientation of each class or group of students. In this age of "all these kids need the exact same experiences so they can score proficient or above," Myers feels that neither her school nor the nursing home could support either of the two "all-kids" options: her own students get the experience or the entire sophomore class does.

In the end, teachers like Myers will continue to find ways to make experiential learning possible for their students. As she put it, "I once heard a football coach say that he learned more on the football field than ever he did in high school classes. While this may or may not be true, the nursing home experience might have been analogous to the football field for many of my students. School should feel more like a performance of skills versus a factory of learning." The opportunity to get out there, meet and learn about people, and then present that to a group of peers is not that dissimilar to the athletic competition of a Friday night football game. She believes, and we concur, that now might be the perfect time for a return to teaching practices by which students gain a multitude of skills and knowledge and not in lock step with their peers down the hall. After the interviews were completed and the projects presented, Myers had her students write thank-you notes to their interviewees; like organic and thoughtful teaching, writing thank-you notes is nearly a lost art too.

Family Writing Projects

The Family Writing Projects (FWPs) in Kansas have grown out of an English teacher education program and the work of a site of the National Writing Project. Kansas State University (KSU), the host institution, is situated in the Flint Hills region of Kansas in an isolated city of around sixty thousand. Being a land grant institution, KSU programs are often expected to carry out research, teaching, and service throughout the state, and the teacher education program is no exception. For example, KSU has agreements with several community colleges for 2 + 2 programs that offer students in rural communities an opportunity to attend a community college for two years and then graduate in two more years at the university in Manhattan, Kansas. In the teacher education program, students are often given the opportunity to complete student teaching in rural areas, sometimes as far as four or five hours away from the university. In an effort to prepare students to work in rural situations and with parents, F. Todd Goodson, professor of English education, devised a comprehensive service learning experience for his preservice English and communication arts teachers. The dynamic initiative asks students enrolled in his teaching methods course to work in a variety of situations including an after-school writing club, an after-school literacy tutoring program, a fluency intervention project, and one of several family writing projects taking place in surrounding communities. Although the programs individually and as a whole are worth discussing, we focus here on the FWPs because of their community-centered focus, wide potential for replication, and robustly defined groundwork.

The concept of the Family Writing Project began, at least officially, with the work of Arthur Kelly, a teacher consultant for the Southern Nevada Writing Project and a veteran Las Vegas middle school teacher. Kelly instigated hands-on projects involving families writing together in the Las Vegas area. He details the project in his book, *Writing with Families: Strengthening the Home/School Connection with Family Scribe Groups* (2006). Essentially, a Family Writing Project is an extracurricular opportunity for students, with parents in tow, to receive extra instruction in writing by developing a writing community among members of a family unit. Typically, FWPs ask students and parents to commit to meet several times throughout the course of a semester or year. From the perspective of a classroom teacher, this commitment makes a lot of sense since it promotes bonds critical for student success to be developed between teacher and parents and provides an extra opportunity to discuss and place value on the writing experience and process with their students.

In Kansas, the Family Writing Project, having originated with an Arthur Kelly presentation, began in 2004 at Wamego Middle and High School, with Lori Goodson as site codirector, and quickly spread to sites in Junction City, Fort Riley, Riley, and Manhattan. Simultaneously, Todd Goodson's two worlds—the writing project and English education—coalesced in a situation where savvy National Writing Project (NWP) trained teachers could work with his wet-behind-the-ears future teachers. As part of their service-learning experience, the preservice teachers both helped to facilitate various aspects of the FWP and participated as writers with parents and students—for many preservice teachers their first interaction with parents in a school setting.

The goals of this project were multifaceted, with each participant—student, parent, teacher, preservice teacher—potentially seeking and gaining completely different notions or concepts; the participants were interconnected, potentially benefitting from and relying on each of the others. At the core of the work, of course, was the school student, who volunteered to participate and had to secure at least one adult's commitment to participate. In cases when parents or guardians weren't available, the teachers involved in each of the sites matched school students with community members, and on special occasions, with preservice teachers. For these school students, the goals were clear: to become better writers through the experience of writing for and sharing with family members, other students, college students, and community members. Parents and community members benefited chiefly from the experience of writing with young adults and secondarily from experiencing positive interactions in a school setting—an outcome that happens too infrequently. The preservice teachers got to see an experienced writing teacher leading a special program over a period of time, work with students in small group settings, and gain a firsthand experience of interacting with parents before it officially "counted" during student teaching or in their first year. Finally, the in-service teacher involved benefited greatly too, having the opportunity to work with all of these stakeholders in the educational pursuit of better writing. In many instances, student teaching matches were forged through this and other service projects.

From the finite goals of a classroom to some of the potentially larger issues addressed with work like this, FWPs are a way for parents and others to become cognizant of literacy issues, to excel as members of the school community, and to ultimately see their place in the educational process. The literacy practices occurring in the homes of these students were, of course, one of the most reliable predictors of the student's ultimate success or failure in reading and writing. When parents, guardians, and community members worked with students, all parties began to see themselves as literate members of a writing community, an idyllic microcosm of the larger community. As this sense of community developed, all stakeholders shared a common bond, language, and sense of belonging.

In a 2009 address at Columbia Teacher's College, Arne Duncan, US Secretary of Education, cited Arthur Levine's 2006 report on schools of education, noting Levine's criticism of schools of education for not doing enough to provide preservice teachers with opportunities to observe and practice teaching before being expected to perform it. Goodson's project addresses this issue and the Family Writing Project incorporates another too oft-forgotten element of the educational community, the parental or community involvement in the school. When these folks have the opportunity to experience a successful writing classroom community, they are less likely to vote down school bonds or criticize teachers and more likely to take an active role in the educational process.

Two additional aspects of FWPs distinguish them. A key to the relevance and success of FWPs is the diverse—racially, socioeconomically, and geographically—settings in which these programs can find homes. Kelly's project started in inner city Las Vegas, whereas the FWP in Riley, Kansas, was held in a K–12 building housing only ninety-four rural students, many of whose parents were deployed overseas with the military. In addition, FWPs are ultimately portable: they can occur anywhere, with any age students, and are relatively cost free to hold.

As the various sites of Family Writing Projects continue to revolve around the work of the Flint Hills Writing Project, a wonderful opportunity is provided for everyone involved; they are ultimately value-added experiences for the communities. While a site of the National Writing Project and a potentially collaborative university aren't necessarily resources available to most schools in the country, we contend any school could make a Family Writing Project work in its context. Parents vary in their involvement, but sometimes they never get an invitation into a positive school setting. Although we support athletics in schools, few of our public or private school students will do much with what they learn on Friday nights. They will need reading and writing abilities on all the other days that end in "y" as well.

Students Involved in Sustaining Their Arkansas: The Future of ADOHP

As should be clear from the preceding chapters, ADOHP was not flawless. We made our share of mistakes, and we think we dealt with them adequately and fairly. But if there was one aspect of ADOHP that was particular troublesome, it was the potential for the project to become *excessively* nostalgic. As we argue in chapter 2, the work of Ursula Kelly convinced us of the efficacy of embracing a modicum of nostalgia in the ADOHP, that modicum being the window into traditions and values worth maintaining in a reinhabitation of the Delta. But when ADOHP descended inescapably into the realm of "oh, for a return to the good old days," which it did on rare occasion, it threatened to move away from its grounding principles of youth cultural studies, critical pedagogy of place, and authentic intellectual work.

The desire to avoid such an uncritical descent into the past has motivated us to develop the next iteration of ADOHP, a new project called Students Involved in Sustaining Their Arkansas—SISTA for short. The project combines what we think are the best features of ADOHP: the students' inquiry, via oral history, into vital issues for their hometowns and region; the tapping into the resources of "place" for teaching and learning; and the fostering of authentic intellectual achievement. SISTA adds to this mix a new focus on promoting sustainability and growth in the Arkansas Delta. In SISTA, high school juniors, designated as SISTA fellows, spend a year working with a University of Arkansas mentor, developing fully fleshed-out proposals for projects that will, in some way, revitalize and sustain the quality of life in their hometowns and regions.

SISTA was initially going to be called simply Students Involved in Sustaining Arkansas, or SISA, but our frequent collaborator, Kassie Misiewicz, the artistic director of Trike Theatre, said, "Brother, you need a T in there to make it SISTA." In the pilot version of SISTA, a handful of students at two small, predominantly rural high schools in rural Arkansas, Brinkley and Southside, both ARCare communities, spent a year developing proposals for their sustainability projects. Prior to launching the pilot in these two communities, the Brown Chair, with the help of two partner organizations, a bank and ARCare, set up citizen-support committees in each community, with the understanding that these committees would receive the proposals when the students had completed them and, if feasible, find funding to carry them out.

A University of Arkansas graduate student served as a mentor at each of the two participating schools, and the tasks for completing the project were sequenced over the academic year:

- By September 1, 2014, a 250-word proposal was due, addressing the following questions: What project are you proposing? What are two things you know about the problem/issue/topic already? What are two questions you think you will need to answer? Why is it an important project for you and your community?
- By October 10, 2014, a 1,250-word-maximum "oral history of the topic" document was due, addressing the following questions: What is the oral history of the topic that the project takes up? What do people say about it? What stories do they tell about it? Why do people who have lived in the community for a substantial amount of time say the topic is important? What is the history of the community (both written and oral), and how does the history of the topic fit within the community's history? How does the writer (i.e., the student, the project proposer) connect to the topic of the proposal?
- By November 14, 2014, a 750-word-maximum "quality of key personnel" document was due: Who are the personnel that will be involved in carrying out the project and what is the experience and expertise that qualifies them to work on it?
- By December 19, 2014, a 1,000-word-maximum timeline was due: What duties will each person involved carry out and when will he or she do the work? In other words, what is the timeline or schedule for the project's development and start-up?

Students were given the month of January to inspect carefully and revise everything they had done so far.

- By February 20, 2015, a 500-word-maximum budget estimate was due: What will the project cost for it to get up and running? How can you explain and justify these costs?
- By March 13, 2015, a 1,000-word-maximum evaluation description was due: How will the project be evaluated to determine its effectiveness after it is up and running? How will the operation of the project be sustained for long-term operation after it has been developed and implemented?
- By April 10, 2015, a 250-word-maximum executive summary was due.

On May 5, 2015, students submitted their completed proposals to the Brown Chair.

Three proposals emerged from one of the sites, Brinkley: a proposal for a community bakery and healthy nutrition center, where adults will teach students how to bake and the products will be sold at a rejuvenated farmers' market on the town square; a proposal for a community pottery and fine arts studio, where people of all ages will not only learn how to make pottery but will also teach and take music lessons; and a proposal for a community recreation center with a swimming pool as its central feature. Two proposals emerged from the other site, Southside: one for a new community and civic center, featuring office and meeting space for the town, which has just recently been incorporated; and one for a community livestock barn where students and townsfolk will be able to show and auction the animals they maintain.

Lessons from the SISTA Pilot: Moving Students toward Citizenship

We see SISTA working with the same nodus of theoretical concepts that ADOHP embodied: students tap into community resources as research sites, create nontraditional (for most high school classes, at least) genres that call for new writerly identities, engage in authentic intellectual work by constructing new knowledge, and contribute to the reinhabitation of their hometowns and regions. The students, moreover, learn some very practical things: they work on college-level writing projects, they practice writing persuasively, they learn how to articulate a problem and its solution in writing. Because the project is so multifaceted, they also have to develop organizational skills, learn how to develop an idea, and then be flexible when that idea evolves; they develop creative problem-solving skills by evaluating the needs in a specific situation, breaking the problem down in detail, and establishing goals and a plan for meeting all the practical needs in that situation; they learn the importance of conducting extensive research and developed their abilities to conduct that research; and they learn specifically how to write a project proposal.

But perhaps more important than these academic skills are the abstract, personal parts of what they learned. SISTA invites them to function as citizens of their community and stresses the importance and the benefit of being involved in one's community. By requiring the students to evaluate their community's needs and then come up with an idea to fit those needs, SISTA helps them to begin thinking as municipal officials and as concerned citizens who want to see their communities improve and thrive. It encourages them to avoid the apathy about community that often prevails. Moreover, SISTA gives them confidence in their own ideas, their own visions. Because the project is not strictly an intellectual exercise but includes the possibility of their ideas coming to fruition, it gives them a sense of power: the power to make change happen, as well as the desire to make change happen. The process of developing their proposal instills in them confidence that their ideas are solid and valuable. The experience of confidence and power directed at improving their communities for themselves and for others is good for their own well-being and is potentially good for every community they will be part of in the future. Because they have worked to improve a community once, and have received encouragement that their ideas are both worthwhile and possible, they are more likely to do it again. Ideally, that sense of ambition, power, and confidence will follow them forever.

We hope that confidence, ambition, and power will transfer into their writing and work in college as well. All of us on the SISTA team are experienced composition teachers, so we frequently note among our students a lack of confidence in their own ideas and, on a very deep level, an unwillingness in many of them to develop their own original ideas. Among some of our students, there seems to be a sense that they can't make any changes in the status quo, so why bother? This notion gives us pause both as citizens and educators. In SISTA, we hope, education is not only about telling students a bunch of facts, but is about encouraging emerging citizens to think and act for themselves so that our communities' collective knowledge grows over time and our communities' collective well-being and quality of life improve over time.

We must continuously acknowledge, however, that taking on these powerful roles as self-motivated, self-actualized students and forceful, emerging students can represent a frightening prospect to high school juniors from a small rural town in the Delta, especially when we ask them to present and defend their ideas to folks associated with the big state university located four hours away in prosperous Northwest Arkansas. In March 2015, we brought all the participating students from the two sites to Fayetteville for a two-day working session, and one of us carved out special personal conversation time with them. Two of the young women from the smaller town have visions of themselves as a surgeon and a lawyer, respectively, and they wanted to meet University of Arkansas students currently studying in those fields. Both seemed a bit impatient to get on with their futures right now. But at fifteen and sixteen years of age, they also seem afraid to leave their hometowns and their families. "Will you go far away to school?" they were asked. They responded with knitted brows. What if there's a tornado? What if someone gets sick? What if I get sick?

These two high school juniors are the young pillars of their homes, pinched tightly between brothers and sisters. SISTA is moving them toward becoming pillars of their community as well. They frequently feel themselves negotiating the two attitudes one often finds in small towns: *get me out of here* and *let me stay*. Ideally, SISTA will help them live through that tension. As they chronicle the history of their Arkansas and scope out future prospects, maybe they will generate a place for new families who will want to stick around.

SISTA Turns Two: We Continue, as We Hope You Do, Too

As we complete this chapter, we have just appointed a new group of SISTA fellows—twelve students from five high schools in different regions throughout the state. Their proposed projects are rich in potential:

- A student from Watson Chapel High School proposes to create a paddle-boat business on Saracen Landing, a public pavilion that was completed in 2007 with a walking trail, grill area, wildlife observation decks, a public fishing area, and splash park.
- A team of five students from Mountain Home High School Career Academies proposes to create a plan to restore a local hiking trail and install selections created by local artists.
- Two students at Buffalo Island Central High School propose designing an outdoor market for the Buffalo Island community, bringing together several small towns in an area where there is no grocery store.
- Another student from Buffalo Island Central High School proposes to create an irrigation system using piping in order to assist farmers in the Buffalo Island area.
- A student from Springdale Har-Ber High School proposes to create a project that assists women escape sex trafficking in Arkansas, focusing on the creation of a safe house.
- Two students from Armorel High School propose to create a nonprofit tourism organization for Mississippi County, drawing attention to its histories in farming and Native American culture.

The new SISTA fellows are already linked with their University of Arkansas mentors and are hard at work on the initial oral history stage of their yearlong endeavor.

Reflecting on these new SISTA initiatives and the projects that have grown from the ADOHP seed, we hope that readers will put down this book and think about ways of creating dialogue between rural (and other) communities and their schools. Literacy-in-use-in-context can take myriad forms, isolated in a single classroom or community-wide, but the point of all these projects remains the same:

student-involved experiential literacy education built on personal and interpersonal experience and contributing to social, political, economic, and cultural capital. Connecting community or region to a group of students holds tremendous potential for all parties involved. Creating authentic and challenging learning experiences like these should be a larger, more central part of the nature of school. If we are to create sustainable situations in rural America, the schools must play a critical role and projects like these may help edify and retain teachers, create more insightful and connected students, and ultimately bridge the gap between academics and community. Henry Adams's (1919) words sum up the hopes of the Arkansas Delta Oral History Project, the Family Writing Project, the Telling Their Stories Project, and SISTA: "a teacher affects eternity—he can never tell where his influence stops."

Appendixes

Works Cited

Index

About the Authors

APPENDIX A

ADOHP Staff's Introductory Communication to High School Partners

TO: Colleagues and friends at Forrest City High School, Marvell High School, Lee County High School, McGehee High School, Pine Bluff High School, Great River Educational Cooperative, Delta Cultural Center

FROM: David Jolliffe, Professor of English and Brown Chair in English Literacy
Anne Raines, codirector, Arkansas Delta Oral History Project
Krista Jones, codirector, Arkansas Delta Oral History Project

RE: Planning for the Arkansas Delta Oral History Project

DATE: May 15–16, 2006

First of all, please accept our thanks for agreeing to participate in this exciting new project. The Arkansas Delta Oral History Project will provide the opportunity for University of Arkansas faculty and undergraduate students to work collaboratively with teachers and students in five high schools in the Arkansas Delta, capturing, writing about, and perhaps even performing stories about the rich historical, social, cultural, economic, and political backgrounds of their communities, neighborhoods, homes, and families.

We have two goals for our May 15–16 visits: to meet personally the teachers and administrators with whom we'll be working, and to begin planning a project that will fit most effectively within the curriculums of the five high schools. We aim not to add a troublesome wrinkle to what you're already doing. We are trying, instead, to enrich a curricular or co-curricular project you would already normally take up by adding an oral history component to it. We envision being available to work with you as necessary at regular intervals in the summer and fall of 2006.

As we have envisioned it, the project itself will begin in the middle of January 2007 (perhaps January 19–20), with a two-day workshop at the Delta Cultural Center in Helena, led by Charles Morrissey, former president of the Oral History Association. At this workshop, we hope to organize the students into six-person working groups: one student from the University of Arkansas and one from each of the five participating high schools. Over the course of the second semester, we hope that these working groups can share drafts, revise, and present to one another projects about the essential elements of oral history, the characteristics of an oral history archive, and methods of planning and conducting an oral history interview. The final project for each student would be an original essay based on an oral history interview he or she has conducted. It is these projects that we would like to articulate as closely as possible with your curricular plans.

Once during the semester (perhaps March 9–11), we hope to bring all the participating students to the University of Arkansas at Fayetteville for a weekend consisting of a face-to-face group work, cultural activities, fun, and learning. At the end of the semester (perhaps May 18–19 or thereabouts), we hope to convene the entire group of participating students at the Delta Cultural Center again for two days of sharing the final projects. Ideally, we will be able to archive these projects both in print and electronically. We hope that this event might constitute the first instance of what would become the annual Arkansas Delta Oral History Festival.

Through the generosity of two organizations, the Brown Foundation and the Walton Family Charitable Support Foundation, the University of Arkansas at Fayetteville is able to sponsor the Arkansas Delta Oral History Project so that students can participate at no cost. We will arrange for students' and teachers' transportation to and from the Delta Cultural Center at the beginning and end of the project and to and from Fayetteville during the middle of it. We will also provide food and lodging during these three weekends.

Please feel free to get in touch with us regularly. You may call David Jolliffe at 479-575-2289. You may write to us at these three e-mail addresses:

David Jolliffe: djollif@uark.edu
Anne Raines: anner@uark.edu
Krista Jones: kmj03@uark.edu

APPENDIX B

ADOHP Student Manual

1) What Is Oral History?

The term "oral history" refers to a historical method that uses recorded interviews that preserve firsthand memories, accounts, interpretations of a person's life, an event, a place, a way of life or period. The oral historian is a person who uses all sorts of sources and records—spoken memories of historical significance—to explain the past.

Oral Historian as Problem Solver

The oral historian is a problem solver who uses history to help us understand the problems society confronts.

The oral historian interviews a person and makes the tapes available for teaching. Then students of later generations can profit from others' experiences learning from their mistakes and successes.

1. Experience: everything that happened in the past →
2. Evidence: pictures, story, diary, questionnaire, archeology, the evidence →
3. Survive: What is left after fire, flood, disasters, bombings →
4. Archived: What is saved for future use; protected →
5. Accessible: What people can get to.

The Process

Throughout the entire process, remember you are a professional oral historian. Professionalism is key.

You are a co-creator of historical record. Don't seek to verify your own preconceived notions.

2) How Do You Focus on Potential Topics and Interview Candidates?

- Consider the history of the region.
- Consider chronology: think about the timeline of a person's life.
- Create a "decision tree": identify major turning points in the history of an organization or a person's life.
- Think about turning points in the region: events, lives, power structures.
- Who has had a strong effect on others? On towns? On education?
- What stories do you want to hear?
- Always know why you are doing the interview with someone. You need genuine, authentic, historic, significant reasons for interviews.
- Document the undocumented.
- Ignore a hierarchy. Look for people who are knowledgeable.
- Ask yourself: Is this the best person to interview, considering what I want to find out? Can this person tell me all parts of the story? Are there other people who might tell me other parts of the story?

3) How Do You Arrange for the Oral History Interview?

- Write a one-page letter explaining what you want to do and why.
- Use simple language.
- Do not use jargon.
- Start on the outside and work in to get a key interview.
- Follow up the letter with a phone call or visit to schedule the interview.
- Make sure that they know they are co-creating history. This is a collaborative process.
- Phrases to use when persuading interviewee to participate in project:
    - Do it for your grandchildren.
    - Your story is worth telling.
    - We want the project to be representative of all people involved, not just the major players.

4) How Do You Do Background Research?

- Do your homework.
- Investigate your subject.
- Find out what you can on your own first, so you can ask informed questions.

Remember the Paper Trail!

There are frequently newspaper stories, legal documents like birth certificates, contracts, and wills, and often letters that you can consult to learn more about the story you're investigating.

- Follow the paper trail first; don't assume it does not exist.
- Trace the paper trail, and then use oral history to fill in the gaps.
- Be skeptical of the paper trail. Paper trails can be constructed to hide something. A paper trail and an oral history interview work in tandem.
- When consulting the paper trail, you may run into sensitive areas of the story you're investigating. Make note of them and hope your interviewee will enlighten you on why they are sensitive. But don't bring up these sensitive subjects in the interview until your rapport with your interviewee is HIGH.

Suggestions for Background Research:

- Consult newspaper archives.
- Read *Who's Who* for the appropriate years.
- Look for minutes from meetings, in-house letters, grant applications.
- Interview people about what you don't know, not what you know.
- Research a collection for what questions you should ask. Look for gaps or contradictions in the paper trail.
- Triangulate: use more than one source.
- Ask yourself: What was life like for these people?
- Plan to bring copies of paper-trail documents with you to the interview to use as props.
- The best sources are those created contemporaneously with events.

5) How Do You Plan the Interview?

- Don't disrupt the lives of older people—go to their houses.
- Plan to use a quiet room—dining rooms are good.
- Master your equipment before the interview (see equipment suggestions below).
- Be ready to "go with the flow" of the interview.
- **LISTEN** to the answers; the next question often comes from the answer.

6) How Do You Develop Effective Questioning Techniques?

- *Tips for Writing Questions*
  - Use neutral language—it is critical to success.
  - Ask simple questions—short, sweet, clear.
  - Ask one question at a time.
  - Ask open-ended questions.
  - Do not offer alternatives—let the subject find the answer, don't answer for her.
  - Words to use in questions: describe, tell, explain, elaborate, how, speak to.
  - Identify the most important question(s) to ask.
  - Identify the most sensitive question(s) to ask.
  - Always ask: Did you keep a diary?
  - Do not assume people did not keep paper trails—journals, notes.

Big Six for Interviews:

- Who?
- What?
- When?
- Where?
- **Why?***
- How?

*"Why" is most essential and hardest to ask or answer.

If the interviewee asks for a list of questions, give a list of topics. Many questions will grow from the answers they give.

Questioning Techniques:

Two-sentence format uses a first sentence to serve as an introduction for a more difficult or sensitive second question:

This is why I need to ask *X: X.*

Example: "A future historian would fault me for not asking this question: Why you did not assist George in his plans?"

Today Show format moves from present to past. You are trying to get information about their memories, not what they think about today's events.

Example: "There is great concern today about the American presence abroad. With respect to President Johnson's policy toward Vietnam, how did you view that?"

An *evocation question* is when you ask the interviewee to tell you "how it felt" or "what was it like" to be in a situation.

An *influence question* asks "Why was X such an influential presence in your life?

A *meaning* question: If the interviewee suggests something, follow up with a question: "What meaning did that experience have for you?" "What meaning do you attach to that?"

A *who else* question: Find out who else could have been there to corroborate the story.

Your last two follow-up questions should always be:
  Is there anything I am failing to ask?
  Is there anything you want to go back to and say something more about?

7) How Do You Role-Play a Mock Interview before the Real Interview?

Set up mock interviews and have students observe one another. Always have some students turn their backs and listen for sounds that would be intrusive on the tape recording. Have students evaluate interviews for the Big Six, checking for the paper trail, neutral language, one question at a time.

In some interviews, create problems that the students may have to deal with in an actual interview. (Interruptions, background noise, answers to questions that are not vocalized, doorbells, ringing phones.)

Have a volunteer from the community come in for the students to practice interviewing.

Point to Ponder: William Warner Moss, head of the Kennedy Library Oral History Project, points out: "Just as no two interviewees are alike, so no two interviewers are alike, and success depends to a great extent on the capability and interest of the people involved rather than a structured application of designed questions."

8) How Do You Conduct the Actual Interview?

Building Rapport: Your First Goal!

- Never argue or interrupt.
- Try to put your interview subject at ease. He or she may be very nervous.
- Go to where the subject is comfortable: his or her home, if possible.
- Ask what divides me from the person I am interviewing (age, class, accent, gender, race)?
- Ask what do I share with the interviewee?
- Don't rush folks. Visit with them as well as interview them.
- In interview, start slow. Ask an easy question first to get things started. Ask short and simple questions. Save more probing and aggressive questions for the end of the interview.

Asking Tough Questions:

- If the question is historically significant, you must ask it.
- When is the best time to interview someone? Wait until they are out of office. Dale Bumpers's book was written when he was no longer senator.
- Sensitivity: money is the most sensitive issue.
- Wait to ask the tough questions when the rapport is highest in the interview.

Additional Points:

- Go for individual stories.
- Make sure the person answers all of the Big Six.
- If the subject stumbles on a detail, move on—you can always get the date from another source.
- Dig for details: Ask for examples, details, and specifics.
- Keep yourself in the role of questioner. Save your answers for after the interview.
- Interviewee is the teacher and interviewer is the student.
- Remember visual clues: "This picture is of you in a cheerleader outfit in 1947."
- Note visual communication: nods and gestures.
- Don't interrupt course of interview. Make notes and ask about names and spelling later.

- Remember outcome determines recollection. The game is remembered in terms of score, win, loss.
- If you are ever in doubt as to the meaning the subject is trying to convey, ASK!
- Pursue complexity. Ask for more reasons "why" and more examples and details.

Concluding Questions and Comments:

- Is there anything I have failed to ask you that you would like to talk about?
- Is there anything you want to go back to and add to? Say more about?
- When we send the transcript back for you to review, if you have any further thoughts, just note them in the margins. [Note: Think of the transcript as a chance for more information]

Always end by saying "Thank you" and then turn off the tape recorder, but do not unplug yet. The subject may get started again and you need to be ready.

Remember: Your interviewee is a collaborator. Go back or call to ask for clarification or help.

9) How Do You Record the Interview?

- Basic tape recorder is fine.
- Open tape cases before interview.
- Load cassette before interview.
- Always take more tape than what you think you will need.
- Bring extension cords, always.
- Use an external microphone for better sound recording.
- Think about ideal recording environments, avoid background noises and interruptions.
- Dining rooms usually are the best places.
- Use 60-minute tapes, 30 minutes per side.

Recording Interviews:

- Tape recorders hear but do not see.
- Think about how the transcriber will hear interview.

- Get people to articulate verbally.
- If people object to the tape recorder, say, "It gives a more accurate record of what you say."
- If your equipment fails, take notes and dictate the transcript to a tape recorder immediately after the interview. The longer you wait the less you remember.
- If interviewees ramble, let them go on, don't interrupt.
- Always bring more tape than you think you will need.
- Pre-interviewing dubbing: interviewee's name, location, time, etc.

Importance of Language:

- Connotative vs. denotative meanings.
- Be mindful the words you hear may not be the meanings the speaker intends.

At beginning of interview, visit with the interviewee, explaining who you are and why you're there. Once rapport is building and the interviewee breaks into a good story, say, "Oh this is exactly the type of info I was hoping you'd share with me. Rather than have you repeat yourself, let me plug this in. Turn back to your tape recorder and note time on pad. You have 29 minutes before turning over tape.

Master Your Equipment

- Practice with your equipment prior to interview.
- When switching tapes, just say, "Pardon me while I turn this tape over. Now you were just saying. . . ."
  -or-
  "Let me just turn this tape over. I certainly appreciate your helping us with the oral history."
- The trick is to keep talking while you change the tape, so the subject does not say anything. That way you don't lose anything.
- Label tapes before interview. After interview, be sure to identify tapes clearly.
- Use only stop and record buttons.
- Always make sure the microphone is on. Know that the red record light works even when some machines are paused.
- At beginning of tapes, delay 2–3 seconds before speaking.

- Take a pad of Kleenex to rest the microphone on—the pad will absorb noise.
- Learn to live with interruptions. Just smile.
- If the subject moves away from the table to get something, repeat what he said while he's walking away and back. Microphone may not pick up words.
- After interruptions, subject will ask, "Where were we?" Make notes of topic at interruption.
- Never play a tape, unless the person asks specifically. People don't like how they sound on tape.

10) What Should You Do Immediately after the Interview?

- As soon as you can, look over your notes from the interview. Write out any fragmentary notes into full sentences. Doing this will help you when you transcribe the interview later on.
- Write a substantial paragraph to yourself describing what you learned from the interview. Explain the two or three things you learned in the interview that struck you as most important, most newsworthy. Explain two questions that still remain to be answered before you can write a story or an essay about the interview.
- Always send a thank-you note to the interviewee for his time.
- When you send the transcript, follow up with a call to be sure the subject is reviewing the transcript and will return it.
- If the interviewee is slow to return the transcript, try these suggestions:
    - Would it be helpful if I reviewed the transcript and submitted my suggestions to you? Then be sure to note that transcription or editorial situation in the introduction to the transcript.
    - Is there anything I can do to help you?
    - Our quarterly report is due, and I would love to report your transcript is completed.
    - My assignment is due, and I would love to turn in the transcript to my teacher.

11) How Do You Create a Transcript of the Interview?

The transcript is the typed record of the recorded interview. Transcription requires careful listening and more careful typing. Write an introduction to each transcription explaining the language used and what was omitted or changed.

Tips on Transcription:

- Transcribers—work two hours at a time.
- A potential problem is getting behind on transcription. The more time passes the more people lose interest.
- Generally, for every hour of recorded material it will take three hours of transcription.
- Transcribe for meaning and clarity, but do not fabricate words.
- Be clear about time-bound references: "As we are aware of today"—what does "today" mean?
- Keep the future user of the interview in mind.
- Get nonverbal communication (nods, gestures) into words.
- Avoid transcribing such words as "um," "ahem," "mmm," and so on.
- Don't clutter transcripts with repetition.
- Transcribe for intended meaning. ("I didn' do nuttin" becomes "I did nothing.")
- Keep in mind that transcribed material should be used for research purposes. Dialect and tonality would prompt the researcher to listen to the oral history.
    - Transcribers transcribe in generalized English.
    - Sometimes dialect and tonality are kept in transcripts for emphasis.
        - Ex: WPA slave narratives

Check Your Transcript

After the tape is transcribed, listen to the tape while reading the transcript.

12) How Do You Compose and Revise a Story, Essay, or Other Work Based on the Interview?

To Write a Story Based on the Interview

Set the scene for the story. Provide an inciting incident that sets a conflict in motion. Develop a series of scenes in which the conflict pushes the action forward. Provide a final scene in which the conflict turns in a specific direction and the plot moves toward resolution. Throughout the story, use dialogue—have real, believable language come out of real, believable people's mouths. Throughout the story, show, don't tell. Have people's emotions, beliefs, and attitudes primarily become evident in what *they* do and say, not completely from what *you* say as you tell the story.

To Write an Essay Based on the Interview

Provide some context on the issue, problem, or question you will develop so that your reader will be interested enough to read on into your essay. Make a commitment to the reader to develop and support an important, central idea. Divide this idea into sensible units that you can develop. Develop each subdivided unit by making a general claim about it and then supporting your claim with evidence—stories, examples, details, reasons—that you learned during your interview. Anticipate possible objections to the points you're making and refute them in advance. Conclude by addressing the "so what" question: So what is so important about the points you make in the essay? So what should your readers feel, think, believe, and do with the material you have written about in the essay?

Works Cited

"250 Blacks Confront School Officials at Marianna." 1972. *Arkansas Gazette*, January 18.

Achebe, Chinua. 1958. *Things Fall Apart*. London: William Heinemann.

Adams, Henry. 1919. *The Education of Henry Adams*. Boston, MA: Houghton.

Angelou, Maya. 1969. *I Know Why the Caged Bird Sings*. New York: Random House.

Arkansas Center for Health Improvement. 2006. "Tracking Progress: The Third Annual Arkansas Assessment of Childhood and Adolescent Obesity." Little Rock: Arkansas Center for Health Improvement.

"Arkansas Delta Byways: Soil and Soul." http://www.arkansasdeltabyways.com. Accessed September 4, 2012.

"Arkansas-Delta-Made." http://www.arkansas.com/attractions/detail/. Accessed September 4, 2012.

Arnett, Jeffrey Jensen. 2000. "Emerging Adulthood: A Theory of Development from the Late Teens through the Twenties." *American Psychologist* 55, no. 5: 469–80.

Azano, Amy. 2011. "The Possibility of Place: One Teacher's Use of Place-Based Instruction for English Students in a Rural High School." *Journal of Research in Rural Education* 26, no. 10: 1–12. http://0-search.proquest.com.library.uark.edu/docview/889925596?accountid=8361. Accessed December 2, 2011.

Bawarshi, Anis. 2000. "The Genre Function." *College English* 66, no. 3: 327–52.

Baxter, Batsell Barrett. 1995. "Who Are the Churches of Christ and What Do They Believe In?" The Churches of Christ Internet Ministries. http://church-of-christ.org/who.html. Accessed August 24, 2010.

Bennett, John W., Harvey L. Smith, and Herbert Passin. 1942. "Food and Culture in Southern Illinois: A Preliminary Report." *American Sociological Review* 7, no. 5: 645–66.

Berlin, James. 1988. "Rhetoric and Ideology in the Writing Class." *College English* 50, no. 5: 477–94.

Bolsterli, Margaret. 2000. *Born in the Delta: Reflections on the Making of a White Southern Sensibility*. Fayetteville: Univ. of Arkansas Press.

Bomer, Randy, Joel E. Dworin, Laura May, and Peggy Semingson. 2008. "Miseducating Teachers about the Poor: A Critical Analysis of Ruby Payne's Claims about Poverty." *Teachers College Record* 110, no. 12: 2497–531.

Brandt, Deborah. 1998. "Sponsors of Literacy." *College Composition and Communication* 49, no. 2: 165–85.

Brantley, Max. 2012. "Appeals Court Reinstates Race Claim against Lee County Schools." Arkansas Times.com, February 28. http://www.arktimes.com/ArkansasBlog/archives/2012/02/28/appeals-court-reinstates-race-claim-against-lee-county-schools. Accessed July 28, 2012.

Britton, Nancy. 2010. "Religion." *The Encyclopedia of Arkansas History and Culture*. http://www.encyclopediaofarkansas.net/encyclopedia/entry-detail.aspx?entryID=396. Accessed August 23, 2010.

Carney, George O., ed. 1998. *Baseball, Barnes, and Bluegrass*. Lanham, MD: Rowman and Littlefield.

Carnine, Douglas. 2000. *Why Education Experts Resist Expert Practices*. Washington, DC: Thomas Fordham Foundation.

Carr, Patrick J., and Maria Kefalas. 2009. *Hollowing out the Middle: The Rural Brain Drain and What It Means for America*. Boston: Beacon Press.

Carter, Shannon. 2007. "Living Inside the (Bible) Belt." *College English* 69, no. 6: 572–95.

Center for Health and Health Care in Schools. 2013. "The Arkansas Story—Requiring BMIs of All Students." http://www.healthinschools.org/News-Room/EJournals/Volume-7/Number-3/The-Arkansas-Story_Requiring-BMIs-for-All-Students.aspx.

Centers for Disease Control and Prevention. "Overweight and Obesity." http://www.cdc.gov/obesity/. Accessed June 20, 2012.

Champagne, Catherine M. 2004. "Dietary Intake in the Lower Mississippi Delta Region: Results of Our Delta Study." *Journal of the American Dietetic Association* 104, no. 2: 199–207.

Corbett, Michael. 2007. *Learning to Leave: The Irony of Schooling in a Coastal Community*. Halifax, NS: Fernwood Books.

Covey, Stephen. 1989. *The Seven Habits of Highly Effective People*. New York: Free Press.

Cromartie, John, and Shawn Bucholtz. 2008. "Defining the 'Rural' in Rural America." *Amber Waves* 6, no. 3: 28–34.

Crossan, John Dominic. 2011. "The Search for the Historical Paul: Which Letters Did He Really Write?" *The Huffington Post*, July 5. http://www.huffingtonpost.com/john-dominic-crossan/apostle-paul-letters_b_890387.html. Accessed March 15, 2012.

Cunningham, Michael, and Craig Marberry. 2000. *Crowns: Portaits of Black Women in Church Hats*. New York: Doubleday.

"Curfew Ends in Marianna." 1972. *Arkansas Gazette*, January 18.

Darling-Hammond, Linda. 2003. "Keeping Good Teachers." *Educational Leadership* 60, no. 8: 6–13.

Dean, Pamela, Toby Daspit, and Petra Munro. 1998. *Talking Gumbo: A Teachers' Guide to Using Oral History in the Classroom*. Baton Rouge: Harry T. Williams Center for Oral History, Louisiana State Univ.

Delta Bridge Project. 2009. "Phillips County, Arkansas, 2010-2020 Strategic Community Plan." https://banksouthern.com/downloads/2010-2020-Phillips-County-Strategic-Community-Plan.pdf.

Delta Bridge Project. 2012. http://www.deltabridge.com. Accessed September 4, 2012.

Dennis, Jane. 2011. "Brinkley (Monroe County)." *The Encyclopedia of Arkansas History and Culture*. http://www.encyclopediaofarkansas.net/encyclopedia/entry-detail.aspx?entryID=941.

Donehower, Kim. 2013. "Why Not at School? Rural Literacies and the Continual Choice to Stay." In *Rethinking Rural Literacies: Transnational Perspectives*, edited by Bill Green and Michael Corbett, 35–52. New York: Palgrave Macmillan.

———. 2014. "Connecting Literacy to Sustainability: Revisiting Literacy as Involvement." In *Literacy, Economy, and Power: Writing and Researching after Literacy in American Lives*, edited by John Duffy, Julie Nelson Christoph, Eli Goldblatt, Nelson Graff, Rebecca S. Nowacek, and Bryan Trabold, 97–110. Carbondale: Southern Illinois Univ. Press.

Donehower, Kim, Charlotte Hogg, and Eileen E. Schell, eds. 2007. *Rural Literacies*. Carbondale: Southern Illinois Univ. Press.

———. 2011. *Reclaiming the Rural: Essays on Literacy, Rhetoric, and Pedagogy.* Carbondale: Southern Illinois Univ. Press.

DuFour, Richard, and Robert Eaker. 1998. *Professional Learning Communities at Work: Best Practices for Enhancing Student Achievement.* Bloomington, IN: National Educational Service.

Duncan, Arne. 2009. "Policy Address on Teacher Preparation at Columbia Teacher's College." October 22. http://www.tc.columbia.edu/news.htm?articleID=7195.

During, Simon, ed. 1993. *The Cultural Studies Reader.* London: Routledge.

Eifling, Sam. 2010. "Issue 68: Sam Eifling Asks What Do Arkansans Eat?" *Oxford American*, April 15.

Ellis, Lindsay, Anne Ruggles Gere, and L. Jill Lamberton. 2003. "Out Loud: The Common Language of Poetry." *English Journal* 93, no. 1: 44–49.

Fairclough, Norman. 1993. *Discourse and Social Change.* Cambridge, UK: Polity.

Ferris, Marcie Cohen. 2009. "The Edible South." *Southern Cultures* 15, no. 4: 3–27.

Fitts, Leroy. 1993. "National Baptist Convention, U.S.A." In *Encyclopedia of African American Religions*, edited by Larry G. Murphy, J. Gordon Melton, and Gary L. Ward, 537–38. New York: Garland.

Flower, Linda. 2008. *Community Literacy and the Rhetoric of Public Engagement.* Carbondale: Southern Illinois Univ. Press.

Gallup, George Jr., and Robert Bezilla. 1992. *The Religious Life of Young Americans.* Princeton, NJ: George H. Gallup International Institute.

Gates, Laine. 2010. "Negotiating Identity and Creating Spaces of Agency in Arkansas Public Schools." Master's thesis, Univ. of Arkansas.

Gatewood, Willard B. 1993. "The Arkansas Delta: The Deepest of the Deep South." In Whayne and Gatewood, *Arkansas Delta*, 3–29.

Gee, James Paul. 2001. "Reading as Situated Language: A Sociocognitive Perspective." *Journal of Adolescent and Adult Literacy* 44, no. 8: 714–25.

———. 2002. "Millennials and Bobos, Blue's Clues and Sesame Street: A Story for Our Times." In *Adolescents and Literacies in a Digital World*, edited by Donna Alvermann, 51–61. New York: Peter Lang, 2002.

Giroux, Henry A. 1994. "Doing Cultural Studies: Youth and the Challenge of Pedagogy." *Harvard Educational Review* 64, no. 3: 278–308.

Goering, Christian Z., David A. Jolliffe, Kelly Riley, Hilary Swanton, and Laine Gates. 2011. "The Arkansas Delta Oral History Project:

Understanding Poverty in a Literacy Outreach Project." In Donehower, Hogg, and Schell, *Reclaiming Rural Literacies*, 285–309.

Gordon, Fon Louise. 1993. "From Slavery to Uncertain Freedom: Black in the Delta." In Whayne and Gatewood, *Arkansas Delta*, 98–127.

Gorski, Paul. 2006. "The Classist Underpinnings of Ruby Payne's Framework." *Teachers College Record*, February 1.

Grisham, John. 2001. *A Painted House*. New York: Doubleday.

Green, Bill, and Michael Corbett. 2013. "Rural Education and Literacies: An Introduction." In *Rethinking Rural Literacies: Transnational Perspectives on Its Questions, Methods, and Knowledge*, 1–13. London: Palgrave Macmillan.

Gruenewald, David A. 2003. "'The Best of Both Worlds': A Critical Pedagogy of Place." *Educational Researcher* 32, no. 4: 3–12.

Gutierrez, Kris, Betsy Rymes, and Joanne Larson. 1995. "Script, Counterscript, and Underlife in the Classroom: James Brown versus *Brown v. Board of Education*." *Harvard Educational Review* 65, no. 3: 445–71.

Harrill, James Albert. 1995. *The Manumission of Slaves in Early Christianity*. Tubingen, Germany: Mohr.

Hawkins, B. Denise. 1997. "Cultural Attitudes and Body Dissatisfaction." *Black Issues in Higher Education* 21, no. 25: 27.

Heath, Shirley Brice, and Milbrey McLaughlin. 1993. *Identity and Inner-City Youth: Beyond Ethnicity and Gender*. New York: Teachers College Press.

Herzberg, Bruce. 1994. "Community Service and Critical Teaching." *College Composition and Communication* 45, no. 3: 307–19.

Holmes, William F. 1973. "The Arkansas Cotton Pickers Strike of 1891 and the Demise of the Colored Farmers's Alliance." *The Arkansas Historical Quarterly* 32, no. 2: 107–19.

Irvin, Matthew J., Judith L. Meece, Soo-yong Byun, Thomas W. Farmer, and Bryan C. Hutchins. 2011. "Relationship of School Context to Rural Youth's Educational Achievement and Aspirations." *Journal of Youth and Adolescence* 40, no. 9: 1225–42.

Jerald, Craig. 2009. *Defining a 21st-Century Education*. Alexandria, VA: Center for Public Education.

Johnson, James. 2013. "Pine Bluff, Arkansas: America's Most Dangerous Little Town." *Inquisitr*, February 19. http://www.inquisitr.com/532225/pine-bluff-arkansas-americas-most-dangerous-little-town/.

Jolliffe, David A. 2010a. "The Arkansas Delta Oral History Project: A Hands-On, Experiential Course in School-College Articulation." In

Going Public: The WPA as Advocate for Engagement, edited by Shirley Rose and Irwin Weiser, 50–67. Logan: Utah State Univ. Press.

———. 2010b. "The Community Literacy Advocacy Project: Civic Revival through Rhetorical Action in Rural Arkansas." In The *Public Work of Rhetoric*, edited by John Martin Ackerman and David Coogan, 267–82. Columbia: Univ. of South Carolina Press.

———. 2012. "Shakespeare and the Cultural Capital Tension: Advancing Literacy in Rural Arkansas." *Community Literacy Journal* 6, no. 2: 77–87.

Jones, Krista. 2012. "'It Was Awful, but It Was Politics': Crittenden County and the Demise of African American Political Participation." Master's thesis, Univ. of Arkansas.

Joos, Martin. 1962. *The Five Clocks: A Linguistic Excursion into Five Styles of English Usage*. New York: Harcourt.

Jordan, Wayne. 1969. "4-Member Medical Society Blocks VISTA Doctor." *Arkansas Gazette*, November 16.

Kelly, S. Arthur. 2006. *Writing with Families: Strengthening the Home/School Connection with Family Scribe Groups*. Gainesville, FL: Maupin House.

Kelly, Ursula A. 2009. "Learning to Lose: Rurality, Transcience, and Belonging (a Companion to Michael Corbett)." *Journal of Research in Rural Education* 24, no. 11: 1–4.

Kennedy, George A. 1994. *A New History of Classical Rhetoric*. Princeton, NJ: Princeton Univ. Press.

Kenniston, Kenneth. 1971. *Youth and Dissent: A Rise to a New Opposition*. New York: Harcourt Brace Jovanovich.

King, Kendra. 2010. *African-American Politics*. Cambridge, UK: Polity.

Latshaw, Beth A. 2009. "Food for Thought: Race, Region, Identity, and Foodways in the American South." *Southern Cultures* 15, no. 4: 106–28.

Levenstein, Harvey A. 2003. *Paradox of Plenty: A Social History of Eating in Modern America*. Berkeley: Univ. of California Press, 2003.

Levine, Arthur. 2006. "Educating School Teachers." The Education Schools Project. http://www.edschools.org/pdf/Educating_Teachers_Exec_Summ.pdf.

Lewis, Johanna Miller. 2008. "Implementing *Brown* in Arkansas." In *With All Deliberate Speed: Implementing Brown v. Board of Education*, edited by Brian J. Daugherity and Charles C. Bolton, 1–19. Fayetteville: University of Arkansas Press.

Liburd, Leandris D., Lynda A. Anderson, Timothy Edgar, and Leonard Jack, Jr. 1999. "Body Size and Body Shape: Perceptions of Black Women with Diabetes." *Diabetes Educator* 25, no. 3: 382–88.

Lincoln, Yvonna, and Egon Guba. 1985. *Naturalistic Inquiry*. Beverly Hills, CA: Sage, 1985.

Long, Elenore. 2008. *Community Literacy and the Rhetoric of Local Publics*. West Lafayette, IN: Parlor Press.

"Main Street West Memphis." http://www.broadwaywestmemphis.com. Accessed September 4, 2012.

Maira, Sunaina, and Elisabeth Soep. 2004. "United States of Adolescence? Reconsidering US Youth Cultural Studies." *Young: Nordic Journal of Youth Research* 12, no. 3: 245–69.

Manatt, Amanda, and Louise Mitchell. 2009. "Consolidated White River Academy." http://www.encyclopediaofarkansas.net/encyclopedia/entry-detail.aspx?entryID=5351. *The Encyclopedia of Arkansas History and Culture*. Accessed May 7, 2011.

"Marianna Blacks Protest at School; 22 Are Arrested." 1972. *Arkansas Gazette*, January 14.

Mathieu, Paula. 2005. *Tactics of Hope: The Public Turn in English Composition*. Portsmouth, NH: Heinemann.

McCollum, Jason. 2011. "Progressive Farmers and Household Union of America (PFHUA)." *The Encyclopedia of Arkansas History and Culture*. http://www.encyclopediaofarkansas.net/encyclopedia/entry-detail.aspx?entryID=3027. Accessed March 27, 2013.

McMillen, Neil. 2007. "The White Citizens' Council and Resistance to School Desegregation in Arkansas." *The Arkansas Historical Quarterly* 66, no. 2: 125–44.

Mississippi Delta Grassroots Caucus. 2007–12. http://www.mdgc.us.

Moje, Elizabeth Birr. 2002. "Re-framing Adolescent Literacy Research for New Times: Studying Youth as a Resource." *Reading Research and Instruction* 41, no. 3: 211–29.

Moje, Elizabeth Birr, and Allan Luke. 2009. "Literacy and Identity: Examining the Metaphors in History and Contemporary Research." *Reading Research Quarterly* 44, no. 4: 415–37.

National Public Radio. 2005. "Brinkley, Ark., Discovers the 'Lord God Bird.'" July 6. http://www.npr.org/2005/07/06/4721675/brinkley-ark-embraces-the-ord-god-bird. Accessed May 8, 2011.

National Research Center on Rural Education Support. 2011. "Rural Aspirations Study." https://ies.ed.gov/ncer/RandD/details.asp?ID=131. Accessed September 4, 2012.

Newmann, Fred, and Associates. 1996. *Authentic Achievement: Restructuring Schools for Intellectual Quality*. San Francisco, CA: Jossey-Bass.

Newport, Frank. 2009. "State of the States: Importance of Religion." Gallup, Inc. January 28. http://www.gallup.com/poll/114022/state-states-importance-religion.aspx.

Ng, Jennifer C., and John L. Rury. 2006. "Poverty and Education: A Critical Analysis of the Ruby Payne Phenomenon." *Teachers College Record*, July 1.

Osei-Kofi, Nana. 2005. "Pathologizing the Poor: A Framework for Understanding Ruby Payne's Work." *Equity and Excellence* 38, no. 4: 367–75.

Payne, Ruby. 2005. *A Framework for Understanding Poverty*. 4th ed. Highlands, TX: aha! Process.

Perelman, Chaim, and Lucie Olbrechts-Tyteca. 1991. *The New Rhetoric: A Treatise on Argumentation*. Notre Dame, IN: Univ. of Notre Dame Press.

Petraglia-Bahri, Joseph, ed. 1995. Reconceiving Writing: Rethinking Writing Instruction. Hillsdale, NJ: Lawrence Erlbaum.

Pew Research Center. 2013. "Religion in American Culture—Pew Forum on Religion and Public Life." http://www.pewforum.org. Accessed April 20, 2014.

"Private Schools: The Last Refuge." 1969. *Time Magazine*, November 14.

Public Broadcasting Service. 2004. *The Tradition of Hats in the African American Church*. February 13. http://www.npr.org/templates/story/story.php?storyId=876404. Accessed August 26, 2011.

Rand, Lizabeth A. 2001. "Enacting Faith: Evangelical Discourse and the Discipline of Composition Studies." *College Composition and Communication* 52, no. 3: 349–67.

Regnerus, Mark, Christian Smith, and Melissa Fritsch. 2003. *Religion in the Lives of American Adolescents: A Review of the Literature*. Chapel Hill, NC: National Study of Youth and Religion.

Robert Wood Johnson Foundation. 2012. "New Report Finds Adult Obesity Rates Could Exceed 60 Percent in 13 States by 2013." September 18. http://www.rwjf.org/en/library/research/2014/09/the-state-of-obesity.html. Accessed on June 14, 2013.

Rosenfield, Lawrence W. 1980. "The Practical Celebration of the Epideictic." In *Rhetoric in Transition: Studies in the Nature and Uses of Rhetoric*, edited by Eugene E. White, 131–55. State College: Pennsylvania State Univ. Press.

Russell, David R. 1994. *Writing in the Academic Disciplines, 1870–1990*. Carbondale: Southern Illinois Univ. Press.

Salomon, Gavriel, and David N. Perkins. 1989. "Rocky Roads to Transfer: Rethinking Mechanisms of a Neglected Phenomenon." *Educational Psychologist* 24, no. 2: 113–42.

Schlechty, Phillip. 2004. *Shaking Up the Schoolhouse: How to Support and Sustain Educational Innovation*. San Francisco, CA: Jossey-Bass.

"School, City Reported Quiet at Marianna." 1972. *Arkansas Gazette*, January 15.

Schrock, Earl, Jr. 1992. "Traditional Arkansas Foodways." In *An Arkansas Folklore Sourcebook*, edited by W. K. McNeil and William Clements, 172–211. Fayetteville: Univ. of Arkansas Press.

Schwartz, Marvin. 1988. *In Service to America: A History of VISTA in Arkansas, 1965–1985*. Fayetteville: Univ. of Arkansas Press.

Semmes, Clovis E. 1996. *Racism, Health, and Post-Industrialism: A Theory of African-American Health*. Westport, CT: Praeger.

Settersten, Richard, Jr., and Barbara Ray. 2010. *Not Quite Adults: Why 20-Somethings Are Choosing a Slower Path to Adulthood, and Why It's Good for Everyone*. New York: Random House.

"Shadden—Obituary." 2010. *Helena Daily World*, May 24. www.helena-arkansas.com/news/20100521/wayne-shadden-obituary. Accessed September 12, 2013.

Sheard, Cynthia Miecznikowski. 1996. "The Public Value of Epideictic Rhetoric." *College English* 59, no. 7: 765–94.

Sims, Norman, ed. 1984. *The Literary Journalists: The New Art of Personal Reportage*. New York: Ballantine.

Sisserson, Kendra, Carmen Manning, Annie Knepler, and David A. Jolliffe. 2002. "Authentic Intellectual Achievement in Writing." *English Journal* 91, no. 6: 63–69.

Smart, Juanita M. 2005. "Frankenstein or Jesus Christ? When the Voice of Faith Creates a Monster for the Composition Teacher." In Vander Lei and Kyburz, *Negotiating Religious Faith*, 11–23.

Smith, Christian, Melinda Lundquist Denton, Robert Faris, and Mark Regnerus. 2002. "Mapping American Adolescent Religious Participation." *Journal for the Scientific Study of Religion* 41, no. 4: 597–612.

Smith, Michael, and Jeffrey Wilhelm. 2002. *Reading Don't Fix No Chevys: Literacy in the Lives of Young Men*. Portsmouth, NH: Heinemann.

Snow, Malinda. 1985. "Martin Luther King's 'Letter from Birmingham Jail' as Pauline Epistle." *Quarterly Journal of Speech* 71: 318–84.

State of Arkansas, 84th General Assembly. 2003. "Act 1220 of 2003: An Act to Create a Child Health Advisory Committee; to Coordinate Statewide Efforts to Combat Childhood Obesity and Related Illnesses; and to Improve the Health of the Next Generation of Arkansans." Little Rock: Arkansas General Assembly.

Stockley, Grif. 2001. *Blood in Their Eyes: The Elaine Race Massacres of 1919*. Fayetteville: Univ. of Arkansas Press.

———. 2009. *Ruled By Race: Black/White Relations in Arkansas from Slavery to Present*. Fayetteville: Univ. of Arkansas Press.

Stoecker, Randy. 2016. *Liberating Service Learning and the Rest of Higher Education Civic Engagement*. Philadelphia, Pennsylvania: Temple Univ. Press.

Street, Brian. 2003. "What's 'New' in New Literacy Studies? Critical Approaches to Literacy in Theory and Practice." *Current Issues in Comparative Education* 5, no. 2: 77–91.

Taylor, Edward. 1998. "A Primer on Critical Race Theory." *The Journal of Blacks in Higher Education* 19: 122–24.

Taylor, Kieran. 1999. "'We Have Just Begun': Black Organizing and White Response in the Arkansas Delta, 1919." *The Arkansas Historical Quarterly* 58, no. 3: 264.

Taylor, Orville W. 1984. "Arkansas." In *Encyclopedia of Religion in the South*, edited by Samuel S. Hill, 54–55. Macon, GA: Mercer Univ. Press.

Theobald, Paul. 2005. "Urban and Rural Schools: Overcoming Lingering Obstacles." *Phi Delta Kappan* 87, no. 2: 116–22.

Tillotson, James. E. 2004. "America's Obesity: Conflicting Public Policies, Industrial Development, and Unintended Human Consequences." *Annual Review of Nutrition* 131, no. 6: 617–43.

Tolbert, Jason. 2001. "Lessons from the Gillett Coon Supper." *Arkansas News*, January 17. http://arkansasnews.com/jason-tolbert/lessons-from-the-gillett-coon-supper. Accessed August 14, 2013.

United States Census Bureau. 2000– . "Monroe County, Arkansas." *American Fact Finder*. http://factfinder.census.gov/faces/nav/jsf/pages/community_facts.xhtml?src=bkmk. Accessed May 7, 2010.

University of Arkansas Division of Agriculture. 2015. *Profile of Rural Arkansas 2015*. Little Rock: Univ. of Arkansas Press.

Vander Lei, Elizabeth, and Bonnie Kyburz, eds. 2005. *Negotiating Religious Faith in the Composition Classroom*. Portsmouth, NH: Heinemann.

Varnell, Cannon, ed. 2013. *Keeping a Moment: Through the Lens of Billie J. Seamans*. Fayetteville, AR: Brown Chair in English Literacy.

Vernon-Feagans, Lynne, Kathleen C. Gallagher, and Kirstin Kainz. 2010. "The Transition to School in Rural America: A Focus on Literacy." In *Handbook of Research on Schools, Schooling, and Human Development*, edited by Judith L. Meese and Jacquelyne S. Eccles, 163–84. New York: Routledge.

Vickers, Brian. 1988. *In Defense of Rhetoric*. Oxford: Clarendon Press.

"Violence Follows Trial at Marianna." 1971. *Arkansas Gazette*, August 6.

"VISTA Is Welcome in Arkansas." 1971. *Arkansas Gazette*, November 27.

Waller, Jeannie, ed. *Veterans of Woodruff County: Stories and Memories of Service to One's Country*. 2012. Fayetteville, AR: Brown Chair in English Literacy.

Whayne, Jeannie. 1996. *A New Plantation South: Land, Labor, and Federal Favor in Twentieth-Century Arkansas*. Charlottesville: Univ. Press of Virginia.

Whayne, Jeannie, and Willard B. Gatewood, eds. 1993. *The Arkansas Delta: Land of Paradox*. Fayetteville: Univ. of Arkansas Press.

Whitman, Glenn. 2004. *Dialogue with the Past: Engaging Students and Meeting Standards through Oral History*. Lanham, MD: AltaMira.

Wiggins, Grant. 1999. "Assessment: Authenticity, Context, and Validity." *Phi Delta Kappan* 75, no. 3: 200–214.

Wigginton, Eliot. 1974. *Moments: The Foxfire Experience*. Rabun Gap, GA: The Foxfire Fund.

Williams, Bronwyn T. 2005. "Taken on Faith: Religion and Identity in Writing Classes." *Journal of Adolescent and Adult Literacy* 48, no. 6: 514–18.

Index

About the Authors

James A. Anderson Jr. is an assistant professor of English and English education at Lander University in Greenwood, South Carolina, where he teaches writing and literature and coordinates the program in secondary English education. While completing a doctorate at the University of Arkansas, he wrote his dissertation on rural teachers' perceptions of advocacy and writing in a rural institute of the Northwest Arkansas Writing Project. Since relocating to the Piedmont area of South Carolina, Anderson continues to focus his research on rural schools and rural literacies, while preparing future teachers to work in the region's many rural schools.

Christian Z. Goering is an associate professor of English Education at the University of Arkansas, where he directs the Northwest Arkansas Writing Project and the licensure programs in English education and theater and communications. He attended a rural Kansas high school and thus part of his mission as a professor includes expanding opportunities for rural teachers and students. In 2016, Goering coedited *Recontextualized: A Framework for Teaching English with Music* and released an extended-play recording as a singer-songwriter called *Big Engine*.

David A. Jolliffe is professor of English and, by courtesy, curriculum and instruction at the University of Arkansas at Fayetteville, where he is the initial occupant of the Brown Chair in English Literacy. Since 1976, Jolliffe has taught at two public high schools in his native state of West Virginia, four large public universities, a large private university, and a small liberal arts college. His scholarship over the years has considered the history and theory of rhetoric, the preparation of writing teachers, writing assessment, and literacy in rural America.

Krista Jones Oldham is the college archivist and records manager at Haverford College, where she is responsible for managing and overseeing the appraisal, accession, description, and preservation of college records, as well as supporting and promoting their use. She has an MIS from the University of Tennessee, Knoxville, and earned both an MA and BA in history from the University of Arkansas, Fayetteville. In 2016, Oldham became a Society of American Archivists Digital Archives Specialist.